D0070733

About the author

Boaventura de Sousa Santos is Professor of Sociology at the University of Coimbra in Portugal and a Distinguished Scholar of the Institute for Legal Studies at the University of Wisconsin-Madison. He is a leading Portuguese social theorist and has written and published widely on issues of globalization, sociology of law and the state, democratic theory, social movements and epistemology.

BOAVENTURA DE SOUSA SANTOS

The rise of the global left

The World Social Forum and beyond

Zed Books

LONDON | NEW YORK

The rise of the global left: the World Social Forum and beyond was first published by Zed Books Ltd, 7 Cynthia Street, London N1 9JF, UK and Room 400, 175 Fifth Avenue, New York, NY 10010, USA, in 2006

<www.zedbooks.co.uk>

Cover designed by Andrew Corbett
Set in Arnhem and Futura Bold by Ewan Smith, London
Index: <ed.emery@britishlibrary.net>
Printed and bound in Malta by Gutenberg Press Ltd

Distributed in the USA exclusively by Palgrave Macmillan, a division of St Martin's Press, LLC, 175 Fifth Avenue, New York, NY 10010.

A catalogue record for this book is available from the British Library.
US CIP data are available from the Library of Congress.

ISBN   1 84277 800 5 | 978 1 84277 800 5 hb
ISBN   1 84277 801 3 | 978 1 84277 801 2 pb

Contents

Tables and figures

Preface

In the course of the last thirty years, conservative thought believed it had gained immortality. In the political and social domain, a certain kind of thought gains the appearance of immortality when it pronounces its rival thoughts dead, and makes this credible for large sectors of the population. The end of history, the death of the state, the end of the left/right cleavage, the obsolescence of revolution and the Third World are some of the obituaries that have allowed conservative thought to flag its immortality. The truth is that, as the Greek philosopher Epicharmus once admonished us, 'mortals should have mortal, not immortal thoughts'. That is perhaps the reason why the last decade has witnessed a kind of revenge of the dead thoughts. Resurging under new forms, many of these thoughts led to the conclusion that several of the deaths had been pronounced prematurely. One of them was the left/right cleavage. As neo-liberal globalization – the avant-garde of conservative thinking – was being confronted all over the world with movements of resistance credible enough to configure the emergence of an alternative, counter-hegemonic globalization, it became clear that the left/right cleavage was emerging in new ways. So new were they that it could actually be said that the cleavage was being reinvented. The emergence seems obvious today, and the major features of the reinvention are as follows: its global scale, comprising local and national struggles; its huge political and cultural diversity, and the celebration of such diversity; a new concept of politicization, not grounded in the polarization of differences, as before, but rather in the depolarization of differences; its call for high-intensity forms of democracy, both in society and the state, and inside movements and organizations. The World Social Forum (WSF), whose first meeting took place in Porto Alegre (Brazil) in January 2001, is today one of the most eloquent manifestations of the emergence of counter-hegemonic globalization, hence of the reinvention of the left/right cleavage.

The aim of this book is twofold. First, I want to make the WSF better known and highlight its newness in the context of the struggles for social emancipation of the last two hundred years, particularly in the last forty years. Second, I want to highlight the role of the WSF in the renewal or even reinvention of left thinking and practice and in the construction of an emerging global left politics at the beginning of the twenty-first century.

The WSF is one of the pillars of the global movement, which, for the last few decades, has been questioning neo-liberal globalization, the apparent expression of the historical triumph of capitalism. By questioning the historical destiny that neo-liberal globalization claimed to symbolize, the movement of protest and formulation of alternatives presented itself from the start as an alternative, counter-hegemonic kind of globalization. This counter-hegemonic globalization is based on the links between local, national and global struggles, conducted by social movements and non-governmental organizations united by the belief that another world is possible. This idea contains in a nutshell the aspiration of a set of highly diversified subsidiary social groups worldwide that pursue a socially, politically and culturally more just society, a society liberated from the forms of exclusion, exploration, oppression, discrimination and environmental destruction that by and large characterize capitalism and which neo-liberal globalization has helped to aggravate. After 2001, the WSF became the organization that most eloquently articulated the emergent counter-hegemonic globalization.

Neo-liberal globalization is not a completely new phenomenon, since historical capitalism was global from the start and, before it, there were many other non-Western (Persian, Chinese and Indian) globalizations. But it does pose new problems as regards strategies of resistance and the formulation of alternatives, not only because those that in the past guided the anti-capitalist struggles failed, but also because, for the first time in modern Western history, capitalism presents itself as a global civilizational model, which submits practically all aspects of social life to the law of value. To confront this model in all its dimensions is a new challenge, not only in organizational and agency terms, but also in terms of scale and types of collective action and political strategy, and even in terms of the forms and processes of knowledge that must guide emancipatory practices. The WSF is the expression of the novelty of this challenge, of its demands as well as of its dimensions.

In the Introduction, I present a brief history of left politics in the last forty years, thereby setting the context within which I will analyse the WSF in all its political and organizational novelty. In Chapter 1, I situate the WSF in the tradition of modern utopian thinking and characterize it as a critical utopia of a new type. In Chapter 2, I argue that the diversity of knowledges (political and otherwise) that circulate in the WSF announces the emergence of a new epistemology or set of epistemologies that is very distinct from the epistemology that prevailed both in capitalist and in socialist societies throughout the twentieth century. I call this epistemology an epistemology of the South, and analyse its main traits. Chapter 3 is dedicated to identifying in very broad strokes the political orientations that direct the WSF process. I call the set of these orientatîons a new insurgent cosmopolitan politics. In Chapter 4, I analyse the organizational make-up of the WSF and how it has evolved since the first event in 2001. My main argument in this chapter is that the WSF has proved to have an enormous capacity to reform and to transform itself. In Chapter 5, I focus on the issues of political representation within the framework of the WSF, pondering both the question of who represents the WSF and that of whom the WSF itself represents. Through these questions, both the issue of the real globalness of the WSF and that of its internal and external legitimacy are raised and discussed. In Chapter 6, I identify the main political cleavages inside the WSF process and show how and why such cleavages have not put at risk the main global consensus that keeps the WSF going. In Chapter 7, I analyse the two questions that in my view will decide the future of the WSF as a novelty in the tradition of modern left politics and left thinking: self-democracy and the work of inter-cultural and transpolitical translation. They constitute the alternative to the quest for a supposedly general theory that has led us nowhere except to authoritarianism, factionalism and, in the end, historical defeat. In conjunction with the epistemological challenges discussed in Chapter 2, I analyse in Chapter 8 a proposal presented by myself at the WSF of 2003 concerning the creation of a Popular University of the Social Movements. Finally, in Chapter 9, I reflect upon the impact of the WSF on the future of the politics and thinking of the global left. In my conclusion, I return, from another perspective and in a brief reference, to the questions that will most decisively condition the future of the WSF.

To prepare this book I counted on the assistance of many people. Special thanks are due to Maria Paula Meneses, who contributed a great deal to the revisions, additions and updates that make this book substantially different from its previous editions in Portuguese, Spanish and Italian. My thanks also to my research assistants Margarida Gomes, Sara Araújo and Celeste Benson for their enthusiasm and professionalism. For their comments on earlier versions I also thank Antonio Martins, Arturo Escobar, Cândido Grzybowszki, Francisco Whitaker,

Jai Sen, Jorge Romano, Moema Miranda, Nelson Maldonado Torres, Pedro Santana, Peter Waterman, Teivo Teivainen, Virgínia Vargas, Walter Mignolo and, last but not least, Roberto Molteno from Zed Books. As always, my special thanks to Lassalete Simões for preparing the manuscript for publication.

Preface

to MIR

Introduction: forty years of solitude and the novelty of the World Social Forum

The final thirty or forty years of the last century may be considered years of degenerative crisis in global left thinking and practice. To be sure, there were crises before, but not only were they not global – restricted as they were to the Eurocentric world, what nowadays we call the Global North, and compensated for, from the 1950s on, by the successful struggles for the liberation of the colonies – but they were mainly experienced as casualties in a history whose trajectory and rationality suggested that the victory of the left (revolution, socialism, communism) was certain. This is how the division of the workers' movement at the beginning of the First World War was experienced, as well as the defeat of the German revolution (1918–23), and then Nazism, fascism, *Franquismo* (1939–75) and *salazarismo* (1926–74), the Moscow processes (1936–38), the civil war in Greece (1944–49), and even the invasion of Hungary (1956). This kind of crisis is well characterized in the works of Trotsky in exile. Trotsky was very early on aware of the seriousness of Stalin's deviations from the revolution, to the point of refusing to lead an opposition, as proposed to him by Zinoviev and Kamenev in 1926. But he never for one moment doubted that history went along with the revolution, just as the true revolutionaries went along with history. The author who, to my mind, most brilliantly portrays the increasingly Sisyphean effort to safeguard the historical meaning of the revolution before the morasses of the Moscow processes is Maurice Merleau-Ponty in *Humanisme et terreur* (1947).

The crises of left thinking and practice of the last thirty or forty years are of a different kind. On the one hand, they are global, even though they occur in different countries for specific reasons: the assassination of Lumumba (1961); the failure of Che in Bolivia and his assassination (1966); the May 1968 student movement in Europe and the Americas and its neutralization; the invasion of Czechoslovakia (1968); the response of American imperialism to the Cuban revolution; the assassination of Allende (1973) and the military dictatorships in Latin America in the 1960s and 1970s; Suharto's brutal repression of the left in Indonesia (1965–67); the degradation or liquidation of the nationalist, developmentalist and socialist regimes of sub-Saharan

Africa that came out of independence (1980s); the emergence of a new/old militant and expansionist right, with Ronald Reagan in the USA and Margaret Thatcher in the UK (1980s); the globalization of the most retrograde form of capitalism, neo-liberalism, imposed by the Washington Consensus (1989); the plot against Nicaragua (1980s); the crisis of the Congress Party in India and the rise of political Hinduism (communalism) (1990s); the collapse of the regimes of central and eastern Europe, symbolized by the fall of the Berlin Wall (1989); the conversion of Chinese communism to the most savage kind of capitalism, market Stalinism (starting with Deng Xiaoping in the early 1980s); and finally, in the 1990s, the parallel rise of political Islam and political Christianity, both fundamentalist and confrontational.

Furthermore, the crisis of left thinking and practice of the last thirty or forty years appears to be degenerative: the failures seem to be the result of history's mortal exhaustion, whether because history no longer has meaning or rationality, or because the meaning and rationality of history finally opted for the permanent consolidation of capitalism, the latter transformed into a literal translation of immutable human nature. Revolution, socialism, communism and even reformism seem to be hidden away in the top drawers of history's closet, where only collectors of misfortunes reach. The world is made, and well made at that, the neo-liberal argument goes; the future finally has arrived in the present to stay. This agreement on ends is the uncontested fund of liberalism, on whose basis it is possible to respect the diversity of opinions about means. Since means are political only when they are at the service of different ends, the differences concerning social change are technical or juridical and, therefore, can and must be discussed regardless of the cleavage between left and right.

But the alleged degenerative crisis of the left is grounded in three other factors. The first concerns the concept of a more just and truly human future society, where humanism – the human being for the human being – is no longer a mystification, and rather becomes an experience of concrete life for every human being. This concept, however vague, was consistent enough to serve as an evaluation criterion of the life conditions of the working class, excluded social groups and victims of discrimination. On the basis of this alternative vision and the credible possibility of fulfilling it, it would be possible to consider the present as violent, intolerable and morally repugnant. The strength of Marxism resides in this unique capacity to link the alternative future with the oppositional way of living the present. In the last decades, however, neo-liberal conservatism became so dominant that the left split into two fields, none of them, paradoxically, on the left. On the one hand, there were those who took the eradication of the idea of an alternative society to be such a devastating defeat that there would be space left only for the centrism dominated by the 'more enlightened' right; on the other were those who in the absence of an alternative saw a victory, capable of encouraging a new centrism, this time dominated by the left (the Labour Third Way and its developments in Latin America). These two ways of announcing the death of the left ended up being not easily distinguishable. They both missed something: without a concept of an alternative society and without the politically organized struggle to bring it about, the present, however violent and intolerable, would be depoliticized and, as a consequence, would stop being a source of mobilization for revolt and opposition. This fact has certainly not escaped the right, quite the opposite. Bearing it in mind, the right has based its government, since the 1980s, not on the consensus of the victims, but on their resignation.

The second factor of the left crisis concerns the way the left renounced violence. Not the fact that it renounced violence, I insist, but the way it renounced it. Left thinking always started from the idea that democratic liberal capitalist societies are based on a violent foundational act. Indeed, there is first the original violence of colonization (from genocide to epistemicide, from pillage of natural resources to slavery and forced labour). Second, there is the imposition, on the victims of wage labour exploitation, of a social order in which equality before the law is merely the device that legitimizes substantive inequality, just as civil society is the acting space of an anti-social individual, for whom others are no more than an obstacle to the exercise of the individual's freedom. Negation of the humanity of the colonized peoples, proclamation of formal equality among citizens and the concept of civil society contributed to making violence disappear from the principles, formal procedures and political philosophy, but violence ended up, none the less, being exerted in the real lives of the large majority of the population in a social form (unemployment, unjust salary, social exclusion, racial and sexual discrimination). During a good part of the twentieth century, this foundational violence was taken seriously by the left, so much so that one of the most important divisions among the left had to do with the political consequences of such a realization. Part of the left (the revolutionary left) considered it right to use violence in the struggle against liberal society, whenever political conditions prevented non-violent struggle. That would be legitimate violence, mainly because, unlike liberal violence, it aimed to construct

Introduction

3

a society without violence, as regards both principles and practices, a truly inter-human society. Another part of the left (the reformist left) considered foundational violence to be such a basic contradiction in capitalist society that the latter would not survive a political practice consistently grounded in the non-violent principles and laws that it proclaimed. The Weberian idea of the state's legitimate violence can be interpreted in this light: while recognizing the existence of illegitimate violence in society, it strictly limits the exercise of liberal power. The revolutionary left inspired many of the anti-colonial and anti-imperialist struggles in the Global South, whereas the reformist left prevailed in Europe, especially after the failure of the German revolution.

The crisis of the last decades, although apparently implying a victory for the reformist left, actually implied a defeat both for the revolutionary and the reformist left. This defeat came about because the left, having also accepted the impossibility of an alternative society, accepted as normal or inevitable the violence of the democratic liberal capitalist societies. In fact, it stopped recognizing violence as violence. The discrepancy between principles and practices stopped being an irreducible contradiction to become an organizational dysfunction, susceptible of solution. In such conditions, it became unthinkable that, whatever the circumstances, violence might be legitimate as a political tactic: given the agreement on ends, the diversity of opinions on means must be kept as such, as a mere civilized diversity of opinions. Thus, not only did the left abandon the practice of violence – which is fully justified under the circumstances – but it also stopped having a theory of violence – which incapacitated it politically in confronting the new or renewed manifestations of violence: terrorism and state terrorism; immolation of individual life as a manifestation of extreme loyalty to a collective cause; an increase in criminal violence as a depoliticized form of resistance against the structural violence of capitalist social relations; recourse to the violence of the war of aggression to impose ideas of non-violence, be they democracy, human rights or freedom; intensification of states of emergency and the rise of a new state of exception, in which the distinction between legitimate and illegitimate violence seems to collapse.

This theoretical disarming of the left is related to the third factor in the crisis of the past four decades. I mean the rise, in the countries of the Global South, of movements of resistance, both violent and non-violent, against oppression, marginalization and exclusion, whose ideological bases have nothing to do with those that were the references of the left during the twentieth century (Marxism, socialism, developmentalism, anti-imperialist nationalism). Rather they are grounded in multi-secular cultural and historical identities, and/or religious militancy. It is not surprising, therefore, that such struggles cannot be defined according to the cleavage between left and right. What is actually surprising is that the left as a whole does not have theoretical and analytical tools to position itself in relation to them, and that it does not think it a priority to do so. Without trying to be exhaustive, I mention three such movements, of very distinct political meanings: the indigenous movements, particularly in Latin America; the 'new' rise of traditionalism in Africa; and the Islamic insurgency. In spite of the huge differences between them what these movements have in common is that they all start out from cultural and political references that are non-Western, even if constituted by the resistance to Western domination. The difficulties of political evaluation experienced by the left derive, on the one hand, from not envisioning a future society as alternative to the capitalist liberal society and, on the other, from the North-centric or Eurocentric cultural and epistemological universe that has dominated the left.

In view of this, it is more appropriate to speak of a global crisis of the left than of a crisis of the global left. It is possible to speak of a global crisis, to the extent that we are facing the impact of the globalization of neo-liberal capitalism and the ideology that sustains it on left thinking and practice in different regions of the world. But it is not possible to speak of a global left. On the one hand, because there is no left think-ing or ways of thinking capable of accounting for the world diversity of reasons, means and ends of resistance to hegemonic globalization, and capable of deciding what or who is or is not left; on the other, because the organizational unities and the institutional targets or interlocutors are still national or local, the transnational and translocal articulations being too tenuous to allow one to speak of a global left.

If this were the whole story, the existence of this book would not be justified. Enough has been said already about the crisis of the left, and part of what has been said has worked as self-fulfilling prophecy. The mortal fatigue of history is the mortal fatigue of the women and men who make it in their daily lives. The fatigue increases when the habit of thinking that history is with us inclines us, when it is questioned, to think that history is irremediably against us. History does not know better than we do where it is headed, nor does it use the women and men to fulfil its ends. So, we cannot trust history more than we trust ourselves. To be sure, trusting ourselves is not a subjective act, decon-textualized from the world. For the past few decades, the political and

5

cultural hegemony of neo-liberalism gave rise to a conception of the world that shows it as being either too made, and well made at that, to allow for the introduction of any consequent novelty, or too fragmentary to allow for whatever we do to have consequences capable of making up for the risks taken.

The other side of this hegemony, however, was the hegemonic practices that for the past decades have intensified exclusion, oppression, destruction of the means of subsistence and discrimination of large numbers of people, leading them to situations where inaction or conformism would mean death. Such situations convert the contingency of history into the necessity to change it. The acts of resistance into which these situations were translated, together with the revolution in information and communication technologies that took place simultaneously, permitted the making of alliances in distant places of the world and the articulation of struggles through local/global linkages. Thus an alternative globalization was gradually constructed – alternative to neo-liberal globalization, a counter-hegemonic globalization, a globalization from below. The 1994 Zapatista uprising is an important moment in this construction, precisely because it targets a tool of neo-liberal globalization, the North American Free Trade Agreement, and because it aims to articulate different scales of struggle, from local to national to global, from the Chiapas mountains to Mexico City to the solidary world, resorting to new discursive and political strategies, and to the new information and communication technologies available. In November 1999, the protesters in Seattle managed to paralyse the World Trade Organization (WTO) ministerial meeting, and later many other meetings of the World Bank, the International Monetary Fund (IMF), the WTO and the G8 were affected by the protests of non-governmental organizations (NGOs) and social movements intent on denouncing the hypocrisy and destructiveness of the new world disorder. In January 2001, the World Social Forum (WSF) met for the first time in Porto Alegre (Brazil), and many others followed: global, regional, thematic, national, sub-national and local forums. The WSF may be said to represent today, in organizational terms, the most consistent manifestation of counter-hegemonic globalization. As such, the WSF provides the most favourable context within which to enquire to what extent a new left is emerging through these initiatives – a truly global left, having the tools to overcome the degenerative crisis that has been beleaguering the left for the past forty years. This is the enquiry I propose to undertake in this book.

The WSF is the set of initiatives of transnational exchange among social movements, NGOs and their practices and knowledges of local, national or global social struggles carried out in compliance with the Porto Alegre Charter of Principles against the forms of exclusion and inclusion, discrimination and equality, universalism and particularism, cultural imposition and relativism, brought about or made possible by the current phase of capitalism known as neo-liberal globalization.

The WSF is a new social and political phenomenon. The fact that it does have antecedents does not diminish its newness, quite the opposite. The WSF is not an event. Nor is it a mere succession of events, although it does try to dramatize the formal meetings it promotes. It is not a scholarly conference, although the contributions of many scholars converge in it. It is not a party or an international association of parties, although militants and activists from many parties all over the world take part in it. It is not an NGO or a confederation of NGOs, even though its conception and organization owe a great deal to NGOs. It is not a social movement, even though it often designates itself as the movement of movements. Although it presents itself as an agent of social change, the WSF rejects the concept of a historical subject and confers no priority on any specific social actor in this process of social change. It holds no clearly defined ideology, in defining either what it rejects or what it asserts. Given that the WSF conceives of itself as a struggle against neo-liberal globalization, is it a struggle against a form of capitalism or against capitalism in general? Given that it sees itself as a struggle against discrimination, exclusion and oppression, does the success of its struggle presuppose a post-capitalist, socialist, anarchist horizon, or, on the contrary, does it presuppose that no horizon is clearly defined at all? Given that the vast majority of people taking part in the WSF identify themselves with a politics of the left, how many definitions of 'the left' fit the WSF? And what about those who refuse to be defined because they believe that the left/right dichotomy is a North-centric or West-centric particularism, and look for alternative political definitions? The social struggles that find expression in the WSF do not adequately fit either of the ways of social change sanctioned by Western modernity: reform and revolution. Aside from the consensus on non-violence, its modes of struggle are extremely diverse and appear to be spread over a continuum between the poles of institutionality and insurgency. Even the concept of non-violence is open to widely disparate interpretations. Finally, the WSF is not structured according to any of the models of modern political organization, be they democratic centralism, representative democracy or participatory democracy. Nobody represents it or is allowed to speak

7

in its name, let alone make decisions, even though it sees itself as a forum that facilitates the decisions of the movements and organizations that take part in it.[1]

These features are arguably not new, as they are associated with what is conventionally called 'new social movements'. The truth is, however, that these movements, be they local, national or global, are thematic. Themes, while fields of concrete political confrontation, compel definition – hence polarization – whether regarding strategies or tactics, whether regarding organizational forms or forms of struggle. Themes work, therefore, both as attraction and repulsion. Now, what is new about the WSF is the fact that it is inclusive, both as concerns its scale and its thematics. What is new is the whole it constitutes, not its constitutive parts. The WSF is global in its harbouring of local, national and global movements, and in its inter-thematic and even trans-thematic nature. That is to say, since the conventional factors of attraction and repulsion do not work as far as the WSF is concerned, either it develops other strong factors of attraction and repulsion or does without them, and may even derive its strength from their non-existence. In other words, the 'movement of movements' is not one more movement. It is a different kind of movement.

The problem with new social movements is that, in order to do them justice, a new social theory and new analytical concepts are called for. Since neither the one nor the others emerge easily from the inertia of the disciplines, the risk that they may be under-theorized and under-valued is considerable.[2] This risk is all the more serious as the WSF, given its scope and internal diversity, not only challenges dominant political theories and the various disciplines of the conventional social sciences, but challenges as well scientific knowledge as sole producer of social and political rationality. To put it another way, the WSF raises not only analytical and theoretical questions, but also epistemological questions. This much is expressed in the idea, widely shared by WSF participants, that there will be no global social justice without global cognitive justice. But the challenge posed by the WSF has one more dimension still. Beyond the theoretical, analytical and epistemological questions, it raises a new political issue: it aims to fulfil utopia in a world devoid of utopias. This utopian will is expressed in the slogan 'another world is possible'. At stake is less a utopian world than a world that allows for utopia. In this book, I deal with the WSF as critical utopia, epistemology of the South and expression of insurgent cosmopolitan politics.

8

Notes

1 For a better understanding of the political character and goals of the World Social Forum, see the Charter of Principles, available at <www.forumsocialmundial.org.br>.

2 One of the most paradigmatic examples is the poverty – conceptual hubris coupled with bloodless narrow positivism – of the mainstream US sociology of social movements (McAdam et al. 2001).

1 | The World Social Forum as critical utopia

Ernst Bloch says that 'utopias have their timetable' (1995: 479). The conceptions of and aspirations to a better life and society, ever present in human history, vary as to form and content according to time and space. They express the tendencies and latencies of a given epoch and a given society. They constitute an anticipatory consciousness that manifests itself by enlarging the signs or traces of emerging realities. It is therefore appropriate to ask: does the WSF have a utopian dimension? And, if so, what is its timetable?

The hegemonic conception of our age is that of a linear time (the idea of progress) that presents itself as a timeless linear space (the idea of globalization). Whatever is currently dominant in social and political terms is infinitely expansive, thereby encompassing all future possibilities. Total control over the current state of affairs is deemed to be possible by means of extremely efficient powers and knowledges. Herein lies the radical denial of alternatives to present-day reality. This is the context underlying the utopian dimension of the WSF, which consists in asserting the existence of alternatives to neo-liberal globalization. By 'utopia' I mean the exploration of new modes of human possibility and styles of will, and the use of the imagination to confront the apparent inevitability of whatever exists with something radically better that is worth fighting for, and to which humankind is fully entitled (Santos 1995: 479).

As Franz Hinkelammert says, we live in a time of conservative utopias whose utopian character resides in their radical denial of alternatives to present-day reality (2002). The possibility of alternatives is discredited precisely for being utopian, idealistic, unrealistic. All conservative utopias are sustained by a political logic based on one sole efficiency criterion that rapidly becomes a supreme ethical criterion. According to this criterion, only what is efficient has value. Any other ethical criterion is devalued as inefficient. Neo-liberalism is one such conservative utopia for which the sole criterion of efficiency is the market or the laws of the market. Its utopian character resides in the promise that its total fulfilment or application cancels out all utopias. According to Hinkelammert, 'this ideology derives from its frantic anti-utopianism,

Conservative - utopian - fulfilment of present ideals

the utopian promise of a new world. The basic thesis is: whoever destroys utopia, fulfils it' (ibid.: 278). What distinguishes conservative utopias from critical utopias is the fact that they identify themselves with the present-day reality and discover their utopian dimension in the radicalization or complete fulfilment of the present. Moreover, the problems or difficulties of present-day reality are not the consequence of the deficiencies or limits of the efficiency criteria, but result rather from the fact that the application of the efficiency criteria has not been thorough enough. If there is unemployment and social exclusion, if there is starvation and death in the periphery of the world system, that is not the consequence of the deficiencies or limits of the laws of the market; these result rather from the fact that such laws have not yet been fully applied. The horizon of conservative utopias is thus a closed horizon, an end to history.

This is the context in which the utopian dimension of the WSF must be understood. The WSF signifies the re-emergence of a critical utopia, that is to say the radical critique of present-day reality and the aspiration to a better society. This occurs, however, when the anti-utopian utopia of neo-liberalism is dominant. The specificity of the utopian content of this new critical utopia, when compared with that of the critical utopias prevailing at the end of the nineteenth and the beginning of the twentieth century, thus becomes clear. The anti-utopian utopia of neo-liberalism is grounded in two presuppositions: the illusion of total control over present-day reality by means of extremely efficient powers and knowledges; and the radical rejection of alternatives to the status quo. The WSF questions the totality of control (whether as knowledge or power) only to affirm credibly the possibility of alternatives. Hence the open nature of the alternatives. In a context in which the conservative utopia prevails absolutely, it is more important to affirm the possibility of alternatives than to define them. The utopian dimension of the WSF consists in affirming the possibility of a counter-hegemonic globalization. In other words, the utopia of the WSF asserts itself more as negativity (the definition of what it critiques) than as positivity (the definition of that to which it aspires).

The specificity of the WSF as critical utopia has one more dimension. The WSF is the first critical utopia of the twenty-first century and aims to break with the tradition of the critical utopias of Western modernity, many of which turned into conservative utopias: from claiming utopian alternatives to denying alternatives with the excuse that the fulfilment of utopia was under way. The openness of the utopian dimension of the WSF corresponds to the latter's attempt to escape this perversion. For

11

the WSF, the claim of alternatives is plural, both as to the form of the claim and the content of the alternatives. The affirmation of alternatives goes hand in hand with the affirmation that there are alternatives to the alternatives. The other possible world is a utopian aspiration that comprises several possible worlds. The other possible world may be many things, but never a world with no alternative.

The utopia of the WSF is a radically democratic utopia. It is the only realistic utopia after a century of conservative utopias, some of them the result of perverted critical utopias. This utopian design, grounded on the denial of the present rather than the definition of the future, focused on the processes of intercourse among the movements rather than an assessment of the movements' political content, is the major factor of cohesion of the WSF. It helps to maximize what unites and minimize what divides, celebrate intercourse rather than dispute power, be a strong presence rather than an agenda. This utopian design, which is also an ethical design, privileges the ethical discourse, quite evident in the WSF's Charter of Principles, aimed at gathering consensuses beyond the ideological and political cleavages among the movements and organizations that compose it. The movements and organizations parenthesize the cleavages that divide them, as much as is necessary to affirm the possibility of a counter-hegemonic globalization.

The nature of this utopia has been the most adequate for the initial objective of the WSF: to affirm the existence of a counter-hegemonic globalization. This is no vague utopia. It is rather a utopia that contains in itself the concretization that is adequate for this phase of the construction of counter-hegemonic globalization. It remains to be seen whether the nature of this utopia is the most adequate one to guide the next steps, should there be any next steps. Once the counter-hegemonic globalization is consolidated, and hence the idea that another world is possible is made credible, will it be possible to fulfil this idea with the same level of radical democracy that helped formulate it?

To answer this question, the articulation between the WSF's utopian dimension, the new constellations of knowledges it has made visible, and the political activism it has been giving rise to must be brought into the picture.

2 | The World Social Forum as epistemology of the South

Neo-liberal globalization is presided over by techno-scientific knowledge, and owes its hegemony to the credible way in which it discredits all rival knowledges, by suggesting that they are not comparable, in terms of efficiency and coherence, to the scientificity of the market laws. Since neo-liberal globalization is hegemonic, no wonder that it anchors itself in the knowledge, no less hegemonic, of Western-based modern science. This is why the practices and knowledges circulating in the WSF have their origin in very distinct epistemological assumptions (what counts as knowledge) and ontological assumptions (what it means to be human). Such diversity exists not only among the different movements but also within each one of them. The differences within the feminist movement, for instance, are not merely political. They are differences regarding what counts as relevant knowledge, differences about identifying, validating or hierarchizing the relations between Western-based scientific knowledge and other knowledges derived from other practices, rationalities or cultural universes. They are differences, ultimately, about what it means to be a human being, whether male or female. The practice of the WSF reveals that the epistemological diversity of the world is virtually infinite.

The counter-hegemonic globalization to which the WSF aspires thus immediately confronts the epistemological problem of the ability of that same scientific knowledge to advance the counter-hegemonic struggles. To be sure, many counter-hegemonic practices resort to the hegemonic scientific and technological knowledge, and many of them would not even be thinkable without it. This is true of the WSF itself, which would not exist without the new information and communication technologies. The question is to what extent such knowledge is useful and valid, and what other knowledges are available and usable beyond the limits of utility and validity of scientific knowledge. To approach these problems raises an additional epistemological problem, indeed a meta-epistemological problem: on the basis of which knowledge or epistemology are these problems to be formulated?

The core idea that dominates the epistemological questioning provoked by the WSF is that the knowledge we have of globalization, whether hegemonic or counter-hegemonic, is less global than global-ization itself. Scientific knowledge, however supposedly universal, is almost entirely produced in the countries of the developed Global North and, however presumably neutral, promotes the interests of these coun-tries and constitutes one of the productive forces of neo-liberal global-ization. Science is doubly at the service of hegemonic globalization, whether by virtue of the way in which it promotes and legitimizes it, or the way in which it discredits, conceals or trivializes counter-hegemonic globalization. Hegemony presupposes a constant policing and repress-ing of counter-hegemonic practices and agents. Discrediting, conceal-ing and trivializing counter-hegemonic globalization go largely hand in hand with discrediting, concealing and trivializing the knowledges that inform counter-hegemonic practices and agents. Faced with rival knowledges, hegemonic scientific knowledge either turns them into raw material (as is the case of indigenous or peasant knowledge about biodiversity) or rejects them on the basis of their falsity or inefficiency in the light of the hegemonic criteria of truth and efficiency.[1]

Confronted with this situation, the epistemological alternative pro-posed by the WSF is that there is no global social justice without global cognitive justice. This alternative is grounded in three basic ideas. First, the expansion of Western-based global capitalism was made possible and justified by the supposedly all-powerful and only valid form of rationality and knowledge, modern science. On this basis an immense variety of non-Western, non-scientific knowledges were destroyed, sup-pressed or marginalized and, with them, the peoples whose lives and practices were run according to such knowledges. This destruction of knowledge I call epistemicide, and more often than not it took place concomitantly with genocide. Acknowledging this fact amounts to recognizing that the understanding of the world by far exceeds the Western understanding of the world. Without establishing a more bal-anced (neither relativistic nor imperialist) relationship among rival knowledges, all the policies aimed at promoting social justice will end up furthering social injustice. Second, the objectivity of science does not imply neutrality; science and technology may just as well be put at the service of neo-liberal globalization as at the service of counter-hegemonic globalization. The extent to which science may be resorted to is in general arguable within the movements, and it may vary according to circumstances and practices. Third, whatever the extent to which science is resorted to, counter-hegemonic practices are mainly practices of non-scientific knowledges, practical, often tacit knowledges that must be made credible to render such practices credible in turn.

This third point is more polemical because it confronts the hegemonic concepts of truth and efficiency directly. The epistemological denunciation that the WSF engages in consists in showing that the concepts of rationality and efficiency presiding over hegemonic technical-scientific knowledge are too restrictive to capture the richness and diversity of the social experience of the world, and particularly that they discriminate against practices of resistance and production of counter-hegemonic alternatives. Hegemonic rationality and efficiency thus bring about a contraction of the world by concealing or discrediting all the practices, agents and knowledges that are not accounted for by their criteria. The concealment and discrediting of these practices constitute a waste of social experience, both social experience that is already available but not yet visible, and social experience not yet available but realistically possible.

The epistemological operation carried out by the WSF consists of two processes that I designate as a sociology of absences and a sociology of emergences (Santos 2004b). They are critical sociologies of a new kind built in opposition to hegemonic social sciences and upon alternative epistemological presuppositions. They aim at critically identifying the conditions that destroy non-hegemonic and potentially counter-hegemonic social experience. Through the sociology of absences and the sociology of emergences, social experience that resists destruction is unconcealed, and the space-time capable of identifying and rendering credible new counter-hegemonic social experiences is opened up.

The following description of the sociology of absences and the sociology of emergences represents the ideal type of the epistemological operation exemplified by the WSF. In real life, the practices and knowledges of the different movements and organizations, as well as of the global interactions among them, come more or less close to this ideal type.

The World Social Forum and the sociology of absences

The *sociology of absences* consists of an enquiry that aims to explain that what does not exist is in fact actively produced as non-existent, that is – as a non-credible alternative to what exists. Its empirical object is deemed impossible in the light of conventional social science, and for this reason its formulation already represents a break with it. The objective of the sociology of absences is to transform impossible into possible objects, absent into present objects, invisible or non-credible subjects into visible and credible subjects.

There is no single, univocal way of not existing. The logics and

processes through which hegemonic criteria of rationality and efficiency produce the non-existence of what does not fit them are various.
Non-existence is produced whenever a certain entity is disqualified
and rendered invisible, unintelligible or irreversibly discardable. What
unites the different logics of production of non-existence is that they
are all manifestations of the same rational monoculture. I distinguish
five logics or modes of production of non-existence.

The first derives from the monoculture of *knowledge* and *rigour of
knowledge*. It is the most powerful mode of production of non-existence.
It consists in turning modern science and high culture into the sole
criteria of truth and aesthetic quality, respectively. The complicity that
unites the 'two cultures' (the scientific and the humanistic culture)
resides in the fact that both claim to be, each in its own field, exclusive canons of production of knowledge or artistic creation. All that is
not recognized or legitimized by this canon is declared non-existent.
Non-existence appears in this case in the form of ignorance or lack
of culture.

The second logic resides in the *monoculture of linear time*, the idea
that history has a unique and well-known meaning and direction. This
meaning and direction have been formulated in different ways for
the last two hundred years: progress, modernization, development.
Common to all these formulations is the idea that time is linear and
that ahead of time the core countries of the world system proceed and,
along with them, the dominant knowledges, institutions and forms of
sociability. This logic produces non-existence by describing as back-
ward (pre-modern, underdeveloped, etc.) whatever is asymmetrical
vis-à-vis whatever is declared forward. It is according to this logic that
Western modernity produces the non-contemporaneity of the contemporaneous, and that the idea of simultaneity conceals the asymmetries
of the historical times that converge into it. The encounter between
the African peasant and the officer of the World Bank on his field trip
illustrates this condition. In this case, non-existence assumes the form
of residuum, which in turn has assumed many designations for the
past two hundred years, the first being the primitive or savage, closely
followed by the traditional, the pre-modern, the simple, the obsolete,
the underdeveloped.

The third logic is the logic of social classification, based on the
monoculture of *naturalization of differences*. It consists in distribut-
ing populations according to categories that naturalize hierarchies.
Racial and sexual classifications are the most salient manifestations
of this logic. Contrary to what happens in the relation between capital

16

and labour, social classification is based on attributes that negate the intentionality of social hierarchy. The relation of domination is the consequence, rather than the cause, of this hierarchy, and it may even be considered as an obligation of whoever is classified as superior (for example, 'the white man's burden' in his civilizing mission). Although the two forms of classification (race and sex) are decisive for the relation between capital and labour to stabilize and spread globally, racial classification has been the one most deeply reconstructed by capitalism.[2] According to this logic, non-existence is produced as a form of inferiority, insuperable inferiority because natural. The inferior, because insuperably inferior, cannot be a credible alternative to the superior.

The fourth logic of production of non-existence is the logic of the dominant scale: the *monoculture of the universal and of the global*. According to this logic, the scale adopted as primordial determines the irrelevance of all other possible scales. In Western modernity, the dominant scale appears under two different forms: the universal and the global. Universalism is the scale of the entities or realities that prevail regardless of specific contexts. For that reason, they take precedence over all other realities that depend on contexts and are therefore considered particular or vernacular. Globalization is the scale that in the last twenty years has acquired unprecedented relevance in various social fields. It is the scale that privileges entities or realities that widen their scope to the whole globe, thus earning the prerogative to designate rival entities as local. According to this logic, non-existence is produced under the form of the particular and the local. The entities or realities defined as particular or local are captured in scales that render them incapable of being credible alternatives to what exists globally and universally.[3]

Finally, the fifth logic of non-existence is the logic of productivity. It resides in the *monoculture of the criteria of capitalist productivity and efficiency*, which privileges growth through market forces. These criteria apply both to nature and to human labour. Productive nature is nature at its maximum fertility in a given production cycle, whereas productive labour is labour that maximizes generating profit likewise in a given production cycle. In its extreme version of conservative utopia neo-liberalism aims to convert labour into a productive force among others, subject to the laws of the market, like any other productive force. It has been doing this by transforming labour into a global resource while at the same time preventing at any cost the emergence of a global labour market (via immigration laws, violation of labour standards, union busting, etc.). According to the logic of capitalist productivity, non-existence is produced in the form of non-productiveness. Applied to nature, non-productiveness is sterility; applied to labour, 'discardable populations', laziness, professional disqualification, lack of skills.

There are thus five principal social forms of non-existence produced by hegemonic epistemology and rationality: the ignorant, the residual, the inferior, the local and the non-productive. They are social forms of non-existence because the realities to which they give shape are present only as obstacles vis-à-vis the realities deemed relevant, be they scientific, advanced, superior, global or productive realities. They are, therefore, disqualified parts of homogeneous totalities, which, as such, merely confirm what exists, and precisely as it exists. They are what exists under irretrievably disqualified forms of existing.

The social production of these absences results in the waste of social experience. The sociology of absences aims to identify the scope of this waste so that the experiences produced as absent may be liberated from those relations of production and thereby made present. To be made present means to be considered alternatives to hegemonic experience, to have their credibility discussed and argued for and their relations taken as an object of political dispute. The sociology of absences aims thus to create a want and turn the supposed lack of social experience into a waste of social experience. It therefore creates the conditions to enlarge the field of credible experiences in this world and time. The enlargement of the world occurs not only because the field of credible experiences is widened but also because the possibilities of social experimentation in the future are increased.

The sociology of absences proceeds by confronting each one of the modes of production of absence mentioned above. Because the latter have been shaped by conventional social science, the sociology of absences cannot but be transgressive, and as such is bound to be discredited. Nonconformity with such discredit and struggle for credibility, however, make it possible for the sociology of absences not to remain an absent sociology. Indeed, nonconformity and struggle for credibility are embedded in the practices of transgressive freedom – both practices of transformative action and practices of transformative knowledge – adopted by the organizations and social movements involved in the WSF. The sociology of absences works by replacing monocultures by ecologies.[4] I therefore identify five ecologies.

The ecology of knowledges. The first logic, the logic of the monoculture of scientific knowledge and rigour, must be confronted with the identification of other knowledges and criteria of rigour that operate credibly in social practices. Such contextual credibility must be deemed a sufficient condition for the knowledge in question to have enough legitimacy to participate in epistemological debates with other knowledges, namely with scientific knowledge. The central idea of the sociology of absences in this regard is that there is no ignorance or knowledge in general. All ignorance is ignorant of a certain knowledge, and all knowledge is the overcoming of a particular ignorance (Santos 1995: 25). Learning certain forms of knowledge may involve forgetting others and, in the last instance, becoming ignorant of them. In other words, in the ecology of knowledges, ignorance is not necessarily the original state or starting point. It may be the result of forgetting or unlearning implicit in the reciprocal learning through which interdependence is achieved. Thus at each phase in the ecology of knowledges it is crucial to question whether what is being learned is valuable or whether it should be forgotten or unlearned. Ignorance is only an unqualified form of being and doing when what is being learned is more valuable than what is being forgotten. The utopia of inter-knowledge is learning other knowledges without forgetting one's own. This is the idea of prudence that underlies the ecology of knowledges.

The ecology of knowledges begins with the assumption that all relationship practices between human beings and also between human beings and nature involve more than one form of knowledge and, therefore, of ignorance. Epistemologically, modern capitalist society is characterized by the fact that it favours practices in which scientific knowledge predominates. This means that only ignorance of it is truly disqualifying. This privileged status granted to scientific practices means that the interventions in human and natural reality that they afford are also favoured. Any crises or catastrophes that may result from these practices are socially acceptable and seen as inevitable social costs that may be overcome through new scientific practices.

As scientific knowledge is not socially distributed in an equitable manner, the real-world interventions it favours tend to be those that cater to the social groups that have access to scientific knowledge. Social injustice is based on cognitive injustice. The struggle for cognitive justice will not be successful, however, if it is based solely on the idea of a more equal distribution of scientific knowledge. Apart from the fact that this form of distribution is impossible under the conditions of global capitalism, this knowledge has intrinsic limits in relation to the types of real-world intervention that can be achieved. These limits are the result of scientific ignorance and an inability to recognize alternative forms of knowledge and interconnect with them on equal terms. In the ecology of knowledges, forging credibility for non-scientific knowledge does not involve discrediting scientific knowledge. It simply involves its counter-hegemonic use. It consists, on the one hand, of exploring alternative scientific practices that have been made visible through the plural epistemologies of scientific practices and, on the other hand, by promoting interdependence among scientific and non-scientific knowledges.

This principle of incompleteness of all knowledges is the condition of the possibility of epistemological dialogue and debate among the different knowledges. What each knowledge contributes to such a dialogue is the way in which it leads a certain practice to overcome a certain ignorance. Confrontation and dialogue among knowledges are confrontation and dialogue among the different processes through which practices that are ignorant in different ways turn into practices that are knowledgeable in different ways. All knowledges have internal and external limits. The internal limits relate to the restrictions on the real-world interventions that they allow. The external limits result from the recognition of alternative interventions made possible by other forms of knowledge. Hegemonic forms of knowledge understand only internal limits. The counter-hegemonic use of modern science constitutes a parallel exploration of both internal and external limits. This is why the counter-hegemonic use of science cannot be restricted to science alone. It makes sense only within an ecology of knowledges.

The ecology of knowledges permits one not only to overcome the monoculture of scientific knowledge but also the idea that the non-scientific knowledges are alternatives to scientific knowledge. The idea of alternatives presupposes the idea of normalcy, and the latter the idea of norm, and so, nothing being further specified, the designation of something as an alternative carries a latent connotation of subsidiarity. If we take biomedicine and African traditional medicine as an example, it makes no sense to consider the latter, by far the predominant one in Africa, as an alternative to the former. The important thing is to identify the contexts and the practices in which each operates, and the way they conceive of health and sickness and overcome ignorance (as undiagnosed illness) in applied knowledge (as cure).

Ecology of knowledges does not imply acceptance of relativism. On the contrary, from the point of view of a pragmatics of social emancipation, relativism, as absence of criteria that establish hierarchies among knowledges, is an untenable position, because it renders impossible any relation between knowledge and the objectives of social transformation. If anything is of equal value as knowledge, all projects of social transformation are equally valid or, which means the same, equally invalid. The ecology of knowledges aims to create a new sort of relationship between scientific knowledge and other kinds of knowledge. It consists in granting 'equality of opportunities' to the different kinds of knowledge engaged in ever broader epistemological disputes aimed at maximizing their respective contributions to building 'another possible world', that is to say a more democratic and just society, as well as a more balanced society vis-à-vis nature. The point is not to ascribe equal validity to all kinds of knowledge, but rather to allow for a pragmatic discussion of alternative criteria of validity, which does not immediately disqualify whatever does not fit the epistemological canon of modern science.

The ecology of knowledges focuses on concrete relationships between knowledges and on the hierarchies and powers that are generated between them. The aim of creating horizontal relationships is not incompatible with the concrete hierarchies that exist within the context of concrete social practices. Indeed, no concrete practice would be possible without these hierarchies. What the ecology of knowledges challenges is the universal and abstract hierarchies and powers that have been naturalized by history and reductionist epistemologies. Concrete hierarchies must emerge on the basis of valuing a particular real-world intervention in confrontation with other alternative interventions. Complementarity or contradictions may exist between the different types of intervention and, in every case, the debate between them is governed by both cognitive judgements and ethical and political judgements. The prevalence of cognitive judgements in the construction of any given knowledge practice is therefore derivative, that is to say derived from a previous context of decisions on the production of reality in which political and ethical judgements predominate. The objectivity that presides over the cognitive phase does not clash with the non-neutrality that presides over the ethical-political phase.

The basic impetus behind the emergence of the ecology of knowledges, as the epistemological form of the WSF, lies in the fact that the Forum, while giving voice to the global resistance against global capitalism, has made visible the social and cultural realities of societies on the periphery of the world system where the belief in modern science is more tenuous, where the links between modern science and the designs of colonial and imperial domination are more visible, and where other non-scientific and non-Western forms of knowledge prevail in resistance practices.

The ecology of temporalities. The second logic, the logic of the monoculture of linear time, is confronted with the idea that linear time is
only one among many conceptions of time and that, if we take the world
as our unit of analysis, it is not even the most commonly adopted. The
predominance of linear time is not the result of its primacy as a temporal conception, but the result of the primacy of Western modernity
which embraced it as its own. Linear time was adopted by Western
modernity through the secularization of Judaeo-Christian eschatology,
but it never erased, not even in the West, other conceptions of time
such as circular time, cyclical time, glacial time, the doctrine of the
eternal return, and still others that are not adequately grasped by the
images of the arrow of time. This is the case of the temporal palimpsest
of the present, the idea that the subjectivity or identity of a person or
social group is a constellation of different times and temporalities,
some modern, some non-modern, some ancient, some recent, which
are activated differently in different contexts or situations. More than
any other, the indigenous peoples' movements bear witness to such
constellations of time.

Moreover, different cultures and the social practices they ground
have different rules of social time, different temporal codes: the
relationship between past, present and future; how to define early and
late, short-term and long-term, life cycle, urgency; accepted rhythms,
sequences, synchronies and diachronies, tempos, paces of life. Different cultures thus create different communities of time: some control
time, others live within time; some are monochronic, others poli-
chronic; some focus on time needed to carry out activities, others on
activities to fill the time; some privilege clock time, others event time,
subscribing thus to different conceptions of punctuality; some value
continuity, others discontinuity; for some time is reversible, for others
irreversible; some see themselves evolving in linear progression, others
in non-linear progression. The silent language of cultures is above all
a time language.

The need to take into account these different conceptions of time
derives from the fact, pointed out by Koselleck (1985) and Marramao
(1985), that societies understand power according to the conceptions
of temporality they hold. The most resistant relations of domination
are those based on hierarchies among temporalities. Domination takes
place by reducing dominated, hostile or undesirable social experience
to the condition of residuum. Experiences become residual because
they are contemporary in ways that are not recognizable by the dominant temporality. They are disqualified, suppressed or rendered unintel-

ligible because they are ruled by temporalities that are not contained in the temporal canon of Western capitalist modernity.

In this domain, the sociology of absences starts from the idea that different cultures generate different temporal rules and that societies are constituted of various times and temporalities. It aims to free social practices from their status as residuum, devolving to them their own temporality and thus the possibility of autonomous development. Once these temporalities are recuperated and become known, the practices and sociabilities ruled by them become intelligible and credible objects of argumentation and political debate. For instance, once liberated from linear time and devolved to its own temporality, the activity of the African or Asian peasant stops being residual and becomes contemporaneous with the activity of the high-tech farmer in the USA or the activity of the World Bank executive. By the same token, the presence or relevance of the ancestors in one's life in different cultures ceases to be an anachronistic manifestation of primitive religion or magic to become another way of experiencing contemporaneity.

The time diversity of the movements and organizations participating in the WSF is inviting the development of a new kind of time literacy, which I would call multitemporality. Building coalitions and organizing collective actions across different time rules is no easy task. As I will show later on, some of the debates and cleavages within the WSF derive from unacknowledged differences as to social time conceptions and rules. Movements and organizations embedded in clock time, monochronocity, discontinuity, time as a controlled resource and linear progression have difficulties in understanding the political and organizational behaviour of movements embedded in event time, polichronocity, continuity, time as controlling, non-linear progression and vice versa. Only by learning from each other and thus through multitemporal literacy will such difficulties be overcome.

The ecology of recognitions. The third logic of production of absences is the logic of social classification. Although in all logics of production of absence the disqualification of practices goes hand in hand with the disqualification of agents, it is here that the disqualification affects mainly the agents, and only subsequently the social experience of which they are the protagonists. The coloniality of Western modern capitalist power mentioned by Quijano (2000) consists in collapsing difference and inequality, while claiming the privilege to ascertain who is equal or different. The same can be said of the unequal sexuality of modern capitalist power. The sociology of absences confronts coloniality and un-

23

equal sexuality by looking for a new articulation between the principles
of equality and difference, thus allowing for the possibility of equal differences – an ecology of differences comprised of mutual recognition. It
does so by submitting hierarchy to critical ethnography (Santos 2001a).
This consists in deconstructing both difference (to what extent is difference a product of hierarchy?) and hierarchy (to what extent is hierarchy
a product of difference?). The differences that remain when hierarchy
vanishes become a powerful denunciation of the differences that hierarchy reclaims in order not to vanish. The feminist, the indigenous
and the Afro-descendants movements have been in the forefront of the
struggle for an ecology of recognitions.

The ecology of recognitions has become a structural innovation of
the WSF owing to the social and cultural diversity of the collective subjects that participate in it, the different forms of oppression and domination they fight against and the multiplicity of scales (local, national
and transnational) of the struggles they engage in. This diversity has
given a new visibility to the processes that characterize the differentiated and unequal dynamics of global capitalism and the ways in which
they generate different types of contradictions and struggles, not all of
which may be simply integrated into or subordinated to class struggle,
and which do not necessarily take the nation as their privileged arena.
More than that, it has shown that the Eurocentric assumptions about
world history, development and emancipation do not allow for a sufficiently wide-ranging circle of reciprocity capable of capturing the new
called-for balance between the principle of equality and the principle of
recognition of difference. On the basis of such assumptions the 'political' has been defined according to a narrow principle of superordination
which condemns many forms of sociability, contradiction, opposition,
resistance or struggle to the past or to marginality. It obscures, for example, the fact that during the process of creating capitalist relations
of production in the colonies it was not only class relations which were
reproduced but also hierarchical relationships that involved regions,
cultures, languages, sexes and, above all, races.

Feminist, post-colonial, peasant, indigenous peoples', ecological,
and gay and lesbian struggles have brought into the picture a wide
rage of temporalities and subjectivities and have converted non-liberal
conceptions of culture into an indispensable resource for new modes
of resisting, formulating alternatives and creating insurgent public
spheres. In their struggles, the 'cultural' incorporates and shapes
alternative rationalities, without constituting a differentiated sphere
of social life, as in the liberal conception. The recognition of cultural

24

difference, collective identity, autonomy or self-determination has given rise to new forms of struggle (for equal access to existing rights or resources; for the recognition of collective rights; the defence and promotion of alternative local or traditional normative frameworks, of communal forms of producing livelihoods or resolving conflicts, etc.). As a result, the idea of individual or collective multicultural citizenship acquires a more exact meaning as the privileged site of struggles for the mutual articulation and activation of recognition and redistribution.

By widening the circle of reciprocity – the circle of equal differences – the ecology of recognitions creates new demands for mutual intelligibility. The multidimensionality of forms of domination and oppression gives rise to forms of resistance and struggle that mobilize different, and not always mutually intelligible, collective actors, vocabularies and resources, and this can place serious limitations on attempts to redefine the political arena. To address the issue of mutual intelligibility, I see emerging in the WSF inter-knowledge exercises which I call procedures of mutual translation, and which I will deal with in Chapter 7. Unlike any general theory of emancipatory action, the procedure of translation maintains intact the autonomy of the different collective subjects and their struggles, since only that which is different can be translated. Making things mutually intelligible means identifying what unites and what is common to entities that are separated by differences. The procedure of translation allows common ground to be identified in an indigenous, a feminist and an ecological struggle, etc., without effacing the autonomy and difference that sustain each one of them. Autonomy and difference presuppose that the movements condition their mobilization on having their own reasons to mobilize. That is why the procedure of translation is also fundamental in order to link the diverse and specific intellectual and cognitive resources that are expressed through the various modes of producing knowledge about counter-hegemonic initiatives and experiences.

The ecology of trans-scales. The sociology of absences confronts the fourth logic, the logic of abstract universalism and global scale, by recuperating both hidden universal aspirations and alternative local/global scales that are not the result of hegemonic globalization. Viewed from the Global South, universalism is the expression of an apparent convergence or reconvergence of the world under the aegis of neo-liberal globalization. It is, therefore, a false universalism. It comprises the following general and abstract principles: free market, democracy, rule of law, individualism and human rights. Their abstraction and generality are of a new type. Rather than being decontextualized or disembedded, these principles are conceived of as being globally embedded, providing the global criteria for the evaluation of the particularities of the world. The convergence of universalism with globalization is thus both the cause and the consequence of the convergence of the world.

The sociology of absences operates here by showing that the world, rather than converging or reconverging, is diverging or rediverging. While uncovering an alternative globalization – the counter-hegemonic globalization, of which the WSF is an embryonic manifestation – the sociology of absences shows that the new universalism is both excessive and fraudulent. Two main absences are thereby made present. The first one relates to the fact that there are alternative universal aspirations, all of them expressed in the WSF: social justice, dignity, mutual respect, solidarity, community, cosmic harmony of nature and society, spirituality, etc. In our world, universalism exists only as a plurality of partial and competitive universal aspirations, all of them embedded in particular contexts. Recognizing the relativity of such aspirations does not involve relativism; it simply broadens the 'conversation of humankind' called for by John Dewey (1960) by both lending credibility to and expanding the scope of localized clashes among alternative universal or global aspirations. Henceforth another absence is made present: there is no globalization without localization, and as there are alternative globalizations there are also alternative localizations.

The local that has been integrated in (and indeed created by) hegemonic globalization is what I designate as localized globalism – that is, the specific impact of hegemonic globalization on the local (Santos 2000: 179).[5] The disempowerment of the local – its being reduced to the expression of an impact – derives from its imprisonment in a scale that prevents it from moving beyond impact and aspiring to globalize itself. The sociology of absences operates here by deglobalizing the local vis-à-vis hegemonic globalization – by identifying what is there in the local which is not reducible to the effect of the impact – and by exploring the possibility of reglobalizing it as a counter-hegemonic globalization. This is done by identifying other local formations in which the same oppositional globalizing aspiration can be detected, and by proposing credible linkages among them. Through such linkages the different local formations delink themselves from the inert series of global impacts and relink themselves as sites of resistance and generation of alternative globalization. This inter-scale movement is what I call the ecology of the trans-scales. In this domain, the sociology of absences amounts to an exercise of cartographic imagination, whether to see in each scale of representation not only what it reveals but also what it conceals, or to deal with cognitive maps that operate simultaneously with different scales, namely to identify local/global articulations (Santos 1995: 456–73; Santos 2001b). Most movements involved in the WSF started as local struggles fighting against the social exclusion brought about or intensified by neo-liberal globalization. Only later, often via the WSF, have they developed local/global linkages through which they reglobalize themselves in a counter-hegemonic way.

The ecology of productivities. Finally, in the domain of the fifth logic, the monoculture of capitalist productivity, the sociology of absences consists in recuperating and valorizing alternative systems of production, popular economic organizations, workers' cooperatives, self-managed enterprises, solidary production, etc., which have been hidden or discredited by the capitalist orthodoxy of productivity. Peasant movements for access to land and land tenure or against mega-development projects, urban movements for housing rights, popular economy movements, indigenous movements to defend or to regain historical territories and the natural resources found in them, low-caste movements in India to protect land and local forests, ecological sustainability movements, movements against the privatization of water or against the privatization of social welfare services – all these movements base their claims and their struggles on the ecology of productivities.

This is perhaps the most controversial domain of the sociology of absences, for it confronts directly both the paradigm of development and infinite economic growth and the logic of the primacy of the objectives of accumulation (over the objectives of social justice and sustainability) characteristic of global capitalism. Invisibility or disqualification of alternative sociabilities and logics of production is here most likely. All the more so as they bear no resemblance to the seemingly only credible alternatives to capitalism experimented with throughout most of the twentieth century, that is the centralized socialist economies.

The scale of these initiatives is as varied as the initiatives themselves. The alternatives range from micro-initiatives undertaken by marginalized sectors in the Global South, seeking to gain control of their lives and livelihoods, to proposals for national and international economic and legal coordination designed to guarantee respect for basic labour and environmental standards worldwide, novel forms of capital controls, revamped systems of progressive taxation and spending, and expansion of social programmes, as well as attempts to build regional economies based on the principles of cooperation and solidarity.

27

These alternative conceptions and practices of production and productivity share two key traits. First, rather than embodying comprehensive blueprints or system-wide alternative economic agendas, they entail in most cases efforts by local communities and workers, often in tandem with transnational advocacy networks and coalitions, to carve out niches of solidary production and political mobilization within the context of global capitalism. They seek to open up spaces for further transformations of capitalist values and socio-economic arrangements. They are not nearly as grandiose as centralized socialism. Also, their underlying theories are less ambitious than the firm, classic Marxist belief in the historical inevitability of socialism. In fact, the very feasibility of these alternatives, at least in the short and medium term, depends to a great extent on their ability to survive in a capitalist context. Aware of such context, their aim is to facilitate the acceptance of alternative forms of economic organization and lend greater credibility to them. Second, their broad notion of the economy includes such key goals as democratic participation; environmental sustainability; social, gender, racial and ethnic equity; and transnational solidarity.

In this domain, the sociology of absences broadens the spectrum of social reality through experimentation in and reflection on real economic alternatives for building a more just society. By embodying organizational values and forms that are opposed to those of global capitalism, the economic alternatives extend the principle of citizenship beyond the narrowly defined political realm, thus keeping alive the promise of eliminating the current separation between political democracy and economic despotism.

In each of the five domains, the objective of the sociology of absences is to disclose and to give credit to the diversity and multiplicity of social practices and confer credit on them in opposition to the exclusive credibility of hegemonic practices. The idea of multiplicity and non-destructive relations is suggested by the concept of ecology: ecology of knowledges, ecology of temporalities, ecology of recognitions, ecology of trans-scales and ecology of productivities. Common to all these ecologies is the idea that reality cannot be reduced to what exists. It amounts to an ample version of realism that includes the realities rendered absent by silence, suppression and marginalization. In a word, realities that are actively produced as non-existent.

In conclusion, the exercise of the sociology of absences is counterfactual and takes place by confronting conventional scientific common sense. To be carried out it demands both epistemological imagination and democratic imagination. Epistemological imagination allows for the recognition of different knowledges, perspectives and scales of identification, analysis and evaluation of practices. Democratic imagination allows for the recognition of different practices and social agents. Both the epistemological and the democratic imagination have a deconstructive and a reconstructive dimension. Deconstruction assumes five forms, corresponding to the critique of the five logics of hegemonic rationality, namely un-thinking, de-residualizing, de-racializing, de-localizing and de-producing. Reconstruction comprises the five ecologies mentioned above.

The WSF is a broad exercise in the sociology of absences. As I have pointed out, it is internally unequal as to its closeness to the ideal type. If it is in general unequivocally noticeable as a refusal of monocultures and an adoption of ecologies, this process is not present with the same intensity in all movements, organizations and articulations. If for some movements opting for ecologies is unconditional, for others hybridity between monocultures and ecologies is permissible. It is often the case, as well, that some movements or organizations act, in some domains, according to a monocultural logic and, in others, according to an ecological logic. It is also possible that the adoption of an ecological logic is decharacterized by the factionalism and power struggle inside one movement or organization, and that it turns into a new monocultural logic. Finally, I offer as a hypothesis the idea that even the movements that claim different ecologies are vulnerable to the temptation of evaluating themselves according to an ecological logic, while evaluating the other movements according to a hegemonic monocultural logic.

The World Social Forum and the sociology of emergences

The sociology of emergences is the second epistemological operation conducted by the WSF. Whereas the goal of the sociology of absences is to identify and valorize social experiences available in the world, although declared non-existent by hegemonic rationality and knowledge, the sociology of emergences aims to identify and enlarge the signs of possible future experiences, under the guise of tendencies and latencies that are actively ignored by hegemonic rationality and knowledge.

Drawing attention to emergences is by nature more speculative and requires some philosophical elaboration. The deep meaning of emergence can be observed in the most different cultural and philosophical traditions. As far as Western modernity is concerned, however, it happens only in its margins, as, for example, in the philosophy of Ernst Bloch. Bloch takes issue with the fact that Western philosophy has been dominated by the concepts of All (*Alles*) and Nothing (*Nichts*), in which everything seems to be contained in latency, but whence nothing new can emerge. Western philosophy is therefore a static philosophy. For Bloch, the possible is the most uncertain and the most ignored concept in Western philosophy (1995: 241). Yet only the possible permits revelation of the inexhaustible wealth of the world. Besides All and Nothing, Bloch introduces two new concepts: Not (*Nicht*) and Not Yet (*Noch Nicht*). The Not is the lack of something and the expression of the will to surmount that lack. The Not is thus distinguished from the Nothing (ibid.: 306). To say No is to say yes to something different. In my view, the concept that rules the sociology of emergences is the concept of Not Yet. The Not Yet is the more complex category because it expresses what exists as mere tendency, a movement that is latent in the very process of manifesting itself. The Not Yet is the way in which the future is inscribed in the present. It is not an indeterminate or infinite future, rather a concrete possibility and a capacity that neither exist in a vacuum nor are completely predetermined. Indeed, they actively redetermine all they touch, thus questioning the determinations that exist at a given moment. Subjectively, the Not Yet is anticipatory consciousness, a form of consciousness that, although extremely important in people's lives, was completely neglected by Freud (ibid.: 286–315). The Not Yet is, on the one hand, capacity (potency) and, on the other, possibility (potentiality). Possibility has a dimension of darkness as it originates in the lived moment, which is never fully visible to itself, as well as a component of uncertainty that derives from a double want: 1) the fact that the conditions that render possibility concrete are only partially known; 2) the fact that such conditions only exist partially. For Bloch, it is crucial to distinguish between these two wants: it is possible to know relatively well conditions that exist only very partially and, vice versa, it is possible that such conditions are widely present but are not recognized as such by available knowledge.

The Not Yet inscribes in the present a possibility that is uncertain, but never neutral; it could be the possibility of utopia or salvation (*Heil*) or the possibility of catastrophe or damnation (*Unheil*). Such uncertainty brings an element of chance, or danger, to every change. At every moment, there is a limited horizon of possibilities, and that is why it is important not to waste the unique opportunity of a specific change offered by the present: *carpe diem* (seize the day). Considering the three modal categories of existence – reality, necessity and possibility – hegemonic rationality and knowledge focus on the first two and neglect the third entirely. The sociology of emergences focuses

Care

on possibility. As Bloch says, 'to be human is to have a lot ahead of you' (ibid.: 246). Possibility is the world's engine. Its moments are: *want* (the manifestation of something lacking), *tendency* (process and meaning) and *latency* (what goes ahead in the process). Want is the realm of the Not, tendency the realm of the Not Yet, and latency the realm of the Nothing and the All, for latency can end up either in frustration or hope.

The sociology of emergences is the enquiry into the alternatives that are contained in the horizon of concrete possibilities. It consists in undertaking a symbolic enlargement of knowledges, practices and agents in order to identify therein the tendencies of the future (the Not Yet) in which it is possible to intervene so as to maximize the probability of hope vis-à-vis the probability of frustration. Such symbolic enlargement is actually a form of sociological imagination with a double aim: on the one hand, to know better the conditions of the possibility of hope; on the other, to define principles of action that favour the fulfilment of those conditions.

The sociology of emergences acts both on possibilities (potentiality) and on capacities (potency). The Not Yet has meaning (as possibility), but no predetermined direction, for it can end either in hope or disaster. Therefore, the sociology of emergences replaces the idea of determination by the idea of care. The axiology of progress and development, which have justified untold destruction, is thus replaced by the axiology of care. Whereas in the sociology of absences the axiology of care is exerted vis-à-vis alternatives available in the present, in the sociology of emergences the axiology of care is exerted vis-à-vis possible future alternatives. Because of this ethical dimension, neither the sociology of absences nor the sociology of emergences is a conventional sociology. But they are not conventional for another reason: their objectivity depends upon the quality of their subjective dimension. The subjective element of the sociology of absences is cosmopolitan consciousness and nonconformism before the waste of experience. The subjective element of the sociology of emergences is anticipatory consciousness and nonconformism before a want whose fulfilment is within the horizon of possibilities. As Bloch says, the fundamental concepts are not reachable without a theory of the emotions (ibid.: 306). The Not, the Nothing and the All shed light on such basic emotions as hunger or want, despair or annihilation, trust or redemption. One way or another, these emotions are present in the nonconformism that moves both the sociology of absences and the sociology of emergences.

Whereas the sociology of absences acts in the field of social

Epistemology of the South

31

experiences, the sociology of emergences acts in the field of social expectations. The discrepancy between experiences and expectations is constitutive of Western modernity and has been imposed upon other cultures. Through the concept of progress, this discrepancy has been so polarized that any effective linkage between experiences and expectations disappeared: no matter how wretched current experiences may be, they do not preclude the illusion of exhilarating expectations. The sociology of emergences conceives of the discrepancy between experiences and expectations without resorting to the idea of progress, seeing it rather as concrete and measured. The issue is not to minimize expectations, but rather to radicalize the expectations based on real possibilities and capacities, here and now.

Western-based expectations have been grandiose in the abstract, falsely infinite and universal. As such they have justified death, destruction and disaster in the name of redemption ever to come. With the crisis of the concept of progress, the future stopped being automatically prospective and axiological. The concepts of modernization and development diluted those characteristics almost completely. What is today known as globalization consummates the replacement of the prospective and axiological by the accelerated and entropic. Thus, direction turns into rhythm without meaning, and if there is a final stage, it cannot but be disaster. Against this nihilism, which is as empty as the triumphalism of hegemonic forces, the sociology of emergences offers a new semantics of expectations. The expectations legitimized by the sociology of emergences are both contextual, because gauged by concrete possibilities, and radical, because, in the ambit of those possibilities and capacities, they claim a strong fulfilment that protects them, though never completely, from frustration. In such expectations resides the reinvention of social emancipation, or rather emancipations.

The symbolic enlargement brought about by the sociology of emergences consists in identifying signals, clues or traces of future possibilities in whatever exists. Hegemonic rationality and science have totally dismissed this kind of enquiry, because they assume that either the future is predetermined, or that it can only be identified by precise indicators. For them, clues are too vague, subjective and chaotic to be credible predictors. By focusing intensely on the clue side of reality, the sociology of emergences aims to enlarge symbolically the possibilities of the future that lie, in latent form, in concrete social experiences.

The notion of *clue*, understood as something that announces what is to come next, is essential in various practices, both human and animal. For example, it is well known how animals announce when they are "clues" (not a good term)

ready for reproductive activity by means of visual, auditory, and olfactory clues. The preciseness and detail of such clues are remarkable. In medicine, criminal investigation and drama, clues are crucial to decide on future action, be it diagnosis and prescription, identification of suspects or development of the plot. In the social sciences, however, clues have no credibility. On the contrary, the sociology of emergences valorizes clues as pathways towards discussing and arguing for concrete alternative futures. Whereas animals' clues carry highly codified information, in society clues are more open and can therefore be fields of argumentation and negotiation about the future. The care of the future exerts itself in such argumentation and negotiation.

As in the case of the sociology of absences, the practices of the WSF also come more or less close to the ideal type of the sociology of emergences. The stronger and more consolidated movements and organizations tend to engage less in the sociology of emergences than the less strong or consolidated. As regards the relations between movements or organizations, the signs and clues given by the less consolidated movements may be devalued as subjective or inconsistent by the more consolidated movements. In this as well, the practice of the sociology of emergences is unequal, and inequalities must be the object of analysis and evaluation.

Notes

1 On this subject, see also Santos (1995, 2000, 2004b).

2 See Wallerstein and Balibar (1991), Quijano (2000) and Mignolo (2000). Quijano considers the racialization of power relations as an intrinsic feature of capitalism, a feature that he designates as the 'coloniality of power' (2000: 374).

3 On the negative dialectics of the global and the local, see Santos (2002b: 163–87).

4 By ecology I mean the practice of assembling diversity by way of identifying and promoting sustainable interactions among heterogeneous partial entities.

5 The global and the local are thus both produced by the processes of globalization. These are sets of unequal exchanges in which a certain artefact, condition, entity or local identity extends its influence beyond its local or national borders and, in so doing, develops an ability to designate as local rival artefacts, conditions, entities or identities. Although these unequal exchanges are played out in many different ways I have distinguished elsewhere four main ones which I have designated as modes of production of globalization: globalized localisms, localized globalisms, subordinate cosmopolitanism and common heritage of humankind (Santos 2002b: 177–82). The first two modes of production are the double face of hegemonic globalization with

core countries specializing in globalized localisms and peripheral countries being forced to specialize in localized globalisms. From the perspective of hegemonic globalization, the world system is a mesh of localized globalisms and globalized localisms. The other two modes of production of globalization refer to the globalization of resistance against globalized localisms and localized globalisms. They are the counter-hegemonic globalization.

3 | The World Social Forum as an insurgent cosmopolitan politics

The novelty of the WSF is more unequivocal at the utopian and epistemological level than at the political level. Its political novelty does exist, but it exists as a field of tensions and dilemmas, where the new and the old confront each other. The political novelty of the WSF resides in the way in which these confrontations have been handled, avoided and negotiated. This will be made clear in the following chapters as I deal with the issues of organization and representation. In this brief chapter I will lay out the broad political orientations that account for the novelty of the WSF. As I will show later on, they are not understood in the same way by all the movements and organizations involved in the WSF process, and their concrete implementation is often a source of tension. None the less, they constitute the general political framework within which conflicts are fought out and solved or put away.

Before I deal with this topic, I will state more clearly what I mean by the WSF. The broad definition presented in the Introduction is adequate to capture the general outlook of the utopian and epistemological dimensions of the WSF, but it is too general to capture the more specific political processes identified with the WSF. Since the latter are my analytical interest in this chapter, I move to a narrower definition. The WSF is the set of forums – world, thematic, regional, sub-regional, national, municipal and local – that are organized according to the Charter of Principles. The WSF is not confined to the five meetings that took place in Porto Alegre (Brazil) in 2001, 2003 and 2005, in Mumbai (India) in 2004, nor to the three meetings of the 'polycentric' WSF in 2006 (Bamako, Caracas and Karachi).[1] It also includes all the other forums that have been meeting alongside the WSF, such as the Forum of Local Authorities (four editions); the World Parliamentary Forum (four meetings); the World Education Forum (three meetings); the World Forum of Judges (three meetings); the World Trade Unions Forum (two meetings); the World Water Forum (two meetings); the World Youth Forum (three meetings); and the Forum of Sexual Diversity. Second, it includes all the national, regional and thematic forums that have taken place over the past five years. These are too numerous to include in a complete list. Among the regional ones, I would emphasize the Pan-

Amazonic Forum (four meetings), the European Social Forum (three meetings), the Asian Social Forum (two meetings), the Africa Social Forum (four meetings), the Social Forum of the Americas (two editions) and the Mediterranean Social Forum. Among the thematic forums, special mention should be made of the Forum on 'The Crisis of Neo-Liberalism in Argentina and the Challenges for the Global Movement', the first thematic forum, held in Argentina in August 2002, the Palestine Thematic Forum on 'Negotiated Solutions for Conflicts' in Ramallah, in December 2002, and the Forum on 'Democracy, Human Rights, War and Drug Trade', held in Colombia in June 2003. Third, national or international meetings of movements or organizations to prepare the aforementioned forums must be also included in the WSF.[2] Finally, although the Charter of Principles prevents the WSF from organizing, in its own name, collective actions, the regional or global actions carried out by the networks of movements and organizations that are part of the WSF must be considered part of the WSF process, as long as they abide by the Charter of Principles. For instance, and although this is not a consensual understanding, the actions agreed upon by the assembly of the Global Network of Social Movements, which meets alongside the WSF, are, in my view, part of the WSF process. The most visible of such actions so far was the global march against the war and for peace on 15 February 2003, decided upon in the assembly that took place during the third WSF. Even though they are not carried out in the name of the WSF, these collective actions are an integral part of the WSF process.[3]

In my opinion, the WSF will increasingly become less and less an event or set of events, and increasingly a process based on the work of articulation, reflection and combined planning of collective actions carried out by the different organizations and movements that are integrated in the WSF. Given this scope, the WSF is a very important component of counter-hegemonic globalization. As we shall see, some of the political tensions concerning the WSF have as their reference a narrower definition of the WSF, namely the five world meetings in Porto Alegre and Mumbai and the three meetings of the polycentric WSF of 2006. The political novelties of the WSF can be condensed in the following general orientations.

The struggles for global social justice must be based on a very broad conception of power and oppression

Neo-liberal globalization has not limited itself to submitting ever more interactions to the market, nor to raising the workers' exploitation rate by transforming the labour force into a global resource, and, at the same time, by preventing the emergence of a global labour market. Neo-liberal globalization has shown that exploitation is linked with many other forms of oppression that affect women, ethnic minorities (sometimes majorities), indigenous peoples, peasants, the unemployed, workers in the informal sector, legal and illegal immigrants, ghetto subclasses, gays and lesbians, children and the young. All these forms of power create exclusion. One cannot ascribe to any one of them, in the abstract, nor to the practices that resist them, any priority as to the claim that 'another world is possible'. Political priorities are always situated and context dependent. They depend on the concrete social and political conditions of each country at a given historical moment. To respond to such conditions and their fluctuations, the movements and organizations must give priority to the articulations among them. This ultimately explains the organizational novelty of a WSF with no leaders, its rejection of hierarchies, and its emphasis on networks made possible by the Internet.[4]

Counter-hegemonic globalization is built upon the equivalence between the principles of equality and recognition of difference

We live in societies that are obscenely unequal, and yet equality is lacking as an emancipatory ideal. Equality, understood as the equivalence among the same, ends up excluding what is different. All that is homogeneous at the beginning tends eventually to turn into exclusionary violence. World experience is highly diverse in its struggle for equality, and such diversity refers as much to means as to ends. This much has been claimed again and again by the social movements against sexual, ethnic, racial or religious discrimination. Under conditions of global capitalism there is no real recognition of difference without social redistribution. And vice versa, the struggle for equality will always run the risk of being discriminatory as long as it does not include the struggle for equality among differences. Indeed, we have the right to be equal whenever difference diminishes us; we have the right to be different whenever equality decharacterizes us.

The WSF grants no abstract priority to either principle and purports to be an open space on equal terms for movements that privilege one or the other principle. Concrete political conditions will dictate to each movement which of the principles is to be privileged in a given concrete struggle. Any struggle conceived under the aegis of one of these two principles must be organized so as to open space for the other principle.

An insurgent cosmopolitan politics

37

Rebellion and non-conformity must be privileged to the detriment of the old strategic options (reform or revolution)

There is no unique theory to guide the movements strategically, because the aim is not so much to seize state power as to confront the many faces of power as they present themselves in the institutions and society at large. Social emancipation does not have a general historical subject. In the struggle comprising the WSF, subjects are all those that refuse to be objects, that is to say to be reduced to the condition of vassals.

The WSF aims at a new internationalism

The internationalism promoted by the WSF represents a stark departure from the old internationalism that dominated anti-capitalist politics throughout the twentieth century. The latter was based on four main premises: a privileged social actor (workers or workers and peasants); a privileged type of organization (trade unions and working-class parties together with their federations and Internationals); a centrally defined strategy (the Internationals' resolutions); a politics originating in the North and formulated according to the political principles prevailing in the anti-capitalist North. The emphasis was on social and political homogeneity as a condition for unity and solidarity and on similar life trajectories and cultures as a condition for the development of strong and lasting ties.

On the contrary, the internationalism aimed at by the WSF celebrates social, cultural and political diversity within the broad limits set out by the Charter of Principles. It encompasses many different types of organizations and sees itself as a meeting ground where organizations and movements can interact freely and as an incubator of new networks generated at the exclusive initiative of those participating in them. It does not subscribe to any specific strategic goal beyond the normative orientation to struggle against neo-liberal globalization, nor to any specific mechanism to carry out such a struggle, except for the refusal of armed struggle. The WSF assumes that it is possible to develop strong ties, coalitions, networks among non-homogeneous groups and organizations and, moreover, that the cultural and political differences are enabling rather than paralysing as sources of political innovation. Finally, the WSF was born in the South, in the Latin American South, drawing on a hybrid political culture growing out of grassroots movements, participatory democracy experiments, liberation theology and struggles against dictatorship, as well as on Western left politics (both old and new).

The WSF process progresses as transversal political terrains of resistance and alternative are identified as an ongoing process

Building a counter-hegemonic globalization demands a broad definition of targets and a pluralistic conception of emancipatory goals. Moreover, the accelerated transformation of political and ideological landscapes requires that such transversality be brought about through constant analytical vigilance and strategic flexibility. This quest for transversality emerges eloquently from a mere enumeration of the focal themes that have framed the debates over the years: the production of wealth and social reproduction; access to wealth and sustainability; civil society and the public arena; political power and ethics in the new society (first and second WSF); democratic sustainable development; principles and values, human rights, diversity and equality; media, culture and counter-hegemony; political power, civil society and democracy; democratic world order, struggle against militarism and for peace (third WSF); democracy, ecological and economic security; discrimination, dignity and rights, media, information and knowledge, militarism, war and peace (fourth WSF); assuring and defending the earth and people's common goods – as an alternative to commodification and transnational control; arts and creation: weaving and building people's resistance culture; communication: counter-hegemonic practices, rights and alternatives; defending diversity, plurality and identities; human rights and dignity for a just and egalitarian world; sovereign economies for and of people – against neo-liberal capitalism; ethics, cosmo-visions and spiritualities – resistances and challenges for a new world; social struggles and democratic alternatives – against neo-liberal domination; peace, demilitarization and struggle against war, free trade and debt; autonomous thought, reappropriation and socialization of knowledge and technologies; movement towards construction of international democratic order and people's integration (fifth WSF).

Contrary to what the corporate media have been suggesting, the concern with concrete alternatives has been central to the WSF.[5] Once the idea of an alternative globalization to hegemonic globalization was consolidated, it became clear that the political strength of the WSF would depend on its capacity to formulate credible proposals and to generate enough political leverage to force them on to the political agendas of national governments and multilateral agencies. Moreover, as the consolidation of the WSF would tend to sharpen the cleavages in strategies and political action, the most fruitful way of discussing and clarifying them would be by focusing on concrete alternatives and proposals.

The design, complexity and technical detail of many of the proposals are of higher quality than many of those presented by the institutions of neo-liberal globalization. The challenge ahead is to force these proposals on to the political agendas of the different states and the international community. It is a long-range challenge because, for these proposals to become part of the political agendas, the national and transnational political institutions must be changed. Many such institutional changes will occur only on the basis of non-institutional struggles. They will require rebellion, non-violent but often illegal direct action.

The struggle for radical democracy must be a struggle for demo-diversity

Just as there is biodiversity, which must be defended, there is also demo-diversity, and it must be defended as well. There is not, therefore, one form of democracy alone, i.e. liberal representative democracy. There are several other forms, such as direct, participatory, deliberative, etc. But outside the Western world and culture there are still other forms of democracy (inter-cultural democracy, consensus democracy), which must be valorized. Take, for example, the autonomous government of the indigenous communities of the Americas, India, Australia and New Zealand, as well as the government of the traditional authorities in Africa or the panchayats in India. The point is not to accept critically any of these forms of democracy but rather to make possible their inclusion in the debates about the deepening and radicalization of democracy.[6]

Transcultural criteria must be developed to identify different forms of democracy and to establish hierarchies among them according to the collective quality of life they provide

Democratic systems of public or private interaction are those that aim to transform power relations into relations of shared authority. This means that the scope of democracy is potentially much broader than what liberal political theory has made us believe. And that there are different degrees of democraticity. The truth is, democracy does not exist, there is only democratization. Democracies must be ranked according to the intensity of the processes of shared authority. The more authority is shared, the more democracy is participatory. According to this criterion, we must distinguish between high-intensity democracies and low-intensity democracies. Representative democracy tends to be low-intensity. This is so for the following reasons: by giving a restrictive definition of the public space, representative democracy leaves intact many relations of power, which it therefore does not turn into shared authority; by relying on ideas of formal and not real equality, it does not guarantee the conditions that make it possible; by juxtaposing citizenship and identity in the abstract, it acknowledges difference surreptitiously from the standpoint of a dominant difference (class, colonial, ethnic, racial, sexual, religious) that becomes the norm – the dominant identity – on the basis of which the limits are set, and within which the other differences are allowed to be exerted, acknowledged or tolerated.

The low intensity of this democracy consists in the fact that, were the demands of capitalism to impose restrictions on the democratic game, this form of democracy would have few conditions to resist. Its surrender takes several forms: banalization of political differences and personalization of leadership; privatization of the electoral processes through campaign funding; mediatization of politics; distance between representatives and represented; corruption; an increase in abstention-ism. In the context of low-intensity democracy, the most important task is to democratize democracy.

In many societies, representative democracy is extremely low-intensity indeed. Democracy is extremely low-intensity when it does not promote any social redistribution. This occurs alongside the dis-mantling of public policies, the conversion of social policies into compensatory, residual and stigmatizing measures, and the return of philanthropy as a form of solidarity not grounded in rights. When social inequalities and hierarchical differences reach such high levels, the dominant social groups (economic, ethnic, religious, etc.) constitute themselves as de facto political powers and assume the right of veto over the minimal democratic aspirations of the majorities or minorities. In this case, social relations are dominated by such power asymmetries that they configure a situation of social fascism. The societies in which such asymmetries prevail are politically democratic and socially fascist (Santos 2002b: 453).

The WSF process must be conceived as promoting and strengthening counter-hegemonic forms of high-intensity democracy that are already emerging

Through more developed states and multilateral agencies, neo-liberal globalization has been imposing forms of low- or extremely low-intensity democracy on peripheral countries. Such an imposition, however, doesn't occur without resistance. Forms of high-intensity

41

democracy are emerging. The popular classes and oppressed, marginalized and vulnerable social groups are promoting forms of participatory democracy in many parts of the world, forms of high-intensity democracy based on the active participation of the populations. Through these forms, which are subject to constant renovation, the populations try to resist social inequality, colonialism, sexism, racism and the destruction of the environment.

The potential of democratic forms of high intensity is enormous, but we have to acknowledge their limitations. The most obvious limitation of local high-intensity democracies is precisely the fact that their ambit is local[7] and they cannot, by themselves, contribute to confronting the anti-democratic nature of the political, social and cultural power exerted at the national and global level. These limitations are not ineluctable and must be engaged. Forms of high-intensity democracy must be devised, both at the local and at the national and global levels, and articulations among the different levels must be promoted.

Whenever feasible, participatory democracy must be deepened through complementariness with representative democracy, a complementariness that is necessarily tense but critical as well. Such complementariness will always be the result of a political process whose earlier phases are not of complementariness but rather of confrontation. The articulations may begin at the local level, but they have the potential to reach the national level.

At the national level, the articulation between forms of participatory and representative democracy must be deepened to prevent them from becoming a trap that permits the state to go on managing the business of capitalism in capitalism's interest as if it were the interest of all. Never before has the state been subjected to a massive privatization process, as happens today. Much of the rhetoric concerning the value of civil society is part of a discourse to justify the dismantling of the state. The crucial tasks are, therefore, the democratic reform of the state; and the public control of the state through the creation of non-state public spheres.

In the long run, local participatory democracy does not sustain itself without participatory democracy at the national level, and neither of them is possible without participatory democracy at the global level. Local or even national high-intensity democracy is not sustainable if forms of global democracy are not evolved. It makes no sense today to speak of global civil society because there is no global mechanism to guarantee global civic rights. But if we none the less want to speak of global civil society, then it is necessary to distinguish between liberal global civil society, which feeds on neo-liberal globalization, and emancipatory global civil society, which promotes counter-hegemonic globalization, the globalization of solidarity of which the WSF is an eloquent expression.

A new democratic institution at the world level must be created, a United Nations of the Peoples capable of refounding the organization of the United Nations as we know it today. The institutions that are responsible today for blocking global or even national democracy, such as the World Bank or the IMF, must be abolished, or else radically changed. In all its scales or dimensions, but particularly at the global scale or dimension, democracy is a comprehensive exigency that is not confined to the political system and does not exist without social redistribution. Global collective actions must be organized, and global institutions must be created to allow for immediate, if minimal, global social redistribution, such as, for instance, debt cancellation for peripheral countries and the Tobin tax.

There is no democracy without conditions of democracy

It is imperative to fight against the perversion of democracy. Democracy, which emerged as government by the people, is today often used as government against the people. That which was the ultimate symbol of popular sovereignty is today the very expression of the loss of sovereignty (as, for instance, when democracy becomes an imposition of the World Bank). In the present context, to speak of conditions of democracy implies speaking of the radicalization of democracy. The democracy that exists in the great majority of countries is false, simply because it is insufficient. Democracy must be taken seriously. To be taken seriously it must be radicalized. There are two ways of radicalizing democracy. First, by deepening authority-sharing and respect for difference in the social domains where the democratic rule is already acknowledged. For example, participatory budgeting is a form of deepening the pre-existing municipal democracy. Second, by spreading democracy to a larger and larger number of domains of social life. Capitalism accepted democracy inasmuch as it reduced democracy to a specific domain of public life, which it designated as political space. All the other areas of social life were left outside democratic control: production, consumer society, community life and international relations. Capitalist societies thus constituted themselves as societies with small islands of democracy in a sea of despotism. To radicalize democracy is to transform it into a principle with the potential to regulate all social relations. In capitalist societies it is not possible to spread this principle to every relation. We must, therefore, start thinking of a post-capitalist world and engage in action to make it possible. Left to itself, capitalism leads only to more capitalism.

The democratic imagination has today in the WSF an eloquent expression, but one that is only just emerging. Its development also requires conditions. The WSF and the regional, thematic and national forums are evolving into the most developed form of our democratic imagination. As it nurtures this imagination, however, the WSF process must itself mind the conditions of its own enlargement and democratization. Two such conditions seem crucial. First, following September 11, the international (dis)order, of which the USA is the most prominent protagonist, aims to criminalize social movements and social protest under the pretext of the fight against terrorism. Indeed, the aim is to criminalize all the actions of popular organizations and movements. Local, national and global struggles must be launched against such criminalization. It was, therefore, important for the 2002 Forum of Local Authorities to state that the cities therein represented are committed to defending the right to public and peaceful demonstrations against neo-liberal globalization. Second, the network of organizations that convene in the WSF are movements of the most diverse features that fight for a more democratic society. For this struggle to be successful, the organizations themselves must be fully and thoroughly democratic. And their democracy must be twofold: internal, that is to say inside every organization or movement; and in the relations between movements and organizations. Hegemonism, sectarism and factionalism must be fought.

The struggle for high-intensity democracy starts with the social forces that fight for it. The WSF process integrates many non-governmental organizations involved in partnerships with the state. On the other hand, many organizations of the countries of the Global South are financially dependent on the organizations of the countries of the Global North. To avoid leaving high-intensity democracy at the door of the organizations, these relations must be transparent and subjected to the control of the members or target publics. Partnerships and agreements must be constructed democratically, and measures must be taken to prevent financial dependency from becoming a form of anti-democratic submission.

There is no global social justice without global cognitive justice

However democratized social practices may become, they are never democratized enough, if the knowledge guiding them is not democratized itself. Anti-democratic repression always includes the disqualification of the knowledge and ways of knowing of those repressed. There is no democracy without popular education. There is no democracy of practices without democracy of knowledges – that is, without the ecology of knowledges (see Chapter 2).

The many names for another possible world – social emancipation, socialism, dignity, etc. – are in the end the name of democracy without end

All the preceding orientations are to be discussed, approved, changed and expanded inside and outside the WSF, in workplaces, cities and villages, inside families and organizations. Their aim is to give some coordination to the movement for an alternative globalization on its way to a fairer and less discriminatory society. The struggle against global capitalism has to emerge from ever more places; it must be made up of very diverse struggles guided by a common principle: participatory democracy without end to bring capitalism to an end.

Notes

1 At the Asian Council meeting of December 2005 (Hong Kong) it was decided to organize another event of the polycentric WSF in 2006 in Bangkok, on 21–22 October.

2 Information regarding the activities carried out under the scope of the WSF can be accessed through the WSF official site at <www.forumsocialmundial.org.br>.

3 The inclusion of these actions in the WSF process is not generally accepted. The International Council (IC) integrates organizations whose representatives on the Council reject any organic relation between the WSF and the actions agreed upon by the Global Network of Social Movements or any other network of movements or organizations. According to these representatives – one of the most prominent is Francisco Whitaker, one of the founders of the WSF (Whitaker 2003) – the comprehensiveness and inclusiveness of the WSF can be preserved only if no action in particular is attributed to the WSF as a whole. See Chapter 6.

4 On this subject, see Waterman (2003a, 2003b); Escobar (2004).

5 Among the different overviews of the alternatives proposed see, for instance, Fisher and Ponniah (2003); Blin et al. (2006).

6 On this subject, see Santos (2002b, 2006b).

7 A few examples: municipal management through participatory budgeting in Porto Alegre and many other cities in Brazil, Latin America and Europe; the peace communities in Colombia, in particular that in São José de Apartadó; the forms of decentralized planning in the states of Kerala and West Bengal in India. On these and other examples see Santos (2005).

45

4 | Organizing fragmented counter-hegemonic energies

My main argument in this chapter and in Chapter 5 is that, contrary to the opinion of its critics, the WSF has shown a remarkable capacity to reform itself. The issues of organization and representation have been the main playing field upon which such capacity has been tested. I will try to demonstrate that the limitations of self-reform have lain so far less in the WSF itself than in the global and national structural conditions under which it unfolds.

In the words of Francisco Whitaker, one of the organizers of the WSF, 'the idea for the WSF was struck among a bunch of Brazilians who wished to oppose resistance to neoliberalism's single way of thinking, so obsessively expressed in the annual meetings of the World Economic Forum in Davos' (Whitaker 2002b). A resistance, that is, which aimed to go beyond protests and rallies. According to Whitaker,

> [...] the idea was, with the participation of all the organizations that were already networking in the mass protests, to arrange another kind of meeting on a world scale – the World Social Forum – directed to social concerns. So as to give a symbolic dimension to the start of this new period, the meeting would take place on the same day as the powerful of the world were to meet in Davos. (Interview, 5 September 2003)

Whitaker himself and Oded Grajew presented the idea to Bernard Cassen, editor of *Le Monde Diplomatique* and president of ATTAC.[1] Cassen was excited by the idea and proposed that the Forum take place in Brazil, in the city then already praised worldwide for its municipal participatory democracy, known as participatory budgeting – Porto Alegre. Soon a Brazilian Organizing Committee (OC) was put together to organize the WSF from 2001 onwards (see Table 4.1).[2] During the first WSF it was decided to set up a loosely structured International Council (IC). It met for the first time after the first WSF, in São Paulo, in June 2001.

In June 2001, a delegation of the organizations presented the Forum to the movements gathered together in Geneva for a parallel summit to the UN 'Copenhagen + 5' summit. The idea was very well received and

TABLE 4.1 Composition of the WSF Organizing Committee

ABONG	Brazilian Association of Non-governmental Organizations
ATTAC–Brazil	Association for the Taxation of Financial Transactions for the Aid of Citizens
CBJP	Brazilian Justice and Peace Commission
CIVES	Brazilian Association of Entrepreneurs for Citizenship
CUT	Central Trade Union Federation
IBASE	Brazilian Institute for Social and Economic Studies
CJG	Centre for Global Justice
MST	Landless Movement

an International Council to support the Forum was promptly created. The first WSF was under way. The programme was put together according to two dynamics. In the morning there would be four simultaneous panels on each one of the four chosen thematic areas: the production of wealth and social reproduction; access to wealth and sustainability; civil society and the public arena; political power and ethics in the new society.

Panellists, invited by the organization, were, in Whitaker's words, 'leading names in the fight against the One Truth' (interview, 5 September 2003). In the afternoon there would be workshops coordinated by the participants themselves to engage in debate and exchange experiences. Sessions were also planned to allow for testimonies from people involved in different kinds of struggles.

This structure was kept in the second WSF. It was somewhat changed in the third, though the basic structure of two kinds of sessions was still there: sessions organized directly by the OC, featuring guest speakers invited by the OC itself and by the IC; and sessions submitted by the participating movements and organizations. In the fourth meeting in Mumbai there were some significant organizational changes: more space was allowed for activities beyond conventional sessions (rallies, artistic, theatrical and literary shows) and part of the plenary sessions were self-managed by the organizations and movements, not by the OC as in the past. Along the same lines but resorting to a more participatory methodology to decide upon changes, more organizational innovation was implemented in the 2005 WSF. I will analyse these changes step by step.

The exciting but also overwhelming and at times traumatic experience of the first three meetings of the WSF was rich enough to identify the main organizational problems and also to show that such problems, although organizational in nature, were political as well. I will analyse these problems under the following headings: internal democracy – the relations between the OC and the IC; transparency and hierarchies in participation; parties and movements; size and continuity; the new organizational challenges – the evaluation of the 2003 WSF; the new organizational models – the WSF in Mumbai and the 2005 WSF (the Mumbai demonstration; the 2005 WSF); the 2006 polycentric WSF.

Internal democracy: relations between the Organizing Committee and the International Council

During the second WSF the decision was taken to confer more power on the IC for the planning of the Forum, while ascribing mainly an executive role to the OC, composed of Brazilian organizations. The first document of the IC was issued by the Brazilian OC after its first meeting in São Paulo in June 2001 and states that

> [...] the creation of the IC reflects the concept of the WSF as a permanent, long-term process, designed to build an international movement to bring together alternatives to neoliberal thinking in favour of a new social order, one that will foster contact among a multiplicity and diversity of proposals. Accordingly, the IC will be set up as a permanent body to give continuity to the WSF beyond 2002, to consolidate the process of taking the WSF to the world level.

Echoing criticisms of an excessive Brazilian influence in the organization and design of the WSF, the statement goes on to emphasize that 'the Council will play a leading role in defining policy guidelines and the WSF's strategic directions. National Organizing Committees will serve as organizers and facilitators in tandem with the IC.' The coexistence of the OC – up until 2004 exclusively Brazilian and now composed of Brazilian and Indian members, successively renamed as the International Secretariat (IS) and, since 2005, as the Facilitation Group (see below) – and the IC is today uncontested, even though it began by giving rise to some tension, both at the organizational level and as regards the representativeness of the Forum.

Both the OC/IS and the IC were put together by co-optation. Their legitimacy derives from their having organized the WSF with relative success. Their members were not elected and they are not accountable to any jurisdiction. The Brazilian OC kept its constitution from the beginning until the meeting of Mumbai. It functioned simultaneously as the local organizing committee and as the IS. After Mumbai, and with the expectation that the WSF would in the future be convened in different countries, the IC decided that in the future the local organizing committees and the IS should be strictly separated and that the latter should integrate representatives of the local OCs of the previous meetings of the WSF.[3] Accordingly, since the Mumbai Forum, the IS integrates some representatives of the India organizing committee. Furthermore, the IC has been in a process of permanent structuring since its creation in 2001 with the objective of becoming more global and balanced in terms of thematic, regional and strategic representation, a process that is far from being completed, as I will show in Chapter 5.

Although, according to the Charter of Principles, nobody represents the WSF, in practical terms the IS has been assuming some kind of representative function, and that has been a source of tension. Among other reasons, the fact remains that the IS is in practice almost exclusively Brazilian, whereas the WSF aims to be global. The IC was actually created to solve this problem, and the tendency has been to strengthen the IC's role in its relations with the IS. This is no easy task. Since the WSF took place for three consecutive years in Porto Alegre, the Brazilian OC/IS tended to play a crucial role in organizational and other kinds of decisions. The difficulties piled up during 2002, when the IC wanted to assume the WSF's strategic leadership and give general recommendations for its organization. In the course of the year, the IC held meetings in Porto Alegre, Bangkok, Barcelona and Florence, important decisions having been made each time, most of them addressing the need to internationalize the WSF more and more. In fact, the IC had declared 2002 as the year of the internationalization of the WSF (among other initiatives, through the organization of regional and thematic forums). It seems that it was not always easy to coordinate the IC's and the IS's work. According to some members of the IC, the IS resisted its loss of autonomy. For instance, the decisions made by the coordinators of the thematic areas were not always respected by the IS, especially as far as the choice of guest speakers was concerned. Without wishing to dismiss this point, I believe that the lack of coordination had a lot to do with conjunctural conditions. The IC became stronger in 2002, at a time when the IS lost some of its effectiveness owing to internal political conditions in Brazil – 2002 was election year, and there were state and federal elections (both legislative and presidential). The Workers' Party (PT),[4] ever a staunch supporter of the WSF in Porto Alegre, at both the organizational and financial levels, lost the elections in Rio Grande do Sul, whose capital is Porto Alegre.[5] This fact not only provoked a financial crisis but also upset the administrative apparatus, which had contributed so much to the success of the two previous forums.[6]

Be that as it may, there emerged a tense climate of mutual accusations of lack of transparency and accountability. Although none of these committees was elected by the movements and organizations that take part in the WSF, the truth of the matter is that the IC has been assuming the position of the most representative structure of the WSF, as well as a promoter of its internal democracy. Furthermore, the IC has been assuming a decisive role in strengthening a broad conception of the WSF, turning it into a permanent process and promoting the continuity among its many initiatives, so as to transform the WSF into 'an incremental process of collective learning and growth', as stated in the resolutions adopted at IC meetings during the 2003 WSF.

At the several IC meetings, other decisions were made with a view to changing the correlation of power between the IC and the IS. One important decision was to hold the 2004 WSF in India. The major reason for this decision was, as stated above, the need to deepen the Forum's global nature, encouraging the participation of movements and organizations from world regions with a hitherto marginal presence in the WSF. But the fact is that this decision deprived the IS of its former centrality, a consequence foreseen and indeed welcomed by some members of the IC. The decision to convene the 2004 WSF in India ended up having other advantages, such as, for example, enlarging the sets of organizations with the experience to put together big events. In this respect, it was interesting to observe how the mistrust of the IC members who had expressed their opposition to Mumbai as a venue (mainly Latin Americans) was gradually overcome as the Indian Organizing Committees went on demonstrating its organizational capacity.[7] The IS, in its turn, contributed with its experience whenever asked by the Indian OC. A relationship of mutual trust was thereby created which is patent today in the fact that both OCs share the IS, even though the original Brazilian OC is charged with the greater burden of the executive tasks.[8]

Relations between the IS and the IC began to change for the better after the meeting in Miami in June 2003. Between 2001 and 2003, the dominance of the IS was almost inevitable, given the IC's lack of operationality. At the Miami meeting measures were taken to increase the IC's operationality. As soon as this process was in place, functional complementarity, rather than political rivalry, between the IS and the IC began to be evident.[9] As I will show below, the organizational innovations of the 2005 WSF were already the result of a new relationship between the IS and the IC, a relationship of productive and not destructive tensions, in contrast to what threatened to happen in the past.

The relationships between the IS and the IC changed qualitatively in the IC meeting of Barcelona on 22/23 June 2005. In light of previous discussions on the need to change the institutional architecture of the WSF, the Brazilian members of the IS (as seen above, the IS is also composed of Indian members) presented a document in which they proposed that the IS should be renamed the 'Facilitation Group'. This change was justified by the need to adapt the technical office of São Paulo (the headquarters of the IS) to the new concept of the IC as an effectively functioning network. The document also proposed that the technical office be based in São Paulo until 2008, moving afterwards to another location. Beyond its concrete proposals this document signalled the willingness of the Brazilian side of the IS to respond once and for all to the criticisms of centralism waged against it. The change of name coupled with the change of venue signified not only a further diminution of the dominance of the IS but also the termination of the central role the Brazilian organizations had played in it. Probably tired of the continuing organizational stress and of the recurrent controversies about their alleged centralizing control, the Brazilian organizations felt that they had done their part to build the WSF and that now other organizations should take over. Taken by surprise, the IC was unable to take a final decision on the document. It was agreed that the new organizational architecture of the WSF would be decided in the IC meetings scheduled for 2006. In the meantime, the polycentric WSF of 2006 would be organized by the local OCs jointly, helped by the commissions on methodology, contents, resources and communication of the IC.[10] It was, however, agreed that the technical office would change venue after 2008. In my view, the debates in Barcelona showed both the genuine effort to democratize the governing structure of the WSF and the operational problems thereby posed. They showed above all a positive evolution in the relationships between the IC and the IS, an evolution that reveals the new organizational and political culture the WSF is poised to create. As I will show in the following, it is a culture based on the priority given to depolarizing tensions through incremental but constant institutional innovation and self-reformability.

Transparency and hierarchies in participation

The issue of internal democracy has other facets. Two of them seem particularly pertinent to me. The first concerns the lack of transparency of some of the decisions, which, seemingly organizational, actually have or could have political meaning. Over the years the criticism has been swelling that important decisions are taken by a very restrictive group, without the least control by the movements and organizations affected. Such decisions may include the rejection or marginalization of proposals submitted by the movements and organizations, without explicit justification. Some groups considered themselves marginalized by the organization of the 2002 WSF, a perception that was deepened in 2003.[11] Again without wishing to question the facts, I believe that, in most cases, the alleged discrimination was rather the result of the near organizational collapse of the 2003 WSF. For reasons already stated and others I shall mention below, the organization of the 2003 WSF was far from reaching the quality that distinguished the organization of the two previous Forums. The organizational changes introduced in the WSF of 2004 and 2005, analysed below, helped to discredit the conspiracy theory behind some of the criticisms raised against the IS in previous meetings of the WSF.

The second dimension of the democracy and transparency issue concerns the hierarchical structure of the various events at the WSF meetings and relates to the choice of guest speakers. This has to do with the already mentioned quality of participation. The distinction between sessions organized directly by the local OCs (in Brazil, with the decisive participation of the IS) and those proposed by the movements and organizations has created some tension. On the one hand, whereas those who participate in the first kind of session are invited by the WSF and have their participation funded (though not always), those who participate in the second kind of session must count only upon funding generated by the movements and organizations themselves. On the other hand, the sessions promoted directly by the organization are considered to be the most important and are granted time and space that the others do not have. Again, it was evident during the 2003 WSF that the most serious organizational problems had a greater effect on the sessions promoted by the movements and organizations than on the sessions promoted by the IS/IC. This issue was at the core of the organizational changes introduced in the WSF's of 2004 and 2005 analysed below.

The idea that all the different kinds of sessions should be treated the same way gained strength after the WSF of 2003. Movements and organizations were encouraged to present proposals aimed at deepening the process of experimentation in horizontal organizational practices based on co-responsibility. As much transpires from the above-mentioned IC resolution of January 2003: 'When holding the forums, to organize discussions and the search for alternatives giving equal weight to the activities scheduled by the organizers and to the seminars and workshops proposed and organized by the participants themselves, as well as to stimulate the international character of these forums.'

Criticism concerning lack of democracy and transparency has also been frequent regarding the selection of invited guests. The criticism is levelled both at the selection process and the specific invitations themselves (or exclusions from lists of potential invitees), namely when well-known personalities are at stake. The proposal to invite well-known names from the left, be they Fidel Castro, Hugo Chavez, Ben Bella or Mário Soares, has also caused controversy.[12] The organizational changes introduced in the WSF of 2004 and 2005, in particular the increased prevalence of self-organized activities, helped a great deal to tone down the criticism and controversy in this regard. They surfaced again in the polycentric WSF of 2006 in Caracas, given the excessive presence of Hugo Chavez, who spoke to participants on two occasions with speeches that lasted for more than two hours each. This dominance became particularly objectionable in the first speech as Chavez took sides in one of the political debates within the WSF – the conception of the WSF as an open space or as a movement[13] – defending the position of those who want to transform the WSF into a structured movement with a well-defined political agenda. More than the specific position taken, it was the interference in the internal life of the WSF which provoked most criticism.

Feminist movements have been particularly critical of the selection process, because women have been scarcely represented on the panels of plenary sessions or in the more visible and well-attended sessions (particularly after the plenary sessions were abandoned in the post-2003 WSFs), even though they constitute such a large proportion of all the participants (in the 2002 WSF, women made up 43 per cent of the delegates and, apparently, 52 per cent of the participants).[14] Faithful to their two mottoes – 'another world is possible' and 'no one single way of thinking' – feminist movements have been claiming a larger presence of women among guest speakers, as well as in the organizational structures, both the IC and the local OCs. In light of the experience of the two first forums, Virginia Vargas of the Flora Tristan Feminist Centre (Peru) and the Marcosur Feminist Articulation said: 'despite women's more visible impact, women have not been proportionally represented in the Conferences organized by the Forum or on the Organizing Committee. This is still one single way of thinking, huddled away amidst strategies for change' (2002: 56).

With reference to the first two meetings of the WSF, other critics mentioned the top-down nature of the conferences and the coexistence in the WSF of a top-down organization, comprising the initiatives of the IC and the OC/IS, and a bottom-up organization, comprising the large majority of the participants. Commenting on the experience at the 2002 WSF, Hebe de Bonafini, of the Argentinean 'Mothers of Plaza de Mayo', criticized the inequality of representation, of which she distinguished three levels: the organizers, the official participants and the 'rank-and-file'. According to her: 'There were three different levels to this WSF. First, there were the small gatherings of those who were in charge, controlling things [...]. Then there were all the commissions and seminars where all the intellectuals, philosophers and thinkers participated. And then there were the rank-and-file folks' (Bonafini 2002).

Viewing herself as part of the last group, she concluded: 'We [Mothers of Plaza de Mayo] participated at that level and discussed with all sorts of people. But the fact is that we were brought to the WSF to listen rather than to participate.' Other participants were likewise critical of the forum's top-down organization. Commenting on the third WSF, Michael Albert (2003), for instance, distinguished it from all the others (regional and thematic forums) that were occurring in different parts of the world, often inspired by the WSF. According to him, whereas the WSF was top-down, the others were bottom-up. 'Without exaggerating the virtues of the forums worldwide,' added Albert, 'they are having positive effects and moving in participatory, transparent, and democratic directions. The WSF, however, is different.' Albert offered several proposals aimed at deepening the WSF's participatory and democratic nature (more on this below).

Curiously enough, the organizers themselves acknowledged many of these criticisms, lending weight to my argument that these organizational tensions were part of the Forum's growing and learning process itself. Some of the criticisms incorporated accusations of less limpid intentions on the part of the OC/IS, and some came even close to conspiracy theories. My analysis of the OC/IS then and in the following years has led me to the conclusion that such criticisms had no grounding. The results of the decisions, some of which were rightly criticizable, had mainly to do with the OC/IS's incapacity to handle an event that became unmanageable because of its dimensions and complexity.[15]

The WSF's organizational structure was the most adequate to launch the Forum and render it credible internationally. For instance, the idea of ascribing to the OC/IS the promotion of some of the sessions and the choice of guests was adopted with a double goal in mind: first, to provide a minimal structure to the themes to be debated (for instance, to make sure that the debates would move from the denouncing discourse of mass protests to the discourse of proposals and alternatives); second, to give international visibility to the Forum by addressing invitations to well-known personalities. The WSF saw itself as an alternative to the World Economic Forum and was ready to engage battle with it for the attention of the global media.[16] To my mind, without this kind of organization, and without the extraordinary devotion of the people charged with it, the WSF would never have accomplished what it has so far. The consolidation of the WSF led it to another phase of development, in which its organizational structure was reconsidered so as to adjust it to its new demands and the tasks ahead. This reconsideration was at the core of the changes introduced in 2004, 2005 and 2006 (more on this below).

Parties and movements

The relations between political parties, social movements and NGOs in the construction of counter-hegemonic globalization is no doubt controversial.[17] In a broad sense, they also affect the WSF. The Charter of Principles is clear on the subordinate role of parties in the WSF.[18] The WSF is an emanation of the civil society as organized in social movements and NGOs. In practice, however, things have always been ambiguous. In the first three meetings of the WSF the role of the Workers' Party (PT) in the organization was hotly debated. The PT, in its capacity as government party in the state of Rio Grande do Sul and in the city of Porto Alegre, gave decisive support to the organization of the WSFs, at both the financial and logistical and the administrative levels. Without such support it would have been impossible, at least in Brazil, to organize the WSF with the ambition that characterized it from the start. To be sure, this kind of support had its price. Particularly during the second Forum, the PT's attempt to use the WSF to spread its message and engage in political propaganda was quite visible. Many participants were ready to criticize the organization on this account. Some of them went so far as to criticize the PT for instrumentalizing the WSF. As I will discuss in Chapter 9, the issue of the relations between parties and movements cannot be decided in the abstract. The historical and political conditions vary from country to country, and may dictate distinct responses in different contexts. In the Brazilian context, the PT itself is an emanation of the social movements, and its history cannot be separated from their history. Since the mid-1980s, the struggles against the dictatorship were conducted by the unions and social movements, and the PT was founded in the midst of this powerful social mobilization. In the ensuing years the PT continued to have a privileged relationship with the social movements. Only after the PT won the presidential elections of 2002 and Lula, the historical leader of the PT, became president of Brazil did this relationship start to be questioned. The support that the PT granted to the first three meetings of the WSF must be understood in this very context. The PT's attempt to use the 2002 WSF in its electoral campaign was rightly condemned (mostly by non-Brazilian participants). Contrary to what some other critics argued, I do believe, however, that the PT did not interfere substantially in the choices of the organization, whether as regards thematic areas or invited guests. The WSF became too big and too diverse for the PT to have a significant impact in this regard.

In the WSF of 2004 the debate on the role of political parties became mainly an Indian debate and focused not on whether the parties should have a role – the participation of the leftist parties in the different organizing committees was public and decisive – but rather on which parties had or should have a more decisive role. The ideological rivalries and divergences among different Indian leftist parties led eventually to the organization of a parallel forum designated as 'Mumbai Resistance'. In this case, the most salient divergence may well have concerned the issue of armed struggle as a political strategy, a form of struggle, which the parties and groups in the Mumbai Resistance refused, as a question of principle, to be considered unlawful, in opposition to what is stated in the Charter of Principles of the WSF. In the WSF of 2005 the PT was no longer the governing party either of the state of Rio Grande do Sul or of the city of Porto Alegre. Deprived of the financial support of the local governments, the WSF underwent a serious financial crisis from which it has not yet recovered. The issue of political manipulation was raised again in the polycentric WSF in Caracas in 2006. Besides the above-mentioned highly visible presence of Hugo Chavez, the financial support was also questioned. It appears that the foundations of the Global North which have been funding previous meetings of the WSF refused to provide the funds requested by the Venezuelan Organizing Committee. Most funding came from the government but, according to Edgardo Lander, of the OC and a very well-known and respected sociologist, with no strings attached and therefore without compromising the autonomy of the OC.

The relations between political parties (especially parties on the left) and the WSF will no doubt continue to be debated in the different countries in which forums will be held. In the majority of cases, the issue is not so much whether such relations should or should not exist, but rather to define the exact terms of such relations. If the relation is transparent, horizontal and mutually respectful, it may well be, in some contexts, an important lever for the consolidation of the WSF. The European Social Forum (ESF), held in Florence in 2002, clearly illustrates this. The strength of Italian social movements made possible horizontal links between them and the parties on the left, particularly the Rifondazione Comunista and the PDS (left democrats). Such links contributed decisively to the Forum's success.[19] The relations between leftist parties and social movements in the European context was heatedly discussed in the three meetings of the ESF to date. The London meeting, in October 2004, was perhaps the one that generated more controversy in this regard. In part for this reason, and also because of the ever tense relations between movements and NGOs, some movements decided to organize a parallel and autonomous event designated as 'Beyond the ESF'. According to one of the organizers of the parallel forum, 'local authorities and political parties were dictating the rules of the Forum through control of the budget' (IPSNews, 10 October 2004).

Size and continuity

As shown above in Table 4.1, the successive meetings of the WSF have been drawing a larger and larger number of participants. In my view, the WSF of 2003 was the watershed. The participation grew from 60,000 in the previous meeting to 100,000. Though the above-mentioned local political conditions affected the OC/IS's efficiency and organizational capacity, the large number of participants led many of them to believe that the WSF was victim of its own success: its size rendered it unmanageable. Had this organizational form reached its limits? The discussions in the IC after 2003 focused on this question and, as shown below, significant changes were introduced in the organization of the WSF in 2004, 2005 and 2006. The 2004 WSF, in Mumbai, drew an even larger number of participants and, in spite of notorious deficiencies (especially in translation services), it was unanimously considered much better organized than the 2003 WSF. The 2005 WSF, an equally well-attended meeting, didn't frustrate expectations in this regard either. The structure of the polycentric 2006 WSF symbolized the most drastic departure from the previous organizational model.

Given that the WSF is a learning process, more and more voices have been supporting the idea that the WSF should increasingly turn into a permanent phenomenon, comprised of many linked meetings. In this way it would be possible to further the internationalization of the WSF, structure and focus the dialogues and debates much better, and strengthen the formulation of alternatives. The number of participants in these other forums would certainly be lower and manageable. In this regard, the IC, in its meeting of January 2003, in Porto Alegre, decided to stimulate the multiplication of regional, national and even local forums, as well as thematic forums, which intercommunicate horizontally and which would not be considered preparatory to a larger world meeting but as meetings with their own political value.

The intention was, thus, to further highlight partial meetings to the detriment of the 'global event' that the WSF had been. Aware that such a change would call for new coordination tasks, the IC decided at the same meeting to take on the task of producing a continued and systematic analysis of the situation in the world and, on the basis of it, to assess

> the continuity of the process, to ensure the respect for its Charter of Principles when holding regional and theme forums, to identify themes for the IC's work, for the world events and for the theme forums to be stimulated, as well as to identify regions of the world in which the process needs to expand, acting in alliance with movements and organizations from these regions.

This policy orientation was sustained in the following years. It led to the decision to organize the WSF of 2006 as a polycentric Forum.

The new organizational challenges: the evaluation of the 2003 WSF

As I mentioned above, the 2003 WSF was the watershed in both organizational and political terms. In this section I will deal with the organizational issues. Of course, all the important organizational problems are political as well. Even though this idea seems self-evident, it is not subscribed to by all the members of the IC, or at least, it is not interpreted in the same way. If some agree that priority must be given to political discussion, lest decisions on organizational matters conceal the power relations within the IC, others think that the political discussion may be paralysing and prevent the timely taking of organizational decisions. According to the latter, it is easier to reach consensus on concrete questions than on questions of principle, and so, they argue, political discussion will be more productive if it occurs in the context of concrete problems, which almost always appear as organizational problems. This latter position has prevailed both in the IS and the IC.

The WSF of 2003 was a decisive turning point in the construction of the WSF process. The preparation and the evaluation of the Forum were resolutely geared to confronting the organizational challenges resulting from the success (well beyond expectations) of the two first meetings of the WSF. The WSF of 2003 set the tone for the intense self-reform impulse that informed the preparation and evaluation of the two following meetings and for that reason deserves a detailed analysis. The organizational innovations aimed at responding to two main problems:

1 how to achieve more balanced participation by organizations and movements of the different regions of the world;
2 how to maximize the effectiveness of such participation – that is to say, how to make such participation a factor of internal democratization.

The answers given to these questions illustrate the WSF's strong will and capacity for self-reform, as I am arguing in this chapter. The questions may be arranged under the following topics: evaluation of the 2003 WSF designated by the IS as 'systematization of past experience'; new organizational models of WSF Mumbai and of the 2005 WSF. I will discuss the first topic in this section.

After the second WSF, and having in mind the third, Cândido Grzybowski, director of IBASE and one of the founders of the WSF, took the initiative of setting up a methodology and systematization team, which he himself coordinated. This team's task was to produce a systematic survey of the activities of the 2003 WSF. The aim was to create a database of the themes discussed at the forum; their distribution throughout lectures, panels, seminars, workshops, testimonies and round tables of dialogue and controversy ('*mesas de diálogo e controvérsia*'); activities organized by the OC and self-managed activities; the profile of guest speakers and participants, and so on and so forth. The issue was to organize the collective memory of the WSF and create the conditions to allow for a systematic assessment of its performance, identifying possible problems and proposing solutions. The technical production of such systematization was charged to IBASE.

The results are extremely revealing as regards the performance of the WSF. The survey was divided into four parts, three of which correspond to the three kinds of activities of the Forum: conferences, panels, and self-managed activities. Part four dealt with the survey of the profile of participants. I next present the main results of the three first parts. Part four will be analysed in Chapter 5 as it mainly refers to questions of representation.

Conferences The conferences took place at the Gigantinho Stadium and gathered close to 12,000 people in one single day. In accordance with WSF methodology, the aim of the conferences was to allow for personalities engaged in civic causes, campaigns or struggles to share their views and analyses with the public at large. The WSF invited people whose reports and opinions would contribute to strengthening a broad public-opinion movement geared to the need, possibility and urgency of building 'other worlds'. Thirty-six people gave talks at the third WSF, taking up ten themes. Although the WSF IS sought a balance of gender, only 27.8 per cent of the speakers were women – ten women and twenty-six men. The best-represented socio-political region was Latin America, with eleven speakers (30.6 per cent). If the count is made according to the country of origin, however, the USA led in representation: the USA had four representatives (one more than Brazil). Seven speakers came from Europe, six from North America (including the four from the USA), six from Asia, five from the Middle East, and only one from Africa.

This led to criticisms of sexual discrimination in the organization of the Forum made by the women's movements. Even though the women constituted the majority of the participants, their intervention, especially in the more visible activities, by no means matched such a proportion. On the other hand, the imbalances as regards regional representation were obvious. Half of the conference speakers came from the North and, among those that came from the South, only one came from the continent that has been most affected by neo-liberal globalization: Africa.

The conferences had been questioned all along for their individualistic and monological character. In the seminar on the evaluation of the systematization of the WSF 2003, which took place in Rio de Janeiro, by IBASE's initiative, on 21–23 May 2003, Virginia Vargas concluded that 'the conferences, however important, did not allow for an exchange of ideas and conceptions among the speakers. There was more narcissistic disputing among them than real collective dialogue' (Vargas 2003).

Panels The panels were introduced in the third WSF to offer an alternative of great visibility vis-à-vis the conferences. Whereas conferences based their visibility on the high profile of the conference speakers, panels had a wider range of participants, giving priority to activists, and depending for their visibility on the quality of the debates – spelling out the differences being highly recommended by the OC/IS – and on the proposals of collective action presented. I reproduce below in some detail the methodology proposed for the panels to underline its innovative character and to show how difficult it was for a new methodology to be appropriated by such a vast and vastly diverse number of participants.

At the meetings of the IC preparatory to the third WSF (Bangkok, Barcelona and Florence), the five thematic axes and panel themes within each axis were decided:

Thematic axis 1 – Democratic and sustainable development
1 Recovering economic sovereignty through debt cancellation and capital control
2 Solidarity economy
3 WTO: the road to Cancun
4 Full employment and labour re-regulation
5 For the right to cities
6 For another economy: subsidiarity, localization, devolution and reproduction
7 Beyond Johannesburg: property, biodiversity control and management, water and energy

Thematic axis 2 – Principles and values, human rights, diversity and equality
1 Struggle for equality between men and women: how to implement real change
2 Fighting intolerance and promoting respect for diversity: solidarity as a transformational force in the struggle against the 'single way of thinking'
3 For the full implementation of rights
4 Beyond national borders: migrants and refugees
5 For full access to water, food and land
6 For full access to the rights to education, health, housing and social security

Thematic axis 3 – Media, culture and alternatives to commercialization and homogenization
1 Globalization, information and communication
2 How to ensure cultural and linguistic diversity
3 Strategies for democratizing the media
4 New technologies and strategies for digital inclusion
5 Culture and political practice
6 Symbolic production and peoples' identity

Thematic axis 4 – Political power, civil society and democracy
1 Democratizing democracy by building new paradigms
2 New and old social movements: the current spaces of confluence and tension among multiple local and global actors
3 Citizens' insurgence against established order
4 New dimensions of the democratic state
5 Strategies for citizens' oversight
6 Future perspectives for the movements: new concepts and pathways in organizing social movements

Thematic axis 5 – Democratic world order, struggle against militarization and for peace
1 Empire, war and unilateralism
2 Resistance to militarization
3 Governance, global economy and international institutions
4 World order: sovereignty, role of governments and the United Nations
5 Democratic strategies for resolving international conflicts
6 Democratic cooperation: integration, multilateralism and peace

According to Jorge Romano (2003), a member of the task force on 'systematization' (called the 'systematization group'), the panels would be held during the Forum's first three days. A final panel on each thematic axis would be held on the fourth day. The IC appointed two coordinators by axis and one facilitator for each panel. The IS appointed a team from the systematization group to do the work of record-keeping and minute-taking (in Portuguese, '*memória*', i.e. the Forum's memory). During the first three days, the panels were to be a space for presentation and defence of proposals by networks, campaigns and coalitions. The idea was to visualize, confront and consolidate proposals for the sub-theme, in terms of alternatives and strategies. Each panel would appoint one person to sit on the final panel. This person could be the facilitator or anyone else appointed by its members. It was expected that each panel would not present a full discussion but limit itself to present the diversity of views and paradigms, issues discussed, diversity of proposals and strategies, with consensuses, disagreements and emerging themes. The idea was to focus the debate on convergences and divergences, pointing out perspectives in terms of emerging themes and issues to work on. Panels would require a preparatory stage, including the presentation of written documents. Based on those documents, which should be broadly disseminated, delegates (always representing a diversified set of civil society actors) would be better qualified to participate actively on each panel.

The final panel was meant for sharing the discussed issues, mapping out the diversity of proposals put forward by delegates during previous panels. This would be an effort to organize the Forum's collective memory, and to record its contributions for building 'other possible worlds'. A methodological and political approach of valuing the inputs was recommended – avoiding their reduction to a single proposal. Otherwise the methodology would run counter to the basic commitment to respect and build on diversity, established in the Charter of Principles.

As one of the planned activities by the OC/IS/IC (the others were conferences, round tables of dialogue and controversy), the final panels were designed as a space for confrontation between activities planned by the IC and the IS, and activities proposed by delegates (workshops, seminars, etc.). Emphasis and the priorities of planned and self-managed activities would be compared. As much information as possible extracted by the Secretariat from self-managed activities at the 2003 WSF was to be used as input for final panels.

Each thematic axis would count on the support of a team from the systematization group throughout the panel process. Each team would be made up of three persons. The main objective of the teams was to gather the material for minutes and systematization work. The teams would also help to organize the final panels.[20] In addition to relying on the systematization group team, panels would also be visited by consultants, who would freely circulate throughout WSF activities. Consultants would be specialists from different areas to help the systematization process, producing documents and providing opinions on the work developed by the team more directly involved in the process.

Specific reports on how the different panels functioned would be prepared, highlighting panel composition, coordinating work, panel dynamics, audience and public participation.

I next present the statistical data on the distribution of panellists by thematic axes according to gender and regional origin. There were a total of 167 presentations by 66 women and 101 men. Panel gender distribution according to thematic area was as shown in Table 4.2. In terms of regional origin, there were more panellists from Latin America and the Caribbean (52) and Europe (48). It should be noted that there was no panellist from Oceania. The following table shows the distribution of panellists according to region (see Table 4.3).

The analysis of these data and of the systematized information on

TABLE 4.2 Members of panels by sex

Thematic axis	Total panellists	Women	Men
1	39	17	22
2	33	14	19
3	30	10	20
4	34	16	18
5	31	9	22
Total	167	66	101

TABLE 4.3 Members of panels by region

Thematic axis	North America	Latin America and the Caribbean	Europe	Asia	Africa	Oceania
1	5	11	10	7	6	–
2	3	9	10	7	4	–
3	5	13	7	4	1	–
4	3	12	11	6	2	–
5	7	7	10	4	3	–
Total	23	52	48	28	16	–

the content and dynamics of the debates permits one to draw the following conclusions:

1. The panels achieved a better general gender balance. Even so, there were were about half as many women as men on the panels of thematic axis 3 (media, culture and alternatives to commercialization and homogenization) and 5 (democratic world order, struggle against militarization and for peace).

2. The regional imbalances could still be observed, the Global North (Europe and North America) providing 42.5 per cent of the panellists.

3. The preparation of the panels was inadequate in general. The work of the coordinators of the axes and of the facilitators of the panels was often deficient, and the coordination between them even more deficient. The final panel seldom used the work of systematization, and the policy guideline concerning promoting the formulation and systematization of action proposals was not accomplished.

4. In most of the panels the discussion and divergences expected by the organizers did not occur. Quite the opposite; there was mainly consensus and repetitive, not at all audacious, analyses.
5. The logistic difficulties that the WSF had to face damaged attendance at the panels. Spaces that could hold 2,000 people never had more than 500.

Self-managed activities For the 2003 WSF it was decided to encourage self-managed activities, that is activities proposed by the networks, movements and organizations participating in the Forum – designated as *oficinas* (workshops) – and promote the fusion of activities about similar themes in order to avoid fragmentation. According to Cândido Grzybowski:

> The workshops are considered to be the factory of the Forum – a kind of global civil laboratory – they are meant to facilitate meetings, exchange of experiences, networking, planning and definition of the strategies of groups, coalitions, networks, movements and organizations, always directed towards present and future actions. Perhaps the main force of the WSF lies in the diversity characterized by this sort of activity. But we wonder: do we really know how to make proper use of all this potential? In this sense and above all else, what we are dealing with here is the Memory of the Forum. The living record of what NGOs, social movements, trade-union institutions, academic centres, religious groups, cooperation agencies, networks and other entities think, debate and propose. More than all this, however, the intention is to try to detect the eventual appearance of something new, all the transgression, irreverence, Utopia and re-enchantment that sometimes do not fit into the circumspect format of the thematic axes agreed upon. (Grzybowski 2003b)

It was estimated that of the 1,619 workshops planned, 1,300 took place. Of these, 288 were the object of systematization, that is to say of a systematic analysis of their content and of how well they fared.[21] From the discussion at the systematization seminar organized by IBASE (Rio de Janeiro) on 21–23 May 2003, the following conclusions can be drawn:

1. As regards content, the workshops fulfilled what was expected of them. They revealed the great diversity of interests and struggles that circulate in the WSF. Above all, however, they revealed that there was a significant discrepancy between the activities organized by the IS

and the self-managed activities. Many of the topics that dominated the conferences didn't seem to be priorities for debate among the organizations and movements, for only seldom were they evident in the workshops.[22] Moreover, themes never debated in conferences or panels were dealt with in the workshops. The theme of spirituality, for example, featured in many of the workshops, even though many of them were proposed by the same network.[23] This means that the workshops rebelled objectively against the choice of the grand themes (the thematic axes) made by the OC/IS and the IC. While, on the one hand, this bears witness to the creativity of the base of the WSF, on the other it reveals some distance between the concerns and interests of the *top* of the WSF and those of its *base*. This had a direct impact on the methodology adopted in the fourth and fifth WSF (more on this below).

2. In spite of the wide space opened for the workshops, the truth is that there was unfair competition between them and the grand events (conferences and panels), since their timetables often coincided. The fact that the workshops and the conferences/panels were scheduled for locations very distant from one another made circulating among them impossible. In a way, parallel forums were created inside the Forum, all of them isolated from one another, with the result that the interaction between the 'big names' and the 'people' of the movements ended up being scarce. The tenacious hierarchies that prevail in contemporary societies seemed to penetrate the Forum insidiously.

3. The decision to give total freedom to the organizations and movements to propose workshops and choose their day, time and often location, increased enormously the fragmentation and atomization of the activities. The fragmentation and atomization were the consequence as well of the impossibility of merging workshops on similar topics, thereby resulting in much overlapping and repetition.

Round tables of dialogue and controversy The two great organizational innovations of the 2003 WSF were the panels and the controversy round tables. The latter also had a pragmatic objective, namely to respond to the pressure for the participation of political personalities and parties, as well as governments and multilateral organizations. According to Cândido Grzybowski:

> The roundtables of dialogue and controversy constituted a methodo-
> logical and political novelty among the various activities planned. As a

specific area within the WSF, their purpose was to confront the views and proposals of delegates with those of representatives of political parties, governments, organizations of the United Nations system and members of parliament. This activity was a formal invitation – as required by the Charter of Principles – that allowed political person-alities to attend the main events in the WSF, thus broadening and enhancing the potential of the debate that interests us. (ibid.: 7)

In all, four round tables of dialogue and controversy were held, one each morning, in the Gigantinho Stadium, which has a capacity of 15,000 participants. Each table dealt with one 'hot' question in which dialogue and controversy, according to rules agreed upon beforehand among the participants, could be used to explain the proposals and strategies of civil society throughout the world. The themes of these tables and the profile of the participants were decided at the meeting of the IC held in Florence in November 2002, as proposed by the OC/IS. To prepare the discussion at each table a 'note of presentation' on the topic was drafted and sent beforehand to each member of the table; these notes served to delimit the question and facilitate the debate. Written in four languages, they were distributed at the door of the gymnasium on the day of the debate. On the eve of the debates, all the participants, together with the respective moderator, were invited to meet with the round table coordinator to set the debating rules and to get to know one another.

In all, twenty-nine persons participated in the round tables, twelve of them from civil society entities and movements, thirteen from parties, governments and the United Nations system, with four functioning as moderators. Of this total, ten were from Latin America and the Caribbean (four Brazilians), two from North America, ten from western Europe, four from Africa, one from the Middle East and two from Asia, thus reproducing the regional imbalances that plagued the Forum. In terms of gender the imbalances were equally shocking, in total contrast with the concerns voiced by the organizers: there were twenty men and nine women (four from movements and entities, four from organiza-tions and one moderator journalist).

The following conclusions could be drawn:

1. The composition of the sessions reflected the regional and gender imbalances already observed in the other activities.
2. The sessions were viewed by some as a 'giving in to the enemy' or as a 'confusion with the enemy', but the truth is that they allowed for the confrontation of ideas, the public and well-argued

presentation of strong divergences, and the strengthening of ideological identities.

3. The traditional monological exposition of panel or conference participants was avoided for the sake of a confrontation of points of view. As one might expect, while the participants coming from official political structures (parties, parliaments, governments, the United Nations) shared a common interest in doing whatever was possible within the limits of the current national and international status quo, the participants coming from movements and NGOs voiced broader and more radical perspectives, clearly guided by ethical values.

The systematization/evaluation was the expression of an internal impetus that I found very healthy and most necessary. As we will see below, one of the cleavages in the WSF relates to whether or not the WSF should become more outward-looking, more concerned with its status in global public opinion and with its specific contribution to bringing about concrete transformations in the most unfair societies in which we live today. An inward-looking moment was most important after three successful meetings of the WSF and the systematization was a useful contribution to that. Now, after six meetings of the WSF, there is a heritage to be shared and valued. It is not clear, however, in what such heritage consists. Without a detailed knowledge of the heritage, it is impossible to make it effective and forward-looking. Through the systematization, the WSF looked at itself, reflected upon its past and set itself to derive from such reflection guidelines and energies for the future.

This comprehensive systematization/evaluation established the model for the evaluation of the subsequent meetings of the WSF (see below), but above all it permitted contextualization of many of the debates launched after the 2003 WSF. Such debates represented the political side of the organizational evaluation conducted by the systematization group. To such debates I turn now.

The debates after the WSF 2003 The third WSF sparked an unprecedented debate within its own ranks. Such debate started in the meeting of the IC held in Porto Alegre at the time of the Forum and continued throughout the year. For some, the debate had mainly to do with the success of the WSF. Having gathered more than 20,000 participants at the first meeting, around 60,000 at the second and more than 100,000 at the third, the question now facing it was how best to channel this tremendous energy. Which new and deeper or more ambitious forms of collective action could be built upon the convening power generated by the WSF? For others, the debate should focus on the problems that were now too visible to be swept under the carpet. Here, very sketchily, I present some of the topics of debate:

GIGANTISM. The WSF grew so fast and so dramatically that it may have become unmanageable. The obvious organizational deficiencies were seen by some as evidence that this format had reached its limits and that something new and different should be proposed for the future. In the IC meeting it was decided that greater priority should be given to the national, regional and thematic forums. Some members even proposed that from now on the dynamics of the WSF should rest on these forums, smaller and closer to people, which would choose the delegates to the WSF. In this way, the WSF would become an emanation or expression of those forums, a much smaller event but none the less more representative. Others suggested that the organization of the WSF takes too much energy (both human and financial), draining the resources of the NGOs and social movements which should be applied to their specific objectives and agendas. Accordingly, it was proposed that the WSF take place every two years and that, in the years it does not take place, local and national forums should be organized around the world simultaneously, on the same days that the World Economic Forum of Davos meets. None of these proposals was approved by the IC. It was rather decided that the 2004 WSF would be held in Mumbai, and the 2005 Forum in Porto Alegre, leaving open the decision as to what to do in subsequent years.

THE GLOBAL DEFICIT. The regional, gender and thematic imbalances were all too evident not to be the object of thorough reflection in the future. The overwhelming participation of Brazilians, NGOs and movements from Latin America and the North Atlantic region was almost unanimously viewed as a problem of credibility undermining the WSF's aspiration to be the embryo of a counter-hegemonic global civil society. Notwithstanding the resistance of some groups (in which the Cuban delegation was particularly vocal), the IC decided that the next meeting would be held in India, and that a special effort should be made to bring in more participants from Africa and also from eastern Europe and the Caribbean.

THE SOCIAL DEFICIT. In spite of its size the WSF was much less inclusive than it proclaimed. The really oppressed people, the unemployed, undernourished, those living in shanty towns, dispossessed peasants, the victims of the worst kinds of new and old forms of exploitation and discrimination, were hardly present. As Peter Waterman (2004: 87) put it, the WSF risked being an expression of globalization from the middle rather than globalization from below. The evaluation of the social profile of the participants conducted by the 'systematisation group' confirmed these risks. This evaluation is presented in Chapter 5.

Related to this was the idea that the radical potential of the WSF was being hijacked by the NGOs that controlled it. Social movements, although present in great numbers, did not have the steering power to keep the WSF close to the grassroots movements. The NGOization of the WSF was seen as a disturbing evolution, likely to bring about its discredit in the near future. This problem was tackled in the multiple ways in which the question 'how open is the WSF?' was asked. The limits of inclusion were discussed both in terms of people and in terms of themes and political postures (radical action versus reasonable reformism).

A DISCRETE EVENT OR A PROCESS. What is left after the WSF ends? For some, not much or nothing compared to the effort put into organizing it and participating in it. For most, the question was how to maximize the tremendous potential of this huge and emotionally unforgettable meeting of peoples, ideas and emotions. How to keep alive the contacts made and inter-knowledge obtained. In a sense, the meetings of the networks and of the social movements – in particular, the assembly of the social movements being held in parallel with the WSF – were partial responses to this question, and indeed many links and collective actions have been forged in these meetings. The point of the debate was whether more and better could be accomplished.

Another aspect of this debate was the internal balkanization of the WSF, the danger that the scale of the event – a remarkable achievement in itself – could favour the emergence of ghettos inside the Forum. The discreteness would thus be double: in between Forums and inside each Forum. If, on one side, the big event created an atmosphere of anonymity that favoured the exercise of freedom to attend whatever meeting with whatever degree of engagement, on the other, it facilitated the formation of exclusive groups that held discussions in closed circles without much connection with the rest of the Forum. As Jai Sen put it, this self-insulation was all the more probable, given

> the tendencies of people belonging to particular streams of thought
> and action to stay within or close to 'their' streams. The tendency of

some (many? most?) streams of thought and action, especially those from old politics but not only those, to organize their events in what amounts to being an exclusive manner: With familiar and reliable speakers, and organized in such a manner that the events 'speak' primarily to those within the streams, in other words with an internal discourse – and so inevitably tending to keep things separate. Inter-cultural differences exist between participants from different countries and contexts, and that is likely to be all the more the case as the Forum matures as an idea and the dominance of people from the host country reduces, whether in Brazil or anywhere else. (Sen 2003b: 8)

COORDINATION AND LINKS. The third WSF raised most dramatically the question of the links between the different activities of the Forum, in particular between self-managed and centrally organized activities, as I mentioned above. The sense of being neglected or even marginalized by the organization was widespread among the organizers of self-managed activities, especially among those who organized multiple activities. Notwithstanding the excesses of those who saw conspiracy where there was only incompetence or organizational collapse due to lack of resources, the debate was an important starting point for the design of new solutions, some of them implemented in the 2004 and 2005 WSFs. The most radical innovation occurred in 2006 with the polycentric WSF meeting in three different continents (more on this below).

THE COMPOSITION AND TASKS OF THE IC AND IS. This topic will be dealt with in Chapter 5. Suffice it to say here that the debate focused on whether the composition of the IC – up until then dominated by Latin American and European organizations – should be discussed in strict terms of representativeness or rather in more general terms of reducing the arbitrariness of its composition. This is a topic that is very much alive in the current discussions in the IC and specifically in its expansion committee.

As for the IS, many resented its enormous executive power, which, they claimed, went far beyond that of a technical body, particularly in light of its exclusively Brazilian composition. Others, however, observed that the dominance of the IS was occurring less by design than by default, as the IC had not been able to improve its operational capacity. Moreover, the IS had accumulated some precious inside knowledge that in no way should be wasted. It was in this context that the IC took upon itself to reshuffle its internal functioning (see Chapter 5), and

71

decided that, after Mumbai, some members of the India Organizing Committee would join the IS.

THE WSF AS A SPACE OR AS A MOVEMENT. This has been the most controversial topic of discussion, as it touches the core issue of defining the political nature and role of the WSF. It became particularly heated after the third WSF, embedded in the evaluations of the WSF that followed, and was also due to some conflicts and tensions that occurred during the Forum between the OC and the assembly of the global network of social movements, as well as inside the IC.

The systematization/evaluation showed that the WSF is a power space. To claim the opposite and defend the idea that the WSF is a totally open space, with no centre and no hierarchies and potentially all-inclusive (within the limits set by the Charter of Principles), seems a bit far-fetched. It is true that many of the concrete limits of inclusion were not the responsibility of the organizers. Nevertheless, crucial organizational options were decided by the OC/IS and by the IC, and they conditioned the types of events that would take place, the high-profile participants that would attend, the themes that would be discussed and the ambit of the discussion. As an illustration, the links between organized activities and self-managed activities – and thus the idea of a centre and a periphery inside the WSF – became highly contentious after the 2003 WSF. The changes introduced in subsequent meetings in this regard bear witness to the WSF's capacity for self-reform.

It is therefore wise to recognize the existence of power relations and submit them to the same criteria as those the WSF wants to see applied in society at large: transparency in the operation of such relations and their submission to the mechanisms of participatory democracy.

The debate on whether the WSF is an open space, a power space or a movement reflects some of the most deep-seated tensions within the WSF. For this reason, I deal with it in Chapter 6, where I discuss the cleavages on strategy and political action.

The new organizational models: the Mumbai demonstration and the 2005 WSF

The Mumbai demonstration The idea of holding the WSF in India emerged very early on – indeed, in 2001. Concerned with the further globalization of the WSF, the Brazilian OC and some members of the IC thought that India – a large country with a great tradition of civil society progressive activism – would be the ideal alternative to Brazil. A first visit to India occurred at the end of 2001. After a first national consultation held in New Delhi in early January 2002, it was decided that India could organize the WSF in 2004, not in 2003. Given the fact that general elections would be held in India in 2004, the WSF would be a precious platform from which to advance the progressive and secular political agenda. As a kind of preparation, it was also decided to organize a regional Forum in 2003, the Asian Social Forum, which was held in January 2003, and whose organization was seen as a great success.

The 2004 WSF took place in a social and political context that was very different from the previous ones, a difference that translated itself into important organizational innovations. The adopted organizational structure itself reflected the need to formalize balances among political forces with divergences that were deeply marked and defined according to party loyalties. Four committees were created, corresponding to four levels of organization: 1) the India General Council, comprising about 140 organizations, to define the broad lines of the 2004 WSF; 2) the India Working Committee, comprising about sixty organizations, to supervise the preparatory activities all over India for organizing the Forum, and to formulate the policy guidelines that form the basis for the functioning of the WSF India process; 3) the India Organizing Committee (IOC), of forty-five members, divided into eight working groups, which was the executive body of the 2004 WSF, ultimately responsible for organizing the event; 4) and the local organizing committee, the Mumbai Committee.

One of the policy guidelines, implying a criticism of the previous WSFs, was to democratize the organization of and participation in the WSF as much as possible, so as to render more visible the social inequalities that characterize India. With this is mind, five national consultations were held with the objective of bringing into the process more organizations representing critical sections of society and the economy from across the political spectrum; thus, in the words of the IOC, 'putting in place a democratic transparent and accountable decision-making mechanism in the WSF India process'. On the other hand, it was decided to strengthen the presence in the event of the self-managed activities of participant organizations, highlighting them on the programme and seeing to it that their schedules would not clash with the activities put together by the organizing committee.[24] Finally, there was an attempt to make the social profile of the participants reflect the significance of the 'social groups that remain less visible, marginalized, unrecognized, and oppressed'. In this respect, particularly significant was the participation of more than 30,000 Dalits, members of the lowest caste (previously called 'the untouchables'), who made up about one-third of all the participants. With the same objective in mind, thirteen languages were considered official, as opposed to the four Indo-European languages adopted in the previous Forums: Hindi, Marathi, Tamil, Bengali, Korean, Malayan, Bahasa, Indonesian, Thai, Japanese, English, French and Spanish.

In spite of the careful preparation and the policy of grounding the design of the Forum in several full national consultations, the organization of the Mumbai WSF met with several criticisms, some constructive and engaging, others radical and confrontational. Among the more constructive criticisms, Sen's stood out. In May 2003, Sen drew attention to the fact that the preparation of the event was a less than open and transparent process, strongly dominated by parties within the organized left and unwelcoming to non-invited people or organizations, a process in which the novelty of the WSF was forced to coexist with the old left political culture still prevailing in India (2003b: 25). Sen ended his analysis with some thoughtful recommendations.[25]

Among the radical criticisms, I will mention the report on 'The Economics and Politics of the World Social Forum' prepared by the Research Unit for Political Economy, based in Mumbai and published in September 2003 (RUPE 2003). It reflects the old rivalries among the old left, and, as such, it confirms, from an opposite perspective, Sen's comment above on the political culture prevailing in the organized left in India. The report starts with a general critique of the WSF:

> The WSF slogan, 'Another world is possible', while vague, taps the widespread, inarticulate yearning for another social system. However, the very principles and structure of the WSF ensure that it will not evolve into a platform of people's action and power against imperialism. Its claims to being a 'horizontal' (not a hierarchical) 'process' (not a body) are belied by the fact that decisions are controlled by a handful of organizations, many of them with considerable financial resources and ties to the very countries that control the existing world order. As the WSF disavows arriving at any decisions as a body, it is incapable of collective expression of will and action. Its gatherings are structured to give prominence to celebrities of the NGO world, who propagate the NGO worldview. Thus, in all the talk on 'alternatives', the spotlight remains on alternative policies within the existing system, rather than a change of the very system itself. (ibid.: 1)

This opening statement – with which many of those involved in the WSF might agree, with some qualifications – is followed by a vicious denunciation of the WSF as an agent of imperialism, of the NGOs in India as a counter-revolutionary force and of the Communist Party of India (Marxist) – CPI (Marxist) – for having betrayed the revolution while becoming the driving force behind the WSF in Mumbai. These criticisms echo the rivalries, within the old communist left, between the Marxist and Marxist-Leninist (Maoist) parties. Indeed, the alternative WSF – Mumbai Resistance – held in Mumbai across the street from where the WSF was meeting was organized by some Marxist-Leninist (Maoist) tendencies (while others actively participated in the organization of the WSF).

In spite of the criticisms and the many deficiencies – exiguous space for so many people, activities organized as large events but drawing little participation, translation problems, impossibility of dialogue in spaces that were much too large – the 2004 WSF was considered an organizational success, thereby setting a higher level of expectancy for the organizers of the 2005 WSF.[26] Here are some of the reasons accounting for the success:

1. In retrospect, one can say that the choice of Mumbai as the venue for the 2004 WSF could not have been wiser. With its population of almost 15 million, Mumbai is the living symbol of the contradictions of capitalism in our time. An important financial and technological centre and the site of India's thriving film industry – Bollywood, producing more than two hundred movies a year for an increasingly global audience – Mumbai is a city whose extreme poverty easily shocks Western eyes. More than half of the population live in slums (roughly 2 million on the streets), whereas 73 per cent of families, usually large, live in one-room tenements. The recent spread of the informal economy has turned 2 per cent of the population into street vendors.

2. Moreover, the Mumbai WSF succeeded in demonstrating that the spirit of Porto Alegre, while being a universal aspiration, would acquire specific tonalities in different regions of the globe. In India, the struggle against inequality gains specific nuances that leave their mark on the Forum. First, on top of economic, sexual and ethnic inequalities there are caste inequalities, which, though abolished by the constitution, continue to be a decisive factor of discrimination. The Dalits made a very strong appearance at the Forum, as I mentioned above. They saw in the Forum a unique opportunity to denounce the discrimination that victimizes them. Second, there is the religion factor. As I said earlier, religion was absent from the

large events in the previous Forums. Seen from the perspective of the organizers – which, as we saw, did not coincide with that of many participants, as revealed through their social profile – this was due to the fact that in Western culture, which underpinned the first three meetings of the WSF, religion tends to carry less weight in view of the secularization of power. Be that as it may, the Mumbai WSF showed that, in the East, religion is a crucial social and political factor. Religious fundamentalism – a plague all over Asia, including India itself with the increasing politicization of Hinduism – was a major topic for debate, as was the role of spirituality in the social struggles for a better world.

3. Having taken place in Asia, the Forum could not help but pay special attention to the struggle for peace, not only because it is in western Asia, from Iraq to Afghanistan, that the USA's war aggression is strongest, but also because today South Asia (India and Pakistan) is a region full of nuclear weapons.

4. At the Mumbai WSF the Western conception of ecological struggles gave way to broader conceptions, so as to include the struggle for food sovereignty, land and water, as well as the preservation of bio-diversity and natural resources, and the defence of forests against agro-business and lumber industry.

By its very success, the Mumbai WSF created new challenges for the WSF process. I single out three main challenges. The first was the Forum's expansion, an issue already touched upon. It was not just a question of geographic expansion, but the expansion of themes and perspectives as well. Meeting in Mumbai, the IC decided to encourage the organization of local, national, regional and thematic forums, in order to deepen the syntony of the 'Porto Alegre Consensus' with the concrete struggles that mobilize such a diversity of social groups across the globe. The second challenge related to memory. The WSF had been collecting an impressive amount of knowledge concerning its organizations and movements, the world we live in and the proposals that go on being presented and implemented to change it. Such knowledge should be carefully evaluated in order to be adequately used and render the Forum more transparent to itself, thus allowing for self-learning for all the activists and movements involved in the WSF process.[27] Finally, as knowledge accumulated and the large areas of convergence were identified, the need for developing plans of collective action was likely to increase, giving rise to new problems and tensions. The issue was not so much to augment the WSF's efficaciousness as a global actor

– efficaciousness is probably not gauged by global as much as by local and national actions – but mainly to prepare responses to the attempts of the World Bank, the IMF and the World Economic Forum meeting in Davos to co-opt the agendas of the WSF and sanitize them in favour of solutions that will leave the ongoing economic disorder intact. This challenge echoed the debate on the political role of the WSF already mentioned. The Mumbai WSF showed that, even if the WSF was to keep its character as an open space – not presenting proposals in its own name – it would have to come up with the institutional changes that facilitate the links between the networks that constitute it, in order to strengthen plans of collective action and put them into practice.

The twofold need to evaluate and spread the accumulated knowledge and prepare plans of collective action with a sound political and techni-cal basis led to more discussion than ever before in previous Forums of the relationship between expert and grassroots knowledge, and, more specifically, between social scientists and popular struggles.[28]

The WSF 2005 On the initiative of the content and methodology com-mittees a new methodology for the 2005 WSF started being discussed from the second semester of 2003 onwards. The idea was to pursue in more intense forms the democratization of the WSF, attuning the themes and methodology of the WSF in a more systematic way to the expectations and interests of the participant organizations and movements, and maximizing the possibility of common links and actions. The new methodology was first formulated at the meeting of the content and methodology committees in Perugia, in November 2003, and was finally approved in the April 2004 meeting of the IC held in Passignano sul Trasimeno, Italy.

The new methodology – called 'Thematic Consultation and Cohesion of Activities' – aimed at two main objectives: 1) to build the whole WSF programme from the bottom up, in such a way that all the activities would be in a strong sense self-managed; 2) to maximize the possibility of links and common action among organizations, by inviting them to engage in a sustained dialogue leading to the cohesion of proposed activities for the Forum. The first practical step was a thematic consulta-tion with all the people of Porto Alegre. A questionnaire was sent to all the movements and organizations involved in the WSF process with the objective of identifying a) the themes, struggles, questions, problems, proposals and challenges that they would like to see discussed at WSF 2005 and in which format; and b) which activities they intended to organize at the Forum. The questionnaire was sent out in May and the *new method*

last responses were received at the beginning of August; 1,863 organizations responded to the questionnaire. The results were subsequently analysed in several meetings of the IC commissions on methodology and contents. Eleven thematic terrains were identified, which were to organize all the proposed activities for WSF 2005 (see Chapter 3).

The eleven thematic terrains would be the privileged terrain for the expression of the diversity and plurality within the WSF. Each terrain would be subdivided into sub-terrains. In order to provide focus for the debates, three transversal axes were identified: social emancipation and the political dimensions of struggles; struggle against patriarchal capitalism; struggle against racism.

The great methodological innovation of WSF 2005 was that all activities were self-managed. When proposing an activity, each organization would link it to one of the eleven thematic spaces. In doing so it would be immediately in contact with all the other organizations proposing activities within the same space. The process of aggregating activities would then start – with the help of facilitators, whenever necessary – seeking to avoid the fragmentation that plagued the Forum in previous meetings (different activities on the same topic being held separately and without any communication among them). As the aggregation proceeded activities would be merged and changed and, as a result, the organizations would be free to re-register their activities, taking into account the new format emerging from the aggregation process. It was expected that this linkage and the mutual knowledge it made possible, which started before the Forum and would continue thereafter, would induce and facilitate the planning of common collective actions and campaigns. Moreover, with the same objective, the OC reserved a daily slot of time (5–8 p.m.) for informal meetings among the organizations active in the same thematic space, in which aggregations might be evaluated and revised and plans for future common collective action might be agreed upon.

This new methodology was much more democratic and participatory. It required a higher degree of engagement on the part of the organizations for a longer period of time.

It was also decided to abandon the site where the first three meetings of the WSF had taken place (the headquarters of the Catholic University) and to build what was called the World Social Territory alongside the Guaiba river bank. Even though the appropriation of the methodology did not always succeed in measuring up to expectations, the 2005 WSF was considered by most a successful event. Along the right bank of the Guaiba river, more than 155,000 people circulated and some 250 tents were set up, where more than 2,500 sessions took place, often in torrid temperatures. The large distances along the river bank and the absence of a central venue where large gatherings could take place and the chances of meeting people would be enhanced gave an impression of fragmentation, a sense that one could easily get lost. The eleven thematic terrains were physically distributed in different tents along several kilometres, which made it difficult to move from one terrain to another, even more so considering the weather conditions. This fragmentation was seen by many as retrogression in relation to the Mumbai meeting.[29] But participants more interested in having in-depth discussions on their particular topics and terrain and in setting up partnerships for future action found the physical separation specifically congenial to their purposes. Significant progress in some areas, such as water, debt and FTAA, was reported. At the end of the Forum, 352 agreed proposals for action were posted on the Wall of Proposals.

Building on the experience of the Mumbai WSF, the innovative methodology adopted in the 2005 WSF, with its emphasis on self-organization, made the event more democratic.[30] It was, however, recognized that more fragile groups and non-central themes could not benefit on equal terms from the new format. In the IC meeting of April in Utrecht, the methodology was critically assessed and some members suggested that self-organization had gone too far, allowing for the political manipulation of the event, for instance through the highly visible interventions of both President Lula and President Hugo Chavez. Some also thought that large gatherings like the conferences created a sense of common belonging that was lost in the new format. Moreover, the transversal axes, which were supposed to inform the work of all the thematic terrains, didn't work, not only because they were too vague and confusing but also because there were no mechanisms to make them effective. It should also be mentioned that the process of cohesion – which was aimed at creating interfaces and interconnections among themes, campaigns and movements, and organizations – didn't work according to expectations, because of either the incompetence of the facilitators or the sheer difficulty of coordinating across so much diversity.

· For very different reasons two incidents during the Forum became polemical and should be mentioned. One was the Manifesto of Porto Alegre subscribed to by nineteen highly visible participants. Because of its relevance in the discussion of the political cleavages inside the WSF, it will be dealt with in Chapter 6. The other consisted of around ninety cases of violence against women in the Youth Camp, the *Acampamento*, where 35,000 young people camped. The seriousness of the crimes committed against women led the campers to organize security units inside the camp, the Brigadas Lilás, and a rally to call the attention of the WSF to this type of violence. Feminist groups saw in this violence further evidence of the absence of feminist concerns and perspectives at the core of the WSF, in both political and organizational terms. According to Ana Elena Obando, of the Women's Human Rights net,

> the common denominator amongst the resistance movements [...] was their general opposition to neoliberal capitalism, militarization, war and the destruction of the environment, and their lack of opposition to one of the expressions of patriarchy that is intertwined with those above: fundamentalisms, particularly religious fundamentalisms. Even though we the feminists have conquered our space in the WSF [...] the fact remains that we go on travelling among ourselves and with ourselves incorporating to a certain extent the agendas and concerns of other movements without seeing the latter reciprocating. (Obando 2005)

The 2006 polycentric WSF

It is consensually acknowledged that the organizational experimentation undertaken in the 2005 WSF showed the enormous capacity of the WSF to transform itself. This capacity was further demonstrated in the preparation of the 2006 WSF.

Throughout 2004, there was some discussion in the IC and IS about the possibility of experimenting with a new format for the WSF, particularly in light of the persistent difficulty in improving the global scope of the WSF. In 2005, and after the planned WSF for Africa was scheduled for 2007 (Nairobi), it was finally decided that the 2006 WSF would be decentralized, 'polycentric', according to the designation adopted. It would take place simultaneously in three continents and the date should as usual and whenever possible coincide with the meeting of the World Economic Forum. Caracas, Bamako and Karachi were chosen as the venues. Throughout 2005 there were several meetings in which the organizers of the polycentric forums met with members of the IC and the IS to discuss common organizational problems and to articulate the diversity that each WSF would express in light of its geopolitical context, with the commonality derived from their being partial realizations of the same WSF. The WSF of Caracas and Bamako took place according to the original schedule. WSF Karachi was postponed until March 2006, owing to the disruption caused by the earthquake that devastated the country in the autumn of 2005.[31]

The analysis of the profound organizational transformations during the years of the WSF's existence seems to provide sufficient evidence for my argument that the WSF has shown an enormous capacity to reinvent itself, to identify problems and seek imaginative solutions for them. Reading the minutes of the many meetings of the IC, one gets an eloquent impression of an immense amount of confrontational dialogue and soul-searching, through which tensions and compromises, arguments and counter-arguments, proposals and alternative proposals are played out with the common purpose of improving the capacity of the WSF to transform our unjust societies into another possible world. It becomes evident that such capacity is premised upon the capacity of the WSF to transform itself, learning from past experience without self-indulgence and looking ahead to the new challenges with open-mindedness. It seems that if and when this capacity for self-transformation is exhausted the WSF will be doomed.

Notes

1 ATTAC was formerly the Association for a Tobin Tax for the Aid of Citizens; later on it became the Association for the Taxation of Financial Transactions for the Aid of Citizens.

2 As I will show in the following, in spite of changes in name and composition this group is still the organizing core of the WSF today.

3 Basically for operational reasons the core of the IS continued to be the original Brazilian Organizing Committee. Meanwhile, whenever the WSF convenes in Brazil, the Brazilian members of the IS will integrate the local organizing committee with consultation functions. In the case of the 2005 WSF, the local organizing committee was composed of twenty-four members representing as many organizations and movements.

4 In Portuguese, 'Partido dos Trabalhadores' (PT).

5 The PT was in power in the municipality of Porto Alegre from 1989 until 2004 and in the Rio Grande do Sul state from 1999 until 2002.

6 This much was recognized by the IC, which, in a note circulated after its meeting in Porto Alegre in January 2003, stated, after generally praising the performance of the IS: 'Notwithstanding this, clear limits can be pointed out in the performance of the Secretariat. The fast expansion of the internationalization process has meant that many times we were surpassed by the events; the Brazilian electoral process affected the organizations included in the Secretariat; the event in Porto Alegre has grown dramatically this year and demanded political investments that had to be organized with lesser local resources; information was not always passed to the IC with the necessary agility. These and other limitations must be overcome.'

7 The meetings of the IC in Miami in June 2003 and in Perugia in November 2003 helped to create a climate of mutual trust between the 'Westerners' and the 'Easterners'. In Perugia, the Indian delegates showed unconditional

willingness to give out information and a great capacity for appeasing the more sceptical about the possibility of a successful WSF in Mumbai.

8 The co-presence required by some of the tasks allotted to the IS makes it impossible for the Indian group to share the executive work on an equal basis.

9 In Chapter 5 I describe some of these measures briefly.

10 These commissions are described in chapter 5.

11 Michael Albert, coordinator of the alternative media network ZNET, who organized a wide group of sessions under the general title of 'Life after Capitalism', considered himself discriminated against by the IS. According to him the sessions did not appear on the programme, room assignment was chaotic (successive room changes, lack of simultaneous translation, etc.), and participation became very difficult as a consequence (personal communication).

12 In the first three meetings of the WSF criticism was also expressed concerning the presence of controversial figures, such as leaders of guerrilla groups.

13 See below, Chapter 6.

14 Grzybowski (2002); on the 2003 WSF, see the *Declaration of the 2003 World Social Forum: Perspective of Women of the World March of Women*, at <www.ffq.qc.ca/marche2000/en/fsm2003.html>; accessed on 19 March 2003, and Lagunas (2003).

15 By way of example, I mention three proposals made by myself with a view to increasing internal democracy and transparency during the 2003 WSF: posting the decisions taken by the OC or IC in designated places; saving some space in the evening for an open debate about organization or other issues; taking advantage of the technologies of electronic democracy to carry out referendums on organizational or strategic decisions during the Forum. The two first proposals would have been easy to put in place, had it not been for an administrative breakdown. Suffice it to say that during this Forum the full programme, including all activities, was never published.

16 The 2001 WSF was attended by some 1,800 journalists, the 2003 WSF by more than 4,000, the 2004 WSF by 3,200 and the 2005 WSF by 5,421.

17 As I will discuss in Chapter 9, it is also a major issue in the broader topic of the emergence of a global left politics.

18 The Charter of Principles was agreed upon by the International Council of the WSF in 2001. Later on, during the preparation of the 2004 WSF, it was discussed in various meetings in India. At one of these meetings (Bhopal, April 2002) a policy document was adopted which modified some of the clauses of the Charter and added new ones with the purpose of adapting it to the specific conditions that prevail in India today. The tale of this policy statement will be analysed in Chapter 6. Here, suffice it to mention the clause that, in contrast with the original Charter of Principles, states that 'in India the WSF Charter has been extended to include social and political realities as they exist in the country today ... This entails the opening of a dialogue within and between the broad spectrum of political parties and groups, social movements and other organizations.'

19 On this subject, see for example, Bertinoti (2002).

20 Proposals and strategies would be transformed into charts based on notes sent in by panel members. These charts could be used by facilitators. During the process, the charts would be reworked and a new version made available to the final panel. Panellists would decide on the use of these charts and notes from the systematization team.

21 According to the systematization group the sample was representative.

22 For instance, the term 'globalization', pervasive in the conference presentations, was hardly mentioned in the topics of the workshops.

23 One of the best-attended events at the Forum was entitled 'Mystics and Revolution'.

24 Already, in the WSF 2002, more space had been given to the self-managed activities.

25 '1 – be concerned and informed about larger political and social developments in India;

2 – for people in other parts of the world, try and visit India during this year for a substantial period of time, and build close working relations with like-minded people and organizations there; encourage others you know to also do this;

3 – encourage people you know in India to fully participate in the Forum – to go into the space; this is the only way to truly democratize and defend open space; equally, encourage people you know in all parts of the world to fully participate in the Forum;

4 – globalize the Forum! Insist on open, internationalist planning of the World Social Forum – which as it happens is taking place this next year in India but where this should be embedded in WSF practice, as a matter of principle and permanent practice; and on the introduction of easy, online participation in planning and policy formation;

5 – resist the likely tendency of the Forum in India itself becoming a platform for building unity, however necessary this might be for some social actors within India; insist that the role of the Forum is only to provide space for this to happen;

6 – insist on the public articulation of a larger, more strategic internationalist perspective for the holding of the Forum in India – for if this articulation is not there, and clear to all, then what is the purpose of not continuing to hold the world meeting in Porto Alegre?

7 – insist on open, inclusive, democratic, and friendly communication both from the WSF secretariat in India and from the International Secretariat in Brazil' (Sen 2003b: 31).

26 For a balanced view of the Mumbai WSF, see Vivas (2004).

27 The project of systematization analysed above was a manifestation of the need to respond to this challenge.

28 I myself organized, through the Centre for Social Studies (CES) of the University of Coimbra, where I work, a workshop entitled 'New Partnerships for New Knowledges'. The participants were social scientists and activists. Immanuel Wallerstein (USA), Aníbal Quijano (Peru), D. L. Sheth (India), Goran Therborn (Sweden), Hilary Wainwright (UK) and myself were among the social

scientists; Jai Sen (India), Irene Leon (Ecuador) and Moema Miranda (Brazil) were among the activists. The discussion concentrated on themes that are at the core of the idea of public sociology: the relationship between expertise and engagement; from critique to plans for action; the reliability of the knowledge underlying social struggles and its critique; the impact on social scientists of their engagement with lay or popular knowledges; activists as producers of knowledge. A proposal for a Popular University of Social Movements was also presented at the workshop. See below, Chapter 8.

29 In an evaluation of the 2005 WSF posted on ZNET on 8 February 2005 Alex Calinicos and Chris Nineham saw in the fragmentation a 'potentially disastrous development', commenting that 'one of the great beauties of our movement ... is the way in which people from all sorts of backgrounds and with the most diverse preoccupations come and mix together, participating in a process of mutual contamination in which we learn and gain confidence from one another'.

30 While in the 2004 WSF there were still a small number of centrally organized sessions (thirteen), in the 2005 WSF all the sessions were self-organized with the exception of the opening cultural event.

31 At the time of writing (early March 2006) it is still too early to evaluate the WSFs of Caracas and Bamako. Indeed, full evaluation of the 2006 WSF will have to wait until after the event takes place in Karachi.

5 | Representing this world as it fights for another possible world

The Charter of Principles contains a double statement in this regard: first, the WSF does not claim to be representative of counter-hegemonic globalization; second, no one represents the WSF nor can speak in its name. These are two separate yet related issues: whom does the WSF represent? Who represents the WSF? In this chapter I address the first question by analysing the socio-political profile of the participants in the WSF, and the second question by discussing the issue of the composition and functionality of the International Council. It will become evident in the following that most of the organizational questions analysed in Chapter 4 are also questions of representation.

Whom does the WSF represent?

The first issue – the WSF's representativeness – has been discussed at different levels.[1] One of them concerns the limits of the world dimension of the WSF. The numbers and the diversity of the geographical origin of participants have been increasing steadily, from the first to the fifth WSF. Here are some statistical data.

TABLE 5.1 WSF in numbers

Year/locale	Attendance	Number of workshops	Number of countries represented
I WSF – 2001, Porto Alegre, Brazil	20,000	420	117
II WSF – 2002, Porto Alegre, Brazil	50,000	622	123
III WSF – 2003, Porto Alegre, Brazil	100,000	1,286	156
IV WSF – 2004, Mumbai, India[2]	115,000	1,200	117
V WSF – 2005, Porto Alegre, Brazil[3]	155,000	2,300	149

Although unquestionably significant, these data conceal the limits of the WSF's geographical scope. To begin with, and as one might expect, nationals of the host country represent a very high percentage of participants: around 70 per cent in 2003, 84 per cent in 2004 and

80 per cent in 2005. Participation from neighbouring countries tends also to be very high: from Argentina, Uruguay and Chile in 2003 and 2005; from Pakistan, Nepal and Bangladesh in 2004. For instance, in the 2003 WSF, of the 100,000 participants it is estimated that more than 70,000 were Brazilian and 15,000 from other Latin American countries. If this is so, then no more than 15,000 participants from the 'rest of the world' could have been there. Participation is self-funded, which explains why participants from the USA, France and Italy are present in large numbers, regardless of where the Forum is held. Most movements and non-governmental organizations (NGOs) have no financial capacity to support their own participation in the WSF. Those that have attended, particularly as regards the first three meetings of the WSF, have often been funded by European and North American NGOs. In such cases, the NGOs claim the right to choose who is to be funded. Thus, even if world participation becomes quantitatively broader and more diverse, the issue of representation will always be there until the selection criteria are more transparent and democratic.

This fact has led some critics to affirm that the WSF is far from having a world dimension. The absences of Africa and Asia in the first three meetings were specifically criticized. The scarce participation from Africa and Asia was negative in itself, but it was even more so if one bears in mind that the absence of movements and organizations from these continents is reflected, in part, in the absence of themes and debates particularly relevant or specific to their realities. A vicious circle may thereby emerge: African or Asian movements do not take part in the WSF because the debates that they most cherish are absent, and they are absent precisely because of the scarce participation of Africans and Asians.

As I mentioned in Chapter 4, with this concern in mind, in its meeting of January 2003 in Porto Alegre, the IC decided to convene the fourth WSF in Mumbai. The decision had been in train since the end of 2001, and the date was selected by the India committees. However polemical, the decision was quite successful in facilitating the presence of Asian movements and organizations. Of the 115,000 participants, the overwhelming majority came from India and other Asian countries.[4] The Mumbai WSF was a decisive step forward towards the globalization of the WSF process. It extended the experience of the WSF to a new and impressive set of movements and organizations coming from countries for which the WSF was still something quite remote. Above all, it showed that the spirit of the WSF – the 'Porto Alegre Consensus' (as it begins to be known, in contrast with the 'Washington Consensus'), based on the belief in the possibility of another, more just and more solidary world, and on the political will to fight for it – can be re-created in other parts of the world besides Latin America. And if it can be re-created in Asia,[5] there is no reason whatsoever why it couldn't be re-created in Africa. The African presence in Mumbai was not much larger than in previous forums. Africa's problem is that the Atlantic Ocean separates it from Latin America and the Indian Ocean from Asia. For this reason, and encouraged by the Mumbai success, the IC decided in its meeting in Mumbai that the WSF to take place after the 2005 meeting – since 2003 scheduled for Porto Alegre[6] – would take place in Africa. In the following meeting, which took place in Italy in April 2004, the African representatives committed themselves to having the 2007 WSF in Africa and the specific location, Nairobi, was chosen at the meeting of the IC in Porto Alegre, during WSF 2005.[7] In another demonstration of the will and capacity to increase the globalization of the WSF, it was decided at the same IC meeting that the 2006 meeting would assume a new format: a polycentric WSF, as it was designated, taking place simultaneously, if possible, in three continents, in the Americas (Caracas), Africa (Bamako) and Asia (Pakistan).[8]

I do not question the relevance of this particular dimension of the issue of representation, and, as just shown, a sustained effort to enlarge and balance the geographical representation of the WSF has been made. Besides having the WSF take place in different regions of the world, other proposals have been made with a view to facilitating the participation of movements and organizations of the Global South. According to one of them, movements and organizations of the wealthier North, besides paying for their own participation, should contribute towards a common fund to support the participation of movements and organizations of the South that would otherwise be unable to participate. I believe, however, that the WSF must not be delegitimized for not being worldwide enough. If that were the case, we would be submitting it to a much more demanding criterion of globality than we apply to organizations and institutions of hegemonic globalization. Moreover, the criterion of geographical representation is only one of the representativeness criteria. There are no doubt others, with perhaps far more relevance from the political standpoint. Consider, for example, the representation of different themes and political philosophies, different kinds of organizations and movements, different strategies and agendas, and so on and so forth. Particularly after Mumbai, all these criteria tended to be taken into account more and more. As I will show in Chapter 6, when I deal with issues of political strategy, the question of how to choose between different strategic alternatives is already in place and drawing heated debate.

I do think, however, that so far the issues of representation have been brought into the discussion in such a way that they fail to raise obstacles to the spontaneous congregation of movements and organizations that have been so decisive in affirming the existence of an alternative kind of globalization. The WSF had its origin in a small group of organizations that represented only themselves. The enthusiasm the idea generated surprised even its authors. It gave voice to the need many movements and organizations felt for an arena or space that would not be confined to contesting institutions of hegemonic globalization, but would rather function as a meeting point for the exchange of experiences, debate on alternatives and elaboration of plans for joint action. The idea's success was gauged by free circulation, celebration of diversity, participation without conditions, and the absence of negotiations that might compromise the movements. It was felt that any restrictive criterion would end up bringing about exclusion at a time when only inclusion would make sense. As a matter of fact, even if one had wanted to resort to criteria, it would have been impossible to identify them, let alone rely on an organization capable of legitimately selecting and decreeing them, and supervising their enforcement. It is, however, understandable that the success achieved by the WSF should have contributed to raising the issue of the representativeness of participation. In the evaluations of all the meetings of WSF this issue cropped up frequently. This was particularly the case with the 2003 WSF. As I discussed in Chapter 4, this meeting of the WSF was submitted to a systematic evaluation. One of its main dimensions was the evaluation of the social profile of the participants. It was believed that the results would provide a realistic assessment of the representativeness of the WSF as a counter-hegemonic global movement. The success of the 'systematization' led the organizers to repeat it with basically the same methodology at the two subsequent meetings of the WSF. There were, however, some methodological variations, and for that reason the results are not always comparable. In the following I analyse the social profile of the 'people of Porto Alegre' as established through the systematization of the 2003 WSF, comparing the latter whenever possible with the systematization of the 2005 WSF.

The people of Porto Alegre in 2003 The social profile of the participants in the 2003 WSF was defined through a survey conducted on a representative and stratified sample of 1,500 interviewees.[9] The enrolled participants were divided into three groups: delegates, non-delegate participants and campers (staying at the Youth Camp and other camps). The questionnaire was divided into three large themes: characteristics of the participants, engagement in the social and political struggle, and opinions on the public debates agenda.

CHARACTERISTICS (MAIN RESULTS). The majority of participants were Brazilians (85.9 per cent). Among the non-Brazilians, 39.7 per cent came from Latin America. The countries with the largest number of participants were the countries neighbouring Brazil, France and the USA: Argentina (13.1 per cent), Uruguay (9.5 per cent), Chile (8.7 per cent), Paraguay (8.4 per cent), France (7.2 per cent), USA (6.6 per cent); 46.3 per cent of the non-Brazilians came from the remaining 133 countries that were represented in the WSF. In the case of the delegates – participants who represent NGOs or movements, 23 per cent of the total number of participants – the presence of France and the USA was even stronger. While the Argentinian delegates represented 6.4 per cent of the total, the delegates from France and the USA made up 8 per cent and 10.4 per cent respectively. These data confirmed the deficit of globality in the WSF and the difficulty of including the bottom in the bottom-up globalization.

Women formed the majority, both of the participants in general (51 per cent) and of the delegates (50.4 per cent). The Brazilian delegates had a stronger feminine presence than the non-Brazilians, 52.7 per cent and 45.7 per cent respectively. As I have already said, the presence of women at the bottom had no reflection at the top of the Forum. As regards sexual preference, 6.1 per cent of the participants stated that they were homosexual, the rest heterosexual (6.1 per cent refused to answer).

As concerns age structure, youth had a strong presence at the Forum: 37.7 per cent of participants were in the age bracket fourteen to twenty-four years. As to delegates, however, only 13 per cent were in that same age bracket. In the camps, the majority were young: 68.5 per cent. The remaining age brackets of participants were as follows: between twenty-five and thirty-four years, 25 per cent; between thirty-five and forty-four, 19.9 per cent; between forty-five and fifty-four, 12.6 per cent; fifty-five years or older, 4.9 per cent.

The strong presence of the young had no expression in the activities organized by the OC, and it was not possible to draw any bridge between the activities of the Forum and the Youth Camp (the was true for all the meetings of the WSF). Hence the criticism of the young, who claimed they were marginalized inside the Forum.

Literacy is perhaps among the most intriguing theme in the data about the social base of the WSF. The level of literacy of participants was very high: 73.4 per cent of the participants held a college degree, whether complete or incomplete, a master's degree or a doctorate. Only 25.7 per cent had between zero and twelve years of schooling; 9.7 per cent of the participants had a master's or doctorate, a percentage that rose to 17.8 per cent in the case of the delegates, reaching 30.1 per cent in the case of non-Brazilian delegates. The criticism frequently addressed to the WSF that it is the expression of an elite among the counter-hegemonic globalization seems to be hereby confirmed.

As regards employment, 62.3 per cent of the participants and 81.2 per cent of the delegates were employed. In terms of their occupation, 43.2 per cent worked for private institutions or NGOs (this percentage reached 44.2 per cent in the case of the delegates) and 36 per cent were public officials; 4.3 per cent worked in manufacturing and 3.3 per cent in agriculture; 12.9 per cent worked in commerce. The tertiary sector (services) was thus the major sector of activity: it employed 79.5 per cent of the participants holding jobs. As regards social class, the waged petty bourgeoisie seemed to prevail.

In terms of religious beliefs, 62.6 per cent of the participants declared they had a religion, the percentage being higher among the Brazilians than among non-Brazilians. The predominant religion was, by far, the Catholic religion, accounting for 61.6 per cent of those who stated they did have a religion. Religiosity was even stronger among the delegates (66.3 per cent). These data seem to point to the important role religion plays among the social groups fighting against neo-liberal globalization, and it may explain one of the ideological differences between the organizers of the WSF and its social base as detected in the other results of the systematization presented in Chapter 4. As we saw above, in the first three Forums the themes of religion and spirituality were never considered important enough by the OC and the IC for organized activities to be dedicated to them, let alone activities with high visibility. The situation changed to some extent in the Mumbai WSF.

ENGAGEMENT IN SOCIAL AND POLITICAL STRUGGLE. The majority of participants (64.9 per cent) were engaged in some organization or social movement, a percentage that unsurprisingly reached 89.1 in the case of the delegates. In view of the data analysed above concerning the occupation of the delegates, we can say that most probably a high percentage were employed by the organization in which he or she was involved. The question about the ambit of the organizations with which they were involved allowed for multiple answers. From the answers given, the conclusion may be drawn that organizations of national and sub-national ambit prevailed overwhelmingly: 33 per cent were local, 35 per cent regional and 36 per cent national. It comes as no surprise that only in the case of the non-Brazilian delegates did organizations of international ambit have a significant weight: 36 per cent, as opposed to 16 per cent in the case of participants in general. These data confirm what I said above about the nature of the WSF: its novelty resides in its having invested in the global links among organizations previously involved in national or local struggles.

As regards the institutional nature of the organizations and movements in which the participants were involved, the strong presence of social movements (25.7 per cent) and NGOs (19.4 per cent) was obvious. Trade unions came next (16.3 per cent). As to the area of action (the question allowed for multiple answers), education was by far the most prevalent, at 47 per cent, followed by popular participation/organization, at 30 per cent, and human rights, at 24 per cent; 35 per cent of the participants declared that they were members of political parties, a percentage that reached 44 in the case of the delegates. The more intense the involvement with NGOs and movements, the less probable was party membership. In the case of trade unionists, however, the majority belonged to a political party. The more leftist the political stance stated, the greater the probability of party affiliation: 46 per cent in the case of those who considered themselves extreme left, and only 28 per cent for those from the centre-left. This may suggest that among the parties on the left it was the extreme left parties which invested most in participation in the WSF. The extreme left position was, however, in the minority among the participants: only 6 per cent identified themselves as extreme left, 15 per cent centre-left, 63 per cent left. Among the delegates, the percentage of those considering themselves left was slightly higher, at 67 per cent.

OPINIONS ON THE PUBLIC DEBATES AGENDA. This is a field in which, in surveys of this nature, it is very risky to draw conclusions with any degree of safety. I selected those answers in which the risk seemed to be smaller. As regards abortion, it was asked whether the participants were totally in favour, totally against or whether 'it depends on the situation': 40 per cent said they were totally in favour, 36 per cent that 'it depends on the situation' and 20 per cent were against. More delegates said they were totally in favour, more non-Brazilian delegates (63 per cent) than Brazilian (40 per cent). Not surprisingly, religion

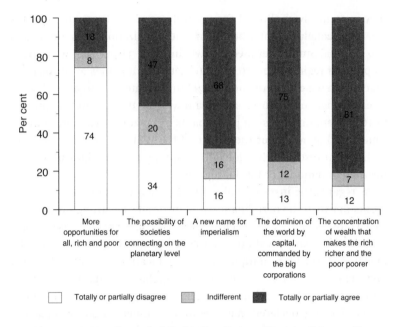

Figure 5.1 Meanings of globalization (Source: Survey of the profile of participants at the 2003 WSF)

seems to be the factor that most colours opinions about abortion: 26 per cent of those professing a religion were totally against abortion, while only 9 per cent of those not professing any religion were of this opinion. Among those participating in the organization of civil society, the proportion totally in favour was significantly lower among the trade unionists (31 per cent).

Several questions were asked concerning the processes of globalization and multilateral institutions. Participants were asked to declare their degree of agreement or disagreement[10] with the following characterizations of globalization: 'a new name for imperialism', 'the concentration of wealth making the rich richer and the poor poorer', 'the possibility of societies connecting on the planetary level', 'more opportunities for all, rich and poor', 'the dominion of the world by capital, commanded by big corporations'. Figure 5.1 presents the results.

Not surprisingly, the opinion most favourable to globalization ('more opportunities for all, rich and poor') was that most rejected. It is, however, significant that this rejection was lower among delegates (71 per cent). Equally interesting was the fact that the most ideologically loaded characterization ('a new name for imperialism') drew a higher rate of

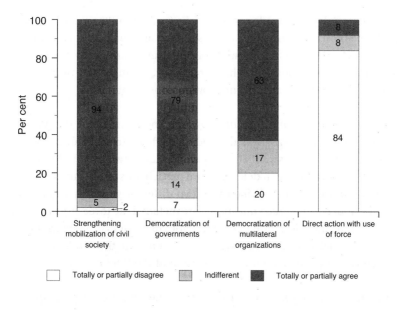

Figure 5.2 Means towards another possible world (Source: Survey of
the profile of participants at the 2003 WSF)

agreement among those active in social movements (72 per cent) than
among those active in NGOs (64 per cent).

The interviewees were asked to express their opinion about the
efficacy of the following mechanisms to bring about 'another possible world': 'strengthening mobilization of civil society on the global,
national, regional and local levels', 'democratization of multilateral
organizations (United Nations, WTO, World Bank, IMF)', 'democratization of governments' and 'direct action with use of force' (see Figure
5.2).

The overall results are not surprising, but there are some significant
differences among different categories of participants. For instance,
Brazilians – obviously under the impact of the then recent victory of
the PT in the presidential elections – had much more confidence in the
democratization of governments (81 per cent) than non-Brazilians (70
per cent). On the other hand, activists in social movements had much
less confidence in the democratization of multilateral institutions (51
per cent) than the members of trade unions or NGOs (68 per cent).
Similarly, the incidence of rejection of direct action with use of force was
much higher among trade unionists (87 per cent) and NGO members
(86 per cent) than among activists in social movements (76 per cent),
and was also much higher among delegates – 87 per cent in the case of

Brazilian delegates and 82 per cent in the case of non-Brazilian delegates – than among the campers, i.e. the students and the participants in the lowest social strata (77 per cent). Not surprisingly, among those who saw themselves as belonging to the extreme left, the incidence of rejection of direct action was significantly lower (67 per cent).

The people of Porto Alegre in 2005 The social profile of the participants in the 2005 WSF was defined through a survey conducted on a representative and stratified sample of 2,540 interviews.[11] This time, the distinction between delegates and participants was eliminated and attendees were rather divided into two different groups: participants and campers.[12] The 2005 questionnaire included the three large themes of the 2003 questionnaire – characteristics of participants, engagement in the social and political struggle, opinions on the public debates agenda – and added a fourth: evaluation of the WSF methodology.

CHARACTERISTICS (MAIN RESULTS). The majority of participants were Brazilians (80 per cent) but less so than in 2003 (85.9 per cent). The countries with the largest number of participants were again the countries neighbouring Brazil, the USA and France:[13] Argentina (13.1 per cent, the same as in 2003), followed by the USA (9.5 per cent, against 6.6 per cent in 2003), Uruguay (7.5 per cent, against 9.5 per cent in 2003), France (4.7 per cent, against 7.2 per cent in 2003) and Chile (4.3 per cent, against 8.7 per cent in 2003). In 2005, 34.7 per cent of the non-Brazilians came from the remaining 134 countries that were represented in the WSF (this corresponds to 46.3 per cent). In terms of the internationalization process of the WSF the two most remarkable facts are, on the one hand, the larger number of participants from the USA[14] and, on the other, the dramatic increase in the participation of Indians: in 2003, they represented a modest 0.6 per cent of the foreign participants; in 2005 this percentage rose to 2.5. This increase is certainly linked to the fact that the WSF was held in India in 2004 and confirms the political success of the strategy of geographical relocation of the WSF, initiated that year to broaden and diversify participation. Another significant factor is that in the Youth Camp (22.6 per cent of the total) campers from Canada and the USA were among the six largest delegations.

Attendance by gender was on average very balanced (49.4 per cent women, 49.6 per cent men). Among non-Brazilian and non-Latin American participants, however, there was a significant imbalance: 46.4 per cent women, 53.6 per cent men. By age group, women tend to be younger: they made up 55.4 per cent of the fourteen-to-twenty-four age group. As regards age structure, the participation of young people has increased significantly: those in the age bracket fourteen to twenty-four represented 37.7 per cent of participants in 2003 and 42.2 per cent in 2005. The differences in the remaining age brackets of participants were not so significant.

The difficulties in drawing bridges between the Forum and the Youth Camp, identified in the previous meetings, remained in the 2005 WSF, even though the Youth Camp had a more central location inside the World Social Territory. Education continued to figure among the most intriguing data about the characterization of the social base of the WSF. The level of education of participants continued to be very high, even higher than in 2003: 77.7 per cent of the participants held a college degree, whether complete or incomplete, a master's degree or a doctorate (73.4 per cent in 2003). Only 22.3 per cent had between zero and twelve years of schooling (25.7 per cent in 2003). The criticism that the WSF is the expression of an elite of the counter-hegemonic globalization, already voiced in 2003, seems to be hereby confirmed.

Concerning occupation, changes in the questionnaire permitted the category student to coexist with other occupations. As a result, 40.8 per cent declared student as their occupation, with considerable variation among the different age groups, as one might expect. Comparison with the 2003 WSF becomes difficult. The most frequently represented occupations are civil servant and employee of NGO/civil society entity/political party/trade union. Almost 30 per cent of the non-Brazilian and non-Latin American participants are in this latter occupational category. Probably more revealing in class terms was the family profile as defined by the father's and mother's occupation. It transpired that the fathers' occupations were mainly civil servants, self-employed and employees of private companies, respectively 20.8, 20.4 and 20 per cent. As far as the mother's occupation is concerned, the data were revealing not only of the sexual division of labour but also of persistent sexual discrimination: 24.7 per cent were unemployed (4.2 per cent in the case of the father), 19.6 per cent maids, 13.5 per cent farmers (8.5 per cent in the case of the father), 12.1 per cent civil servants (20.8 per cent in the case of the father), 5.7 per cent self-employed (20.4 per cent in the case of the father) and 4.8 per cent employees of private companies (20 per cent in the case of the father). It is interesting to note that the father's occupation among Latin American participants deviates considerably from this pattern: 16.4 per cent are farmers (8.5 per cent in total), 18 per cent employers (7 per cent in total) and 12.5 per cent unemployed

(4.2 per cent in total). A preliminary analysis of the data warrants the conclusion that there are no significant changes as to the social class of the participants.

In the case of Brazilian participants, a question was asked concerning race/ethnic group. The great majority considered themselves to be whites (63.3 per cent) while the percentage of blacks and mulattos was basically the same (16 per cent and 15.5 per cent respectively).[15]

ENGAGEMENT IN SOCIAL AND POLITICAL STRUGGLE. In 2005, 23.4 per cent of the participants were affiliated to political parties, which represents a slight but clear drop in relation to the 35 per cent of 2003. There were significant changes in affiliation by gender: 29 per cent of the men, 18.2 per cent of the women. More significant, however, are the comparisons between the 2003 and the 2005 surveys concerning participation in social movements or organizations.[16] In the 2003 survey the majority of participants were engaged in some organization or social movement (64.9 per cent); in the 2005 survey this figure dropped significantly to 55.4 per cent. In part the explanation may lie in the fact that the campers formed a higher percentage of participants in 2005 than in 2003, and it was among them that the participation was lowest: 44.9 per cent. The low incidence of participation in social movements and organizations among campers must be reflected upon. Could it be that the WSF has become a site of international political tourism? Participation in movements or organizations was higher among older participants: 74.4 per cent in the age bracket thirty-four to fifty-four, compared to 40.2 per cent in the age bracket fourteen to twenty-four. The data on participation by occupation showed that participation is higher among civil servants than among employees of private companies, 67.6 per cent and 44.2 per cent respectively. New questions on family participation in movements or organizations revealed some important facts on family influence on activism. The probability of becoming socially and politically active increases significantly if a member of the family is also active: 72.5 per cent of the actives came from active families, while only 47.1 per cent came from non-active families.

Of the participants in movements/organizations (55.4 per cent of the total) the largest percentage participated in NGOs (33.8 per cent), followed by social movements (28.5 per cent), trade unions (15 per cent) and political parties (11.3 per cent). The often-voiced criticism that the WSF is heavily influenced by the general philosophy of NGOs as social actors (the NGOization of the WSF) finds some base here. Moreover, the connection with NGOs (33.8 per cent) rises to 52.7 per cent in the case of non-Brazilian and non-Latin American participants. But in this latter case the travel costs are probably the decisive factor in explaining the difference. What deserves close attention is the comparison between this activism profile and that of the 2003 WSF, where the involvement in social movements was higher than in NGOs, 25.7 per cent and 19.4 per cent respectively. Should we conclude that the trend towards NGOization is deepening? If so, with what consequences? In this context it may be of interest to compare the data on self-identification of political identity. While in 2003 72.1 per cent of the participants considered themselves as belonging to the left and 15.2 per cent to the centre-left, in the 2005 survey these figures were 60.1 per cent and 19.8 per cent respectively.

As to the area of activism, the comparison between 2003 and 2005 is difficult as in 2005 this question was asked only of those who participated in movements/organizations.[17] The only reliable comparison concerns the area of education, which can safely be considered the most prevalent in both meetings of the WSF. Other comparisons are speculative but could be transformed into good working hypotheses as to the future of the WSF. Ranked by decreasing incidence, the following areas were identified in 2005: education, social assistance, combating discrimination, art and culture, popular organization/participation, human rights, environment, agriculture and land issues, defending and promoting rights (advocacy), public policies/public budget. Four variations between 2005 and 2003 might be fertile ground for further analysis: social assistance was second in 2005 and fifth in 2003; combating discrimination was third in 2005 and eighth in 2003; art and culture was fourth in 2005 and seventh in 2003; environment was seventh in 2005 and third in 2003.

In the 2005 survey new questions were asked about use of the Internet and the media. The data on the use of the Internet are relevant in terms of showing the continuing social deficit in the WSF process. Not surprisingly 80 per cent had regular access to the Internet. As we know, the WSF is an Internet-based network. More surprising is the high incidence of access to the Internet at home: 46.6 per cent of all participants, 50.7 per cent of the Brazilian participants. This also serves to confirm the perception that the WSF tends to attract people from higher-income strata.

OPINIONS ON THE LEGITIMACY OF INSTITUTIONS. Some of the questions on the public debates agenda (such as abortion or religion) asked in the 2003 survey were dropped in the 2005 survey.

Several questions were asked concerning the role of organized civil society, processes of globalization and multilateral institutions. In the last two cases it is possible to compare the data with those of 2003. There are no significant variations.

The same can be said concerning opinions about the efficacy of different mechanisms to bring about 'another possible world': 'strengthening mobilization of civil society on the global, national, regional and local level', 'democratization of multilateral organizations (United Nations, WTO, World Bank, IMF)', 'democratization of governments' and 'direct action with use of force'. There is, however, a significant new datum. In contrast with the 2003 survey, the 2005 survey distinguished two types of direct action: 'direct action' and 'direct action with use of force', the latter being the only one used in the 2003 survey. While direct action with the use of force continued to be strongly rejected (76.4 per cent), direct action (without the use of force) was strongly approved (59.3 per cent).

The 2005 survey introduced a new section on the evaluation of the WSF's methodology. The objective was to assess the extent to which the self-reform efforts – that is, the constant movement towards organizational innovation and experimentation – were being perceived and appropriated by the participants in the WSF.[18] The relevant fact in this regard is the growing involvement of the participants in the WSF as a process and not as a disparate event. While in 2003 33.6 per cent had participated in some kind of preparatory event leading to the WSF, this number rose to 54.5 per cent in 2005. As I described in Chapter 4, in 2004 a process of consultation and cohesion was set up to democratize the WSF process (all the activities during the WSF being self-organized; increasing the diversity of themes and facilitating greater dialogue). It is remarkable that 17.6 per cent participated in the process leading up to the 2005 WSF, a figure that rose to 20.4 per cent among non-Latin American participants. The evaluation of the consultation process and of the organizational decisions into which it was translated was clearly positive (62.4 per cent). As mentioned above, the 2005 WSF was organized around eleven thematic terrains or spaces. Half of the participants thought that all the terrains had been clearly defined. Interestingly enough, those who identified some confusing or obscure themes selected the following: 'Ethics, cosmo-visions and spiritualities – resistances and challenges for a new world' (17.8 per cent); 'Autonomous thinking, reappropriation and socialization of knowledge' (13 per cent); and 'Affirming and defending the commonwealth of the Earth and peoples as an alternative to mercantilization and transnational control' (11.7 per cent). One could speculate that the spiritual, the epistemological and the commons are the most challenging grounds for most participants.

SOME REFLECTIONS. This preliminary analysis of the surveys' data is revealing in many ways:

1. The WSF has gradually evolved from a succession of disparate events to a process, and this evolution was accelerated after the 2003 WSF. Both the Mumbai WSF and the 2005 WSF tried to address all the deficits previously identified: the global deficit, the social deficit and the democratic deficit. The Mumbai meeting addressed most decisively the two first deficits, while the 2005 meeting had a very specific impact on the democratic deficit. Nevertheless, the deficits are still there and the social deficit seems particularly resilient.

2. Given the social and political profile of the participants in the WSF – a profile that has seen little variation in the different meetings – the counter-hegemonic nature of the WSF should be viewed by the participants as an open question and should be the object of constant reflection and vigilance. In each specific venue of the WSF, the participation of the most excluded and oppressed social groups should be actively pursued. The progressive activism of the middle classes or of the petite bourgeoisie is a precious political asset and as such must be cherished, but it cannot compensate for the absence of the most oppressed classes and silenced voices. The WSF cannot flourish on the premise that since the Forum exists for the sake of the oppressed the latter don't have to be present.

3. The overwhelming participation of nationals in the WSFs must be acknowledged. This is not a negative feature in itself, since the local impact of the WSF should be viewed as one of the mechanisms through which the local/global linkages are strengthened. The solution for the global deficit problem does not lie in limiting national participation but rather in changing the venue of the WSF.

4. Among the participants there is a basic agreement on several issues, but there are also significant disagreements, which most probably will vary from venue to venue. This raises several issues. First of all, is it possible to link up the different peoples of the WSF as an embryonic form of a counter-hegemonic civil society? Second, how to transform the areas of widely shared consensuses into calls for collective action? Third, how better to explore the implications of both the agreements and the disagreements? Should, for instance,

the latter be the object of specific discussions in the WSF? How should the relationship between participants and organizers (IS, IC and the local OC) be framed? In different venues there will be different emphases, but how to link such diversity with the common core upon which the WSF builds its identity and eventually develops its capacity to act?

5. All these reflections and questions raise the issue of governance. Each meeting of the WSF raises specific governance issues, and both the principle of consensus and the principle of participatory democracy are subjected to specific pressures. But, beyond that, what is at stake are the transparency and democratic nature of the permanent governing structures of the WSF, the IS and the IC. The latter, in particular, because it is in charge of the strategic guidelines and organizational design of the WSF, must be the object of specific scrutiny. To this I turn now.

Who represents the WSF? Composition and functionality of the International Council

The second issue of representation – who represents the WSF? – was touched upon when I dealt with the relations between the IS and IC. It can be discussed from different perspectives. But in my view the discussions about the composition and functionality of the IC are most revealing in this regard.

The IC consisted originally of the groups and organizations invited to the first meeting and all that were admitted afterwards through co-optation. At present, the IC has no fixed number of members. In March 2006 it had 136 members[19] and seven observers (see Annexe I). The imbalances regarding gender, race, age and geography (scarce participation from Africa, Asia and the Arab world) were acknowledged from the very beginning. Equally central was the need to diversify the IC in terms of both the type of organization involved and the focus and scope of the social and political activism. The centrality of these concerns always presupposed the conception of the IC as the embryo of the representative entity of the WSF, the entity in which the diversity of the WSF would arrive at a kind of synthesis, in a body in charge of adopting political-methodological definitions concerning the WSF process.

In view of the serious organizational problems of the 2003 WSF, at the IC meeting that took place during the Forum it was decided to give more responsibility to the IC in planning and organizing the WSF. Accordingly, the following steps were considered necessary: 1) to restructure the IC in order to render it more operational, namely by approving an internal set of rules and by creating committees in charge of specific tasks; 2) to take measures to increase the representativeness of the IC, namely by approving a proactive policy, aimed both at establishing criteria for the admission of organizations and attracting organizations and movements of world regions or thematic areas with weaker representation in the WSF, and in the IC in particular. It was decided that decisions on these matters would be taken in the following meeting of the IC, set for June 2003 in Miami. In Miami, it was not possible to have the internal rules approved, but six committees were created: strategy, expansion, content, methodology, communication and funding committees. The members of the IC chose the committees on which they would like to work, one of the members taking on the role of 'facilitator' in each of them. Each committee was intended to be in office permanently and submit reports to the meetings of the IC. The criterion for creating committees related to the problems previously identified and the felt need to respond to them urgently. Thus, the mission of the *strategy committee* was to analyse the international situation regularly, reflect on its impact on the development of the Forum, and propose new forms of linkage between the WSF and the social movements, namely the general assembly of the social movements that runs parallel to the WSF. The *expansion committee* was charged with proposing measures to enlarge the Forum's territorial and thematic ambit and with establishing criteria for the admission of organizations to the IC.[20] The *content committee* was charged with analysing the written record of the previous WSFs and proposing topics for discussion in future WSFs. In previous meetings of the IC, there had been exchanges on the need to attune the debates to the expectations and interests of participants, prevent the Forum from becoming repetitive, and identify emergent topics not yet approached in previous forums. The task of the *methodology committee* was to reflect on the problems raised by the structure of the Forum and to propose solutions. Some of these problems were: the problematical relationship between the activities organized by the IS and the self-managed activities (organized by the participant organizations themselves); the method of deliberation by consensus; the creation of linked spaces beyond the Forums among the various organizations or movements; the systematization and cohesion of the proposals for activities, so as to prevent fragmentation and overlapping. The *communication committee* was to propose measures to improve the Forum's internal and external communication. It was considered that many of the internal criticisms about the lack of transparency of the decisions of the IS or the IC resulted from a lack of efficient communication channels covering the Forum's base overall. On the other hand, the WSF was finding it difficult to inform the public of its activities and messages. Finally, the *funding committee* was charged with taking care of two complex issues: the criteria for fund-raising and the creation of solidary funding systems to make possible the participation of organizations and movements deprived of resources in the activities of the WSF. The former issue was particularly urgent during preparations for the Mumbai WSF, because the Indian organizing committees refused to accept funding from institutions that had funded the previous WSFs, the Ford Foundation among others.[21] The performance of the committees has varied. The content and methodology committees have been the most active, working in close collaboration. Their work was directly reflected in the new organization model of the 2005 WSF. The work of the expansion committee has also drawn much attention. In fact, concerns over the expansion of the IC and the need to overcome the imbalances in representation have generated much debate at the meetings of the IC in the last three years. It has, however, been very difficult to establish the final criteria for admission to the IC, and as a result new admissions have been decided in the absence of such criteria and only on the basis of recommendations made by the expansion committee. At the meeting in Passignano sul Trasimeno (Italy), in April 2004, the decision was taken to accept as members of the IC nineteen new organizations, namely: Alternatives Russia; Asamblea de los Pueblos del Caribe (APC); Babels; COMPA – Convergencia de los Movimientos de los Pueblos de las Américas; CRID – Centre de Recherche et d'Information pour le Développement; Euromarchés; Federación Mundial de Juventudes Democráticas; Fédération Démocratique Internationale des Femmes (FDIF); Fundació per la Pau/International Peace Bureau (IPB); GLBT South–South Dialogue; Grupo de Trabalho Amazônico (GTA); International Network of Street Papers (INSP); Instituto Paulo Freire (IPF); Peace Boat; Project K; Rede CONSEU (Conferencia de Naciones sin Estado de Europa); UBUNTU – Foro Mundial de Redes de la Sociedad Civil; Unión Internacional de Estudiantes; and the World Association of Community Radio Broadcasters (Amarc).[22]

In April 2005, during the Utrecht meeting of the IC, it was agreed that the well-known imbalances in the IC persisted and needed to be corrected. The plenary committee asked the expansion committee to draft a 'road map' aimed at the restructuring of the IC over an eighteen-month period. During the Barcelona IC meeting (July 2005), a rather lively debate emerged on a proposal to reform the composition of the IC. This debate was a very eloquent expression of the concerns about the global deficit and the need to deepen the representative character of the IC. It also revealed the organization's capacity for self-reform and institutional innovation, and for that reason deserves to be mentioned. The proposal, drafted in the expansion committee, consisted of reviewing the status of all IC members and adopting clearer criteria for the membership of new organizations.[23] The document presented by the expansion committee reinforced the idea that a certain 'weighting would be given to considerations of representativity (on a range of criteria, not just geography, or sector, taken alone), as well as the track record of the organization's participation in the activities of the WSF' (WSF–IC 2005). The debate focused on several issues. With the purpose of avoiding precipitate decisions on admission to the IC, the expansion committee recommended that the slots made available to certain regions or thematic areas should remain vacant as long as the candidate organizations did not meet the criteria to fill them. The form of representation on the IC of continental, regional, sub-regional and local forums was also discussed.[24] The meeting called attention to the very size of the IC. The conclusion was that the 'IC needs to be sufficiently large to ensure diversity, without being so large as to be unwieldy' (ibid.). With the same concern in mind, the expansion committee suggested that the possibility of rotating membership of the IC be considered.

Because the inclusion of new members had traditionally been a rather complex issue for the IC, it was proposed by the expansion committee, and accepted by the IC plenary committee, that six organizations be accepted as new members immediately. The new members of the IC accepted were: Coligação para a Justiça Económica – Mozambique; International Federation Terre des Hommes (IFTDH) – Switzerland; National Network of Autonomous Women's Groups – India; Palestinian Grassroots Anti-apartheid Wall Campaign – Palestine; Réseaux Sous-régional sur la Dette et les DSRP – Mali and Niger; Solidarity Africa Network in Action – Kenya.

It was finally decided that in 2006 (January to April) member organizations of the WSF would be invited to apply for membership of the IC, on the basis of the final criteria to be adopted. Existing members of the IC wanting to continue their membership would also be requested to apply. These applications would have to be made in the prescribed format, and within agreed time frames. The expansion committee proposed three variants of mechanisms to evaluate the candidacies: the

103

TABLE 5.2 Headquarters of the movements/organizations represented on the IC

Region	Number	Percentage
Africa	13	9.6
Arab world	2	1.5
Asia	9	6.6
Asia-Pacific	1	0.7
Australia	2	1.5
Europe	45	33.1
Latin America and the Caribbean	38	27.9
Middle East	4	2.9
North America	17	12.5
Unknown/global	5	3.7
Total	136	100.0

Source: <www.forumsocialmundial.org.br>.

IC could delegate the final decision to a substructure; the substructure would make recommendations to the IC, and the latter would make final decisions; or the substructure would make final decisions on existing IC members (with panel members not participating in decisions concerning their own organizations) but only recommendations in relation to new applicants, which could be finalized by the IC.

A statistical analysis of the composition of the IC reveals the nature and the extent of the imbalances already mentioned, in spite of all the measures to reduce them throughout the period of consolidation of the IC (2003–05). As to the ambit or territorial scale of the activity, the distribution did not change significantly between 2003 and 2005: 49.3 per cent of the organizations operate globally; 33.1 per cent operate regionally; and 17.6 per cent operate nationally. In the latter category I include organizations whose activity is basically national, even though they may have departments of international relations that represent them on the IC (this is the case, for instance, with national federations of trade unions). The regional imbalances can be shown from different perspectives: 61 per cent of the organizations have their headquarters either in Latin America/the Caribbean and Europe (66.6 per cent in 2003), 12.5 per cent have their headquarters in North America, 47.1 per cent have their headquarters in the Global North (Europe, North America and Australia) (see Table 5.2).

Of the organizations whose scale of action is predominantly national,

41.7 per cent are based in Latin America and the Caribbean (47.8 per cent in 2003), while 33.4 per cent are based in the Global North (26 per cent in 2003) (see Table 5.3).

TABLE 5.3 IC organizations operating predominantly at the national level

Region	Number	Percentage
Africa	2	8.3
Arab world	1	4.2
Asia	3	12.5
Australia	1	4.2
Europe	1	4.2
Latin America and the Caribbean	10	41.6
North America	6	25.0
Total	24	100.0

Source: <www.forumsocialmundial.org.br>.

Of the organizations that operate at the regional level, 44.4 per cent operate in Latin America/the Caribbean (52.8 per cent in 2003) and 24.4 per cent in Europe (13.9 per cent in 2003) (see Table 5.4).

TABLE 5.4 IC NGOs/movements operating at the regional level

Region	Number	Percentage
Africa	7	15.6
Arab world	1	2.2
Asia	2	4.4
Asia-Pacific	1	2.2
Australia	1	2.2
Europe	11	24.5
Latin America and the Caribbean	20	44.5
Middle East	1	2.2
North America	1	2.2
Total	45	100.0

Source: <www.forumsocialmundial.org.br>.

Concerning the thematic areas in which the organizations concentrate their activity, the question of imbalances raises complex issues, some related to what balance should mean in this regard, others

TABLE 5.5 The IC by main thematic areas of intervention (2005)

Thematic area	Number	Percentage
Democratization	10	7.4
Economic justice	41	30.1
Ecumenical/religious	5	3.7
Education	4	2.9
Environment	4	2.9
Gay, lesbian, bisexual and transgender	1	0.7
Housing	1	0.7
Human rights	12	å8.8
Indigenous movements	2	1.5
Land/agriculture	5	3.7
Media/press	9	6.6
Peace	2	1.5
Research/knowledge-sharing	10	7.4
Labour/trade unionism	15	11.0
Feminism/women's issues	10	7.4
Youth/students	3	2.2
Unknown	2	1.5
Total	136	100.0

Source: <www.forumsocialmundial.org.br>.

related to the criteria of classification. Many organizations intervene in more than one area and seemingly different areas may be no more than different names for the same area. Not surprisingly, economic justice (development, debt, trade, socio-economic equality, etc.) is the dominant area of activity: 30.1 per cent. It is followed by labour/trade unionism (11 per cent), human rights (8.8 per cent), feminism/women's issues (7.4 per cent) and democratization (participatory, grassroots democracy) (7.4 per cent). If we compare this with the composition of the IC in 2003, the most significant increases occurred in the areas of research/knowledge-sharing, ecumenism/religious issues, media/press and land/agriculture (see Table 5.5).

These data, however preliminary and deserving of more detailed analysis, indicate that the expansion committee of the IC should strengthen even more its proactive stance as regards reducing the regional imbalances. The determination of other types of imbalances (among themes, types of organization, scope and type of intervention) needs to be based on new types of political debates within and outside the IC, broadly defined, systematic, well-prepared debates concerning medium-term and long-term strategies to build another possible world. In the end, the issue of representativeness cannot be solved mechanically. It is a political rather than a technical question, even if its solution has important technical dimensions (funding, for instance). The IC represents the WSF to the extent that it reflects the *in sich* diversity of the WSF and transforms it into a *für sich* diversity.

Notes

1 On the subject of representation at the WSF, see Teivainen (2003).

2 Local participation amounted to 84 per cent of the total.

3 Local participation amounted to 80 per cent.

4 Of special note is the participation of 600 Pakistanis. Apparently many more would have participated if the Indian authorities had not created visa difficulties.

5 'Asia' is a North-centric concept that designates too wide a region to have a homogeneous social, political and cultural content. At the IC's meeting in Mumbai it was, therefore, decided that another WSF be planned in East Asia. In early 2005 it was decided that the 2006 WSF would be polycentric, one of the events taking place in Karachi. At the Asian consultation meeting of the WSF held in Sri Lanka in June 2005 it was decided that another polycentric WSF would be organized in South-East/East Asia, in Bangkok.

6 Holding the 2005 WSF in Porto Alegre was the result of a compromise with those in the IC who were against Mumbai as the venue for the 2004 WSF, arguing that the organizational risks were innumerable and that the existence of the WSF as we know it might thereby be jeopardized. Locating the 2005 WSF in Porto Alegre again aimed to reassure the sceptics that, should anything go wrong in Mumbai, there would always be the possibility of recovery in Porto Alegre. As we know, these pessimistic prophecies were not fulfilled. On the contrary, the exemplary way in which the Mumbai WSF was carried out created a new standard of quality for the 2005 WSF in Porto Alegre.

7 For some time now, the IC has been pondering whether the WSF should continue to convene annually or every two years. The argument in favour of the latter option is that the annual organization demands a tremendous organizational effort that distracts the movements and NGOs from their principal objectives. In favour of the annual event, the argument is that the success of the WSF resides in its symmetry with the World Economic Forum and that, while the latter continues to be annual, the decision to stop convening annually will always be understood as a sign of organizational and political weakness.

8 See note 5 above.

9 On the methodology adopted for the survey, see IBASE (2003: vol. 5).

10 The opinions could be expressed in five degrees from totally agree (1) to totally disagree (5). The responses were then aggregated in terms of 'totally or partially agree', 'totally or partially disagree' and 'indifferent'.

11 There were some methodological changes in relation to the survey of

the 2003 WSF and for that reason not all data are comparable. The results of the 2005 survey can be consulted in IBASE (2006).

12 The sample of participants was stratified according to three groupings: Brazilian participants, Latin American participants and participants from other countries. Participants represented 59.5 per cent of the total. Besides campers (22.6 per cent) there were communicators, volunteers, support services, exhibitors and participants in cultural events.

13 The data must be compared with some caution. In 2005, the countries with a small number of participants (134 countries) were included in a residual category ('other').

14 A trend that continued in the polycentric 2006 WSF in Caracas, where for the first time the US delegation had its own space to give information about its causes and campaigns.

15 In the 2005 survey the questions about religion were eliminated.

16 The real sociological meaning of the data can be revealed only through multivariate analysis, which is impossible at this juncture.

17 Moreover the 2003 questionnaire allowed for unlimited multiple answers while the 2005 questionnaire allowed only up to three options.

18 Only one-third of the participants claimed to know the Charter of Principles, even though another third knew some part of the Charter. It is significant that non-Brazilian and non-Latin America participants claimed a higher knowledge of the Charter.

19 Representing 136 movements and organizations; it also includes the IS, the Brazilian OC and the Indian OC.

20 Actually, in view of pending requests for admission, it was decided to establish a few basic procedural and substantive criteria. As regards procedural criteria, applications were to be submitted to the IS, to then be forwarded to the expansion committee for reviewing and subsequent final assessment by the IC. As to substantive criteria, on the one hand an organization is required to have existed for more than two years and its activities must have an international dimension; on the other, taking part in one of the committees becomes a condition for admission to the IC.

21 The issue of funding sources became polemical in the preparation for the Mumbai meeting but, for reasons already mentioned, it became particularly problematic in the 2005 WSF and in the 2006 polycentric WSF in Caracas, although for different reasons. The costs for the 2005 WSF had been estimated at US$7,547,700 but the actual disbursements totalled US$8,313,016. Resources effectively secured were US$6,793,705, thus leading to the deficit of US$1,573,311 (see van der Wekken 2005). For a list of the organizations that funded the previous meetings of the WSF (up to 2005), see Annexe IV.

22 All these organizations were admitted by recommendation of the expansion committee. All had presented their candidatures to the IC between the meeting in Barcelona, in April 2002, and that in Miami, in June 2003.

23 The Barcelona meeting of the IC also called attention to the need to clarify what constitutes an active and an inactive membership. Based on

preliminary calculations, and assuming that its membership would become inactive if the organization had not attended more than one meeting in the last two years, it could be said that the membership of more than thirty organizations had lapsed. Eighteen organizations had not attended a single meeting, including the first meeting of the IC to which they were invited.

24 As continental forums were initially accorded observer status, it was agreed that this representation should be strengthened and that they be given full delegate status.

6 | Making and unmaking cleavages: strategy and political action[1]

The WSF is characterized, as I have already said, by its claim to the existence of an alternative to the anti-utopian, single way of thinking of neo-liberalism's conservative utopia. It is a radically democratic utopia that celebrates diversity, plurality and horizontality. It celebrates another possible world, itself plural in its possibilities. The novelty of this utopia in left thinking in Western capitalist modernity cannot but be problematical as it translates itself into strategic planning and political action. These are marked by the historical trajectory of the political left throughout the twentieth century. The translation of utopia into politics is not, in this case, merely the translation of long range into medium and short range. It is also the translation of the new into the old. The tensions and divisions brought about by this are no less real for that reason. What happens is that the reality of the divergences is often a ghostly reality, in which divergences in concrete political options get mixed up with divergences in codes and languages of political option. Accordingly, it is not always possible to determine whether the real disputes correspond to real divergences.

It should be stressed, however, that the novelty of the utopia has managed so far to overcome the political divergences. Contrary to what happened in the thinking and practice of the left in Western capitalist modernity, the WSF managed to create a style and an atmosphere of inclusion of and respect for divergences which made it very difficult for the different political factions to exclude themselves at the start with the excuse that they were being excluded. To this the WSF's 'minimalist' programme outlined in its Charter of Principles contributed decisively: emphatic assertion of respect for diversity; access broadly open (only movements or groups that advocate political violence being excluded); no voting or deliberations at the Forum as such; no representative entity to speak for the Forum. It is almost like a tabula rasa where all forms of struggle against neo-liberalism and for a more just society may have their place. In light of such openness, those who choose to exclude themselves find it difficult to define what exactly they are excluding themselves from.

All this has contributed to making the WSF's power of attraction greater than its capacity to repel. Even the movements that are most severely critical of the WSF, such as the anarchists, have not been absent. There is definitely something new in the air, something that is chaotic, messy, ambiguous and indefinite enough to deserve the benefit of the doubt and freedom from manipulation. Few would want to miss this train, particularly at a time in history when trains have ceased to operate. For all these reasons, the desire to highlight what the movements and organizations have in common has prevailed over the desire to underscore what separates them. The manifestation of tensions or cleavages has been relatively tenuous and, above all, has not resulted in mutual exclusions. It remains to be seen for how long this will to convergence and this chaotic sharing of differences will last.

Neither the kinds of cleavages nor the way in which the movements relate to them are randomly distributed inside the WSF.[2] On the contrary, they reflect a meta-cleavage between Western and non-Western political cultures. Up to a point, this meta-cleavage also exists between the North and the South. Thus, given the strong presence of movements and organizations of the North Atlantic and white Latin America, particularly in the first three meetings of the WSF, it is no wonder that the most salient cleavages reflect the political culture and historical trajectory of the left in this part of the world.[3] This means, on the one hand, that many movements and organizations from Africa, Asia, the indigenous and black Americas and the Europe of immigrants do not recognize themselves in these cleavages; on the other, that alternative cleavages which these movements and organizations might want to make explicit are perhaps being concealed or minimized by the prevailing ones.[4] After this caveat, my next step is to identify the main manifest cleavages.

Reform or revolution

This cleavage carries the weight of the tradition of the Western left, even though it can be found elsewhere, most notably in India, to speak only of the countries that have been more directly involved in the WSF process. It is the cleavage between those who think that another world is possible, by the gradual transformation of the unjust world in which we live, through legal reform and mechanisms of representative democracy, and those who think that the world we live in is a capitalist world which will never tolerate reforms that will question or disturb its logic of operation, and that it must therefore be overthrown and replaced by a socialist world. This is also regarded as a cleavage between moderates and radicals. Both fields comprise a wide variety of positions. For instance, among revolutionaries there is a clear cleavage between the old left, which aspires to a kind of state socialism, the anarchists, who are radically anti-statist, and some newer left, rather ambivalent about the role of the state in a socialist society. Although they amount to a very minor proportion of the WSF, the anarchists are among the fiercest critics of reformism, which they claim controls the WSF's leadership (IS/IC).

This cleavage reverberates, albeit not linearly, in strategic options and options for political action. Among the most salient of these should be counted the strategic option between reforming/democratizing the institutions of neo-liberal globalization (the WTO and international financial institutions) or fighting to eliminate and replace them; and the option for political action between, on the one hand, constructive dialogue and engagement with those institutions, and, on the other, confrontation with them.

This cleavage also translates itself into opposite positions, either as regards the diagnosis of contemporary societies, or as regards the evaluation of the WSF itself. As to the diagnosis, according to one stance contemporary societies are viewed as societies where there are multiple discriminations and injustices, not all of them attributable to capitalism. Capitalism, in turn, is not homogeneous, and the struggle must focus on its most exclusionary form – neo-liberalism. According to another stance, contemporary societies are viewed as intrinsically unjust and discriminatory because they are capitalist. Capitalism is an enveloping system in which class discrimination feeds on sexual, racial and other kinds of discrimination. Hence, the struggle must focus on capitalism as a whole and not on any single one of its manifestations.

As to the evaluation of the WSF, the WSF is viewed now as the embryo of an efficacious rebuttal of neo-liberal globalization, confronting neo-liberal globalization at the global level, where more social injustice has been produced, not as a movement which, because it is not grounded in the principle of the class struggle, will accomplish little beyond a few rhetorical changes in dominant capitalist discourse.

What is new about the WSF as a political entity is that the majority of the movements and organizations that participate in it do not recognize themselves in these cleavages and refuse to take part in debates about them. There is great resistance to rigidly assuming a given position and even greater to labelling it. The majority of movements and organizations have political histories in which moments of confrontation alternate or combine with moments of dialogue and

engagement, in which long-range visions of social change coexist with
the tactical possibilities of the political and social conjuncture in which
the struggles take place, in which radical denunciations of capitalism
do not sap the energy for small changes when the big changes are
not possible. Above all, for many movements and organizations, this
cleavage is West-centric or North-centric, and is more useful for understanding the past of the left than its future. Indeed, many movements
and organizations do not recognize themselves, for the same reasons,
in the dichotomy between left and right.

Precisely because for many movements and organizations the priority is not to seize power but rather to change the power relations in
oppression's many faces, the political tasks, however radical, must
be carried out here and now, in the society in which we live. It makes
no sense, therefore, to ask a priori if their success is incompatible
with capitalism. Social conflicts always start out by being fought in the
terms imposed by the dominant or hegemonic forces, and the success
of the struggles for another possible world is measured precisely by
their capacity to change the terms of the conflict as the latter unfolds.
What is necessary is to create alternative, counter-hegemonic visions,
capable of sustaining the daily practices and relations of citizens and
social groups. The work of the movements' leaderships is of course
important, but in no way is it conceived as the work of an enlightened
avant-garde that forges a path for the masses, ever the victims of mystification and false consciousness. On the contrary, as Sub-comandante
Marcos (leader of the Mexican Zapatista Army of National Liberation)
recommends, it behoves the leaderships to 'walk with those who go
slower'. It is not a question of either revolution or reform. It is, for
some, a question of rebellion and construction, for others a question of
revolution in a non-Leninist sense, a question of civilizational change
occurring over a long period of time.

Socialism or social emancipation   vs. Soc e

This cleavage is related to the previous one but there is no perfect
overlap between the two. Regardless of the position taken vis-à-vis the
previous cleavage, or the refusal to take a position, the movements
and organizations diverge as to the political definition of the other
possible world. For some, socialism is still an adequate designation,
however abundant and disparate the conceptions of socialism may be.
For the majority, however, socialism carries in itself the idea of a closed
model of a future society, and must, therefore, be rejected. They prefer
other, less politically charged designations, suggesting openness and

a constant search for alternatives – for example, social emancipation as the aspiration to a society in which the different power relations are replaced by relations of shared authority. This is a more inclusive designation focusing on processes rather than on final stages of social change. But some still have strong reservations as to the heroic tone of the idea of 'social emancipation' and at best accept it if used in the plural, 'social emancipations'.

Many movements of the Global South think that no general labels need be attached to the goals of the struggles. Labels run the risk of diverging from the practices that originated them, acquiring a life of their own, and giving rise to perverse results. As a matter of fact, according to some, the concept of socialism is West-centric and North-centric, while the concept of emancipation is equally prey to the Western bias towards creating false universalisms. Hence many do not recognize themselves in either term of this dichotomy, and don't even bother to propose any alternative.

The state as enemy or potential ally

This is also a cleavage in which movements of the Global North recognize themselves more easily than movements of the Global South. On the one hand, there are those who think that the state, although in the past it may well have been an important arena of struggle, for the past twenty-five years has been transnationalized and turned into an agent of neo-liberal globalization. Either the state has become irrelevant or is today what it has always been – the expression of capitalism's general interests. The privileged target of counter-hegemonic struggles must, therefore, be the state, or at least they must be fought with total autonomy vis-à-vis the state. On the other hand, there are those who think that the state is a social relation and, as such, it is contradictory and continues to be an important arena of struggle. Neo-liberal globalization did not rob the state of its centrality, rather it reoriented it better to serve the interests of global capital. Deregulation is a social regulation like any other, hence a political field where one must act if there are conditions for acting.

The majority of the movements, even those that acknowledge the existence of a cleavage in this regard, refuse to take a rigid and principled position. Their experiences of struggle show that the state, while sometimes the enemy, can often be a precious ally in the struggle against transnational impositions. In these circumstances, the most adequate attitude is, again, pragmatism. If in some situations confrontation is in order, in others collaboration is rather advised. In others still a combination of both is appropriate. The important thing is that, at every moment or in every struggle, the movement or organization in question be clear and transparent regarding the reasons for the adopted option, so as to safeguard the autonomy of the action. Autonomy is, in such cases, always problematical, and so it must be watched carefully. According to the radical autonomists, collaboration with the state will always end up compromising the organizations' autonomy. They fear that collaborationists, whether the state or the institutions of neo-liberal globalization are involved, will end up being co-opted. According to them, an alliance between the reformist wing of counter-hegemonic globalization and the reformist wing of hegemonic globalization will thereby ensue, ending up compromising the goals of the WSF.

National or global struggles

This is the most evenly distributed cleavage in the totality of move-ments and organizations that comprise the WSF. On one side, there are the movements that, while participating in the WSF, believe that the latter is no more than a meeting point and a cultural event, since the real struggles that are truly important for the welfare of the popula-tions are fought at the national level against the state or the dominant national civil society. For instance, in a report on the WSF prepared by the Movement for National Democracy in the Philippines, one can read:

> [...] the World Social Forum still floats somewhere above, seeing and trying yet really unable to address actual conditions of poverty and powerlessness brought about by Imperialist globalisation in many countries. Unless it finds definite ways of translating or even trans-cending its 'globalness' into more practical interventions that address these conditions, it just might remain a huge but empty forum that is more a cultural affair than anything else [...] national struggles against globalisation are and should provide the anchor to any anti-globalisation initiative at the international level. (Gobrin-Morante 2002: 19)

In other words, globalization is most effectively fought at the national level.

On the other side, there are the movements according to which the state is now transnationalized and thus is no longer the privileged centre of political decision. This decentring of the state also brought about the decentring of civil society, which is subjected today to many processes of cultural and social globalization. Furthermore, in some situations the object of the struggle (be it a decision of the WTO, the World Bank or oil drilling by a transnational corporation) is outside the national space and includes a plurality of countries simultaneously. This is why the scale of the struggle must be increasingly global, a fact from which the WSF draws its relevance.

According to the large majority of the movements, this is again a cleavage that does not do justice to the concrete needs of concrete struggles. What is new about contemporary societies is that the scales of social and political life – the local, national and global scales – are increasingly more interconnected. In the most remote village of the Amazon or India the effects of hegemonic globalization and the ways in which the national state engages with it are clearly felt. If this is the case with scales of social and political life in general, it is even more so with the scales of counter-hegemonic struggles. It is obvious that each political practice or social struggle is organized in accordance with a privileged scale, be it local, national or global, but whatever the scale may be, all the others must be involved as conditions of success. The decision as to which scale to privilege is a political decision that must be taken in accordance with concrete political conditions. It is therefore not possible to opt in the abstract for any one hierarchy among scales of counter-hegemonic practice or struggle.

Both the question of the ambit or scope of the struggles to be prioritized and the question of how best to coordinate national, regional and global struggles came to the foreground in the discussions leading to two little-known changes introduced into the Charter of Principles as the WSF process unfolded. The Charter of Principles was agreed upon by the IC of the WSF in June 2001, on the basis of a proposal presented by the OC in April 2001.[5] Later on, during the preparations for the 2004 WSF, it was discussed in various meetings in India. As Sen describes it (2004: 72), the organizations that took the responsibility for organizing the Mumbai WSF came to the conclusion that the Charter of Principles, as it stood, did not fully address social and political conditions in India. Accordingly they decided to modify the charter to suit local conditions. After some months of discussion, a policy document was adopted at a meeting in Bhopal, in April 2002, entitled 'WSF India Policy Statement: Charter of Principles – World Social Forum India'. This document modified some of the clauses of the charter and added new ones with the purpose of adapting it to the specific conditions that prevail in India today. For a while, and because it was posted on the website of WSF-India, it looked like a new version of the Charter of Principles. It included specific clauses that asserted the inclusive character of the Forum, it addressed the question of 'communalism', emphasized the importance of diversity and of local idioms, and allowed for the possibility of political parties participating in the WSF. In the Perugia meeting of the IC (November 2003), the members of the Indian Organizing Committee made it clear that the document had no official character and that in no way could it be seen as an Indian version of the charter. But the official documents on the methodology of the India WSF continued to state that 'in India the WSF Charter has been extended to include social and political realities as they exist in the country today [...]. This entails the opening of a dialogue within and between the broad spectrum of political parties and groups, social movements and other organizations.' In my view, the changes introduced signal an innovative process of local adaptation to global dynamics. Through it, national conditions and struggles are embedded in a broader global context, but at the same time invite the latter to recontextualize itself in light of the specificity of national realities and their ways of inserting themselves in the counter-hegemonic globalization.

The same can be said of the 'Charter of Principles and Values of the African Social Forum', adopted in January 2003 in Addis Ababa. This important document takes an explicit regional stance, focusing on the specific problems confronting the continent as a result of the particularly devastating impact of neo-liberal globalization. It conceives of the Forum as contributing to regional integration (Pan-Africanism) and puts special emphasis on 'the power of democracy as the preferred channel for conflict negotiation within societies and between States'. Worth mentioning is the fact that, as regards the non-admission of violence-promoting organizations, both the African charter and the Indian policy statement adopt the formula (or some variation) of the original version of the Charter of Principles, as proposed by the OC, rather than the formula of the final version. In the OC proposal Clause 11 of the charter stated: 'The meetings of the WSF are always open to all those who wish to take part in them, except organizations that seek to take people's lives as a method of political action.'[6]

Direct or institutional action

This cleavage is clearly linked to the first and third cleavages. It specifically concerns the modes of struggle that should be adopted preferably or even exclusively. It is a cleavage with a long tradition in the Western left. Those for whom this cleavage continues to have a great deal of importance are those who disparage the newness of neo-liberal globalization in the historical process of capitalist domination.

On the one side, there are the movements that believe that legal struggles, based on dialogue and engagement with state institutions or international agencies, are ineffectual because the political and legal system of the state and the institutions of capitalism are impervious to any legal or institutional measures capable of really improving the living conditions of the working classes. Institutional struggles call for the intermediation of parties, and parties tend to put those struggles at the service of their party interests and constituencies. The success of an institutional struggle has, therefore, a very high price, the price of co-optation, betrayal or trivialization. But even in the rare cases in which an institutional struggle leads to legal and institutional measures that correspond to the movements' objectives, it is almost certain that the concrete application of such measures will end up being subjected to the legal-bureaucratic logic of the state, thereby frustrating the movements' expectations. In the end there will be only a hollow hope. This is why only direct action, mass protest and strikes will yield success for the struggles. The working classes have no weapon but external pressure on the system. If they venture into it, they are defeated from the start.

On the other hand, the supporters of institutional struggles assume that the 'system' is contradictory, a political and social arena where it is possible to fight and where failure is not the only possible outcome. In the course of the twentieth century the working classes conquered important institutional spaces, of which the welfare system in the Global North is a good example. The fact that the welfare system is now in crisis and the 'opening' that it offered the working classes is now being closed does not mean that the process is irreversible. Indeed, it won't be so if the movements and organizations continue to struggle inside the institutions and the legal system.

This cleavage is not spread out at random among the movements that make up the WSF. In general the stronger movements and organizations are those that more frequently privilege institutional struggles, whereas the less strong are those that more frequently privilege direct action. This cleavage is much livelier among movements and organizations of the Global North than of the Global South. The majority of the movements, however, refuse to take sides in this cleavage. According to them, the concrete legal and political conditions must dictate the kind of struggle to be privileged. Conditions may actually recommend the sequential or simultaneous use of the two kinds of struggle. One of the most influential movements in the WSF, the MST (the movement of the landless rural workers in Brazil), is known for resorting both to direct action (land occupation) and institutional action (negotiations with the government, judicial action), sometimes within the ambit of the same struggle or campaign. Historically, direct action was the basis of progressive juridico-institutional changes, and it was always necessary to combat the co-optation or even subversion of such changes through direct action.

The principle of equality or the principle of respect for difference

As I have already said, one of the novelties of the WSF is the fact that the majority of its movements and organizations believe that, although we live in obscenely unequal societies, equality is not enough as a guiding principle of social emancipation. Social emancipation must be grounded in two principles – the principle of equality and the principle of respect for difference. The struggle for each of them must be linked with the other; otherwise both will end in defeat. Nevertheless, there is a cleavage among the movements and even, sometimes, within the same movement, as to whether priority should be given to one of these principles, and if so to which. The cleavage is between those who give priority to the principle of equality – for equality alone may create real opportunities for the recognition of difference – and those who give priority to the principle of the recognition of difference, for without such recognition equality conceals the exclusions and marginalities on which it rests, thus becoming doubly oppressive (for what it conceals and for what it shows).

This cleavage occurs among movements and within the same movement. It traverses, among others, the workers', the feminist, the indigenous and the black movements. For instance, whereas the workers' movement has privileged the principle of equality to the detriment of the principle of the recognition of difference, the feminist movement has privileged the latter to the detriment of the former. But the most common position is indeed that both principles have equal priority, and that it is not correct to prioritize either one in the abstract. Concrete political conditions will dictate to each movement which of the principles is to be privileged in a given concrete struggle. Any struggle conceived under the aegis of one of these two principles must be organized so as to open space for the other principle.

In the feminist movement of the WSF, this position is now dominant. Virginia Vargas (n.d.) expresses it well when she says:

> At the World Social Forum, feminists have begun [...] nourishing processes that integrate gender justice with economic justice, while

recovering cultural subversion and subjectivity as a longer-term strategy for transformation. This confronts two broad expressions of injustice: socio-economic injustice, rooted in societal political and economic structures, and cultural and symbolic injustice, rooted in societal patterns of representation, interpretation and communication. Both injustices affect women, along with many other racial, ethnic, sexual and geographical dimensions.

Vargas asks for new feminisms – feminisms of these times – as a discursive, expansive, heterogeneous panorama, generating polycentric fields of action that spread over a range of civil society organizations and are not constrained to women's affairs, although women undoubtedly maintain them in many ways. And she concludes: 'Our presence in the WSF, asking these very questions, is also an expression of this change.'

The WSF as a space or as a movement

This cleavage occurs at a different level from the previous ones. Rather than concerning the political differences of movements/NGOs within the WSF, it concerns their differences about the political nature of the WSF itself. Indeed, this cleavage runs through all the others since differences about strategic goals and forms of action often boil down to differences about the role of the WSF in those goals and actions.

As I have already indicated, this cleavage has been present from the outset. It led, for instance, to some little-known clashes within the Organizing Committee for the first meeting of the WSF. But it was during and after the third WSF that this cleavage gained widespread notoriety and involved a large number of participants. The sheer size of WSF 2003 and the organizational problems it raised prompted the discussion about the future of the WSF. It soon became clear to the broader membership of the WSF that the discussion was not about organization issues but rather about the political role and nature of the WSF. Two extreme positions can be identified in this discussion, and between them a whole range of intermediate positions. On one side is the conception of the WSF as a 'movement of movements'. This conception has been expounded almost from the very beginning by influential members of the global network of social movements whose general assembly meets in parallel with the WSF. The idea behind this conception is that unless the WSF becomes a political actor in its own right it will soon be discredited as a talking shop, and the anti-capitalist energy that it has generated will be wasted. The celebration of diversity, however praiseworthy, if left alone, will have a paralysing effect and will play into the hands of capitalist domination. In order to be enabling, diversity must have an organizational and political core capable of deciding and carrying out collective actions in the name of the WSF. Such decisions should be stated in a final declaration of each meeting of the WSF, and for that the Charter of Principles must be revised. Horizontal organization based on consensus should be replaced by (or at least be linked with) a democratic command capable of acting in the name of the WSF.

On the other side is the conception of the WSF as a space, a meeting ground on which no one can be or feel excluded. The WSF is not a neutral space, though, since its objective is to allow as many people, organizations and movements that oppose neo-liberalism as possible to come together freely. Once together, they can listen to each other, learn from the experiences and struggles of others, discuss proposals of action, and become linked in new nets and organizations without the interference of leaders, commands or programmes. The extreme version of this conception has been expounded by Francisco Whitaker, one of the founders of the WSF and an influential member of the IS and the IC. According to him the nature of the WSF as an open space – he uses the metaphor of the public square – based on the power of free horizontal association, should be preserved at all costs. After counterposing the organizational structure of a space and of a movement, he lashes out against the 'so-called social movements' that want to transform the WSF into a movement:

> [...] those who want to transform it [the WSF] into a movement will end up, if they succeed, by working against our common cause, whether they are aware or not of what they are doing, whether they are movements or political parties, and however important, strategically urgent and legitimate their objectives might be. They will be effectively acting against themselves and against all of us. They will be hindering and suffocating its own source of life – stemming from those associations and initiatives born in the Forum – or at least destroying an enormous instrument that is available for them to expand and to enlarge their presence in the struggle we are all engaged in. (Whitaker 2003)

The second conception is by far the dominant one, both in the IS and in the IC, but it is rarely defended in Whitaker's extreme version.[7] For instance, Cândido Grzybowski, another founder of the WSF whose NGO, IBASE, is a very influential member of the IS, wrote in the first issue of the journal of the Forum, *Terraviva* (2003a):

Making and unmaking cleavages

The Manifesto 2005 →

Six

To try to eliminate contradictions at the core of the WSF and turn it into a more homogeneous space and process for confronting neo-liberalism is the aim of certain forces, inspired by the classic political partisanship of the left. I would even say that this struggle within the Forum is legitimate and deserves respect, given its visions and values. But it destroys innovation of the WSF, what it possesses in terms of potential to feed a broad and diverse movement of the global citizenry in building another world.

Another intermediate position in this cleavage but closer to the movement position has been taken by Teivo Teivainen, a member of the IC, representing NIGD:

> We have to move beyond rigid movement/space dichotomies if we want to understand the role of the WSF. The WSF can play and has played a role in facilitating radical social action. One example is the fact that the massive antiwar protests of 15 February 2003 were to a significant extent initiated and organized from within the WSF process. We should use this example more consciously to counter the claims that the WSF is politically useless. We should also use it as a learning experience, to build more effective channels for concrete action without building a traditional movement (of movements). The WSF should not be turned into a political party or a new International. It should, however, have better mechanisms for exchanging, disseminating and debating strategies of radical transformation. More explicit mechanisms and procedures mean more possibilities for getting things done. (Teivainen 2004)[8]

This cleavage, however intensely promoted among some leading figures in the WSF, does not resonate among the social base of the Forum. The vast majority of the movements/NGOs come to the WSF to exchange experiences, learn about relevant issues and look for possible alliances that may strengthen the struggles in which they are already involved. The contacts made at the WSF may lead them into new struggles or courses of action, but only if they choose to be so led.

This cleavage surfaced with some intensity in WSF 2005 and afterwards in the aftermath of the presentation by some high-profile participants of a declaration entitled 'Manifesto of Porto Alegre'. The idea of drafting a document that would synthesize the major points of agreement among the movements and NGOs participating in the WSF dates back to the second meeting, in 2002. Impressed by the enthusiasm with which so many organizations across the world responded

Teivo
e. g. Feb 15

122

to the call of the WSF and the atmosphere of general consensus on major global issues expressed in so many meetings convened by so many different organizations, some intellectual-activists started discussing the idea of putting together the main points of agreement in a document. The document would have the twofold purpose of providing the participants with an overview of the diversity of the WSF and showing to the outside world that such diversity was neither chaotic nor devoid of concrete orientations for collective global action. The success of the third WSF (2003) was interpreted as providing further justification for the idea of a document in light of the immense range of topics discussed and the generalized view that the lively debates were not being used to generate concrete proposals for action against neo-liberal globalization. In the WSF held in Mumbai, Bernard Cassen, founder of ATTAC, was particularly insistent on the idea that the growing strength of the WSF demanded that the alternative provided by the WSF to the World Economic Forum of Davos be sharpened and made visible worldwide. If the WEF had been for many years the think tank of hegemonic globalization and the legitimizing amplifier for the Washington Consensus, the WSF should present itself to the world as being the major manifestation of a counter-hegemonic globalization and the bearer of an alternative global consensus, the Consensus of Porto Alegre. How to accomplish this, having in mind the informal and horizontal structure of the WSF and the terms of the Charter of Principles? The idea of a manifesto of the WSF was ruled out by the charter. The charter, however, did not prevent the participants from drafting manifestos and from presenting them as expressing the political will of the signatories. The political weight of the manifesto would depend on the number of participants willing to sign it. The manifesto was finally drafted during the fifth WSF, signed by nineteen well-known participants[9] and presented to the media outside the World Social Territory (the grounds where the WSF was convened) as a document open to the subscription of all participants in the WSF. The focus of the document was on concrete proposals, 'twelve proposals for another possible world'.

The document met with strong criticism. Two major types of criticisms can be identified: methodological and substantive. The methodological criticism stated that the manifesto either violated the Charter of Principles or came close to doing so. By presenting their document as the Manifesto of Porto Alegre, the signatories induced the media wrongly to take the terms of the document as an authoritative interpretation of the political will of the WSF. The WSF does not provide for any mechanism by means of which such a political will may be determined, for the simple reason that such determination is ruled out by the spirit and the letter of the charter. In other words, the document violated the idea that the WSF is an open space where different political wills can be formulated. As might be expected, Francisco Whitaker was the most vocal critic, minimizing the importance of the manifesto by viewing it as one among hundreds of proposals being presented at the Forum. When the signatories responded that this was precisely what they had tried to do (to present as a proposal a document to be signed by whoever agreed with its terms), Whitaker argued that, such being the case, they should not have used such an ambiguously all-encompassing title as 'Manifesto of Porto Alegre'.

The second kind of criticism was substantive. It focused on the content of the document, and on the methodology used to produce it. Two different kinds of criticisms should be mentioned, both of them emphasizing the reductionist view of the 'consensus' presented, which allegedly suppressed the diversity and the pluralism present at the Forum. One of the criticisms, originating in the feminist movements and organizations, stated that the document had been drafted and signed by eighteen white men and one African woman. Not surprisingly, it was argued, sexual discrimination was mentioned in only one of the proposals (number 8), among many other forms of discrimination, and there was no trace of a gender perspective in the rest of the document (Obando 2005). The other criticism, originating in the radical leftist groups, alleged that the manifesto was a reformist or neo-reformist document, drafted by a small group of intellectuals (the same old types). Most proposals, even if correct, were limited in scope, so the argument ran, thus contributing to the illusion that imperialism may be success-fully confronted by non-radical measures and struggles.

As one of the signatories of the document, I responded to these criticisms (Santos 2006a: 73–8). Starting with the substantive criticisms, and in a kind of voluntary self-criticism, I fully accepted the feminist critique. As for the anti-reformist criticism, I started from the assumption that social revolution is not on the political agenda (for the time being at least) of short-term or medium-term social transformation. If we bear this in mind, the proposals formulated in the manifesto, both individually and taken together, were very radical indeed. Concerning the methodological criticism, I saw a point in Whitaker's stance, since I fully share his idea that the strength of the WSF lies in the rich diversity of the participants and in the celebration of pluralism and horizontal-ity. But I also emphasized that the strength of the WSF may become its weakness if more and more groups reach the conclusion that the costs of getting involved in the WSF are too high when compared with the real impact of the WSF in making the world less comfortable for global capitalism. The danger of being prey to factionalism is as real as the danger of being dismissed as irrelevant. The manifesto was aimed at addressing the latter danger, even if, as I admit, it was not carried out in a consistent and correct way. Rather than being dismissed, it should be reworked using a new and more participatory and democratic methodology. I also thought that the idea that nobody and no group owns the WSF was a most precious heritage. But it applied both to those who tried to write a manifesto that might be taken as binding on all participants and to those who criticized the initiative on the basis of the seemingly sole authorized and authoritative interpretation of the Charter of Principles. Otherwise the commitment to horizontality might end up a dogmatism like any other.

The 'incident' of the manifesto highlighted the cleavage between those who conceive of the WSF as a social space and those who conceive of it as the embryo of a global civil society, constituted by a wide range of global or globally linked social actors. But, as I said above, this cleavage was confined to a group of high-profile participants. My guess is that most people did not know about or read the manifesto, and that those few who did found it obvious, neither dangerous nor important.

Except for the last one, the tensions and cleavages mentioned above are not specific to the WSF. They belong in fact to the historical legacy of the social forces that for the past 200 years have struggled against the status quo for a better society. The specificity of the WSF resides in the fact that all these cleavages coexist in its bosom without upsetting its cohesive power. To my mind, two factors contribute to this. First, the different cleavages are important in different ways for the different movements and organizations, and none of them is present in the practices or discourses of all the movements and organizations. Thus all of them, at the same time that they tend towards factionalism, liberate potential for consensus. That is to say, all the movements and organizations have room for action and discourse in which to agree with all the other movements or organizations, whatever the cleavages among them. Second, there has so far been no tactical or strategic demand that would intensify the cleavages by radicalizing positions. On the contrary, cleavages have been of a fairly low intensity. For the movements and organizations in general, what unites has been more important than what divides. In terms of union and separation, the advantages of union have overcome the advantages of separation. Third, even when cleavages are acknowledged, the different movements and organizations distribute themselves among them in a nonlinear way. If a given movement opposes another in a given cleavage, it may well be on the same side in another cleavage. Thus, the different strategic alliances or common actions featured by each movement tend to involve different partners. In this way the accumulation and strengthening of divergences that could result from the alignment of the movements in multiple cleavages are precluded. To the contrary, the cleavages end up neutralizing or disempowering one another. Herein lies the WSF's cohesive power.

Notes

1 I will return to some of the questions dealt with in this section in Chapter 9.

2 A good overview of the cleavages and conflicts is available in Fisher and Ponniah (2003).

3 As we saw above, India is not totally immune to this type of political culture and political cleavages.

4 This is well illustrated by the changes introduced in the Charter of Principles, first by the Indian Working Committee of the WSF and later by the African Social Forum, to adapt it to the social, political and cultural realities and cleavages prevailing in South Asia and Africa, respectively (more on this below).

5 There are some significant changes between the original proposal and the final version. The existence of two documents may have caused some confusion (the proposal was taken for the final version by some). On the case of India, see Sen (2004: 72–5). This fact is, however, irrelevant to the argument I am making in this chapter.

6 In Annexe II I reproduce the three documents (the official charter, the Indian policy statement, and the charter of the African Social Forum) and compare the differences between them.

7 During WSF 2003 there were severe tensions within the OC and between the OC and the assembly of the social movements concerning the fact that, by being held on the last day of the WSF and ending with a final document or declaration, the assembly was allegedly trying to present its declaration to the participants and international media as the final declaration of the WSF.

8 On this subject, see also Teivainen, forthcoming.

9 The first signatories were Adolfo Pérez Esquivel, Aminata Traoré, Eduardo Galeano, José Saramago, François Houtart, Armand Matellart, Roberto Sávio, Ignácio Ramonet, Ricardo Petrella, Bernard Cassen, Samuel Ruiz Garcia, Tariq Ali, Frei Betto, Emir Sader, Samir Amin, Atílio Borón, Walden Bello, Immanuel Wallerstein and myself. See the text of the manifesto in Annexe III.

7 | The future of the World Social Forum: self-democracy and the work of translation

In the WSF the new and the old face each other. As utopia and epistemology, the WSF is something new. As a political phenomenon, its novelty coexists with the traditions of left thinking or, more generally, counter-hegemonic thinking, both in its Western and its Southern and Eastern versions. The novelty of the WSF is consensually attributed to its absence of leaders and hierarchical organization, its emphasis on cyberspace networks, its ideal of participatory democracy, and its flexibility and readiness to engage in experimentation.

The WSF is unquestionably the first large international progressive movement following the neo-liberal backlash at the beginning of the 1980s. Its future is the future of hope in an alternative to *la pensée unique* (single thinking). This future is completely unknown, and can only be speculated about. It depends both on the movements and organizations that make up the WSF and the metamorphoses of neo-liberal globalization. For instance, the fact that the latter has been acquiring a bellicose component fixated on security will no doubt affect the evolution of the WSF. In light of this, the future of the WSF depends in part on the evaluation of its trajectory up till now and the conclusions drawn from it, with a view to enlarging and deepening its counter-hegemonic efficaciousness.

Evaluation of the WSF is one of the exercises that best discloses the confrontation between the new and the old. From the point of view of the old, the WSF cannot but be assessed negatively. It appears as a vast 'talk show' that hovers over the concrete problems of exclusion and discrimination without tackling them; a cultural movement without deep social roots, therefore tolerated and easily co-opted by the dominant classes; it has no definite agents or agency, because, after all, it doesn't have any definite enemies either; its inclusiveness is the other side of its inefficaciousness; its efficaciousness, besides having an effect on the rhetoric of hegemonic discourse, has been minimal, since it has achieved no changes as far as concrete policies go, nor contributed to ameliorating the ills of exclusion and discrimination.

In this evaluation, the WSF is assessed according to criteria that prevailed in progressive struggles up until the 1980s. Such criteria do not concern strategies and tactics alone; they also concern the time frames and geopolitical units that are the reference points of their applicability. The time frame is linear time, a time that gives meaning and direction to history; the temporality or duration is that of the state's action, even if the action aims to reform or revolutionize the state. From the standpoint of linear time, the counter-hegemonic experiences and struggles, particularly the most innovative or radical ones, are either unrealistic or residual. They cannot conceptualize the multiple temporalities that constitute these experiences and struggles, from the instant time of mass protests to the *longue durée* of indigenous peoples' struggles for self-rule, not to speak of the infinite temporality of utopia. The same is true of the conventional geopolitical unit of progressive politics. Such a unit is national society, the boundary within which the most decisive progressive struggles of the last 150 years have occurred. On the contrary, as I analysed above, the geopolitical unit of the counter-hegemonic experiences and struggles convened by the WSF is trans-scale: it combines the local, the national and the global.

Let's call the epistemology underlying this evaluation positivist epistemology. It seems obvious that this epistemology is completely different from that I ascribed to the WSF above (Chapter 2). In order to be minimally adequate, the evaluation of the WSF must be carried out according to the epistemology of the WSF itself. Otherwise the assessment will always be negative. In other words, the evaluation must be carried out on the basis of the sociology of absences and the sociology of emergences.

In this light, the evaluation of the WSF cannot but be positive. By affirming and rendering credible the existence of a counter-hegemonic globalization, the WSF has contributed significantly to enlarging social experience. It has turned absent struggles and practices into present struggles and practices, and shown which alternative futures, declared impossible by hegemonic globalization, were after all showing signs of emerging. By enlarging the available and possible social experience, the WSF created a global consciousness for the different movements and NGOs, regardless of the scope of their action. Such a global consciousness was crucial to create a certain symmetry of scale between hegemonic globalization and the movements and NGOs that fought against it. Before the WSF, the movements and NGOs fought against hegemonic globalization without being aware of their own globality.

The decisive importance of this consciousness explains why the WSF, once aware of it, does everything to preserve it. It explains, ultimately, why the factors of attraction and aggregation prevail over those of repulsion and disaggregation. This consciousness of globality was decisive in making credible among the movements and the NGOs themselves the trans-scale nature of the geopolitical unit wherein they acted. By encompassing all those movements and NGOs, however, the WSF incorporated that same trans-scale nature, and that is why its efficaciousness cannot be assessed exclusively in terms of global changes. It has to be assessed as well in terms of local and national changes. Given all the levels involved, the evaluation of the WSF's efficaciousness is undoubtedly more complex, but for that same reason it does not allow for rash assessments derived from positivist epistemology.

The WSF is today a more realistic utopia than when it first appeared. Increased realism, however, poses considerable challenges to utopia itself. The challenges consist in deepening its political existence without losing its utopian and epistemological integrity. I identify two main challenges, one short-range, the other long-range: self-democracy and the work of translation, respectively.

Self-democracy

The first, short-range challenge I designate as self-democracy. The WSF's utopia concerns emancipatory democracy. In its broadest sense, emancipatory democracy is the whole process of changing power relations into relations of shared authority. Since the power relations that the WSF resists are multiple, the processes of radical democratization in which the WSF is involved are likewise multiple. In brief, the WSF is a large collective process for deepening democracy. Since this is the WSF's utopian distinction, it is no wonder that the issue of internal democracy has become more and more pressing. In fact, the WSF's credibility in its struggle for democracy in society depends on the credibility of its internal democracy.

In spite of all criticisms and shortcomings, the organizing structure of all the meetings of the WSF has been, to my mind, the most appropriate in spite of the deficiencies of application. Admittedly, the criteria of representation and participation could have been better attuned to the diversity of the movements and NGOs. But as I showed in Chapters 4 and 5, the successive meetings of the WSF have tried to respond to the criticisms in the most productive way. If the response has not always been satisfactory, I believe the reason has more to do with administrative incapacity than with politically motivated biases. The fourth WSF, in Mumbai, aside from organizational innovation, represented a breakthrough in dramatically expanding the social base of participation, while the fifth WSF, in Porto Alegre, was equally a break-through regarding the bottom-up construction of the programme.

Assuming that the WSF may be entering a new phase, the challenge consists in changing the organizing structure according to the demands of the new phase and in respect of the objective of deepening the internal democracy, a most consensual objective in the IC. Two paths for reaching this goal may be identified, a moderate and a radical one. The first consists in expanding the representativeness of the IC and in transferring the WSF's core from discrete global events to a continuous process consisting of national, regional and thematic forums, taking place around the world according to a planned schedule. The idea is that at more circumscribed levels the issues of representation and participatory democracy are easier to solve, while the recurrence and diversity of the events will allow for the application of multiple criteria of representation and participation. The WSF, as a global event, will continue to affirm the globality of counter-hegemonic globalization, but it will lose some of its centrality. The IS or a coordination/facilitation entity will continue to have an executive and coordinating role, while the IC will continue to be charged with defining the broad strategic, the-matic and organizing options. The democratizing effort must therefore focus on the IC, urging it to go on reflecting on the multiple diversities that congregate in the WSF. As I show in Chapter 5, this path is close to what the majority of the members of the IC have been proposing. It assumes its continuity with the previous phase. The aim is to introduce changes that represent unequivocal gains in terms of representation and participation without putting at risk the extraordinary successes achieved so far.

This path does not claim to solve the issue of participatory democ-racy. That is to say, however representative and democratic the organ-izing structures of the forums may be, the issue of the deliberative participation of the rank-and-file participants will always be there. As I have suggested above, information and communication technologies today offer new possibilities for voting and carrying out referendums during the forums. If it is true in general that cyber-democracy has an individualistic bias in its reducing the citizen's political capacity to merely interacting with a computer terminal, it is no less true that such a bias is neutralized in the meetings of the forum, where the exchange of experiences and points of view is so intense, precisely among the rank and file. Of course, deliberative democracy at the meetings will not solve the problem of the democratic inclusion of movements and organizations eager to participate but unable to do so.

The second, far more radical path would increase the WSF's internal democracy by constructing it from the bottom up. On the basis of the smaller forums or forums of narrower scope, such as local or city forums, representative structures would be created at the different levels in such a way that those in the higher ranks would be elected by the immediately lower ranks. The result would be a pyramidal organization with a forum of delegates at the top.[1] This type of proposal may include measures that aim at correcting a plurality of structural imbalances of representation. It involves, however, a radical break with the organizational model adopted up until now and, even if there is a widespread feeling that the present model needs to be drastically revised, one fears that such a radical break may be throwing away the baby with the bath water. Needless to say, any proposal, especially one so radical, must be debated and ultimately voted on. But by whom? By the current IC, certainly not representative of the whole WSF, let alone democratically elected by its members? By the participants of the forums? Which forums? These questions show that there is no machinery of democratic engineering capable of solving the problem of internal democracy at a single blow. To my mind, such a problem will end up being taken care of through successive partial solutions. Its cumulative effect will be the result of a learning process, which, at each democratization stage, consolidates its force and gathers energy to venture on to a higher stage.

The work of translation

The second challenge is long-range. The challenge of internal democracy concerns the processes of decision-making, rather than the content of the decisions, let alone the practices of struggle that may evolve therefrom. In the long run, evaluation of the WSF will depend on its capacity to transform the immense energy that is gathered within it into new forms of counter-hegemonic agency – more efficacious forms because combining the strength of different social movements and NGOs.

The political theory of Western modernity, whether in its liberal or its Marxist version, constructed the unity of action from the agent's unity. According to it, the coherence and meaning of social change were always based on the capacity of the privileged agent of change, be it the bourgeoisie or the working classes, to represent the totality from which the coherence and meaning derived. From such capacity of representation derived both the need and operationality of a general theory of social change.

The utopia and epistemology underlying the WSF place it in the antipodes of such a theory. The extraordinary energy of attraction and aggregation revealed by the WSF resides precisely in refusing the idea of a general theory. The diversity that finds a haven in it is free from the fear of being cannibalized by false universalisms or false single strategies propounded by any general theory. The WSF underwrites the idea that the world is an inexhaustible totality, as it holds many totalities, all of them partial. Accordingly, there is no sense in attempting to grasp the world by any single general theory, because any such theory will always presuppose the monoculture of a given totality and the homogeneity of its parts. The time we live in, whose recent past was dominated by the idea of a general theory, is perhaps a time of transition that may be defined in the following way: we have no need of a general theory, but still need a general theory on the impossibility of a general theory. We need, at any rate, a negative universalism that may give rise to the ecologies made possible by the sociology of absences.

What is the alternative to the general theory? To my mind, the alternative to a general theory is the work of translation. Translation is the procedure that allows for mutual intelligibility among the experiences of the world, both available and possible, as revealed by the sociology of absences and the sociology of emergences, without jeopardizing their identity and autonomy, without, in other words, reducing them to homogeneous entities.

The WSF is witness to the wide multiplicity and variety of social practices of counter-hegemony that occur all over the world. Its strength derives from having corresponded with or given expression to the aspiration of aggregation and association of the different social movements and NGOs, an aspiration that up until then was only latent. The movements and the NGOs constitute themselves around a number of more or less confined goals, create their own forms and styles of resistance, and specialize in certain kinds of practice and discourse that distinguish them from the others. Their identity is thereby created on the basis of what separates them from all the others. The feminist movement sees itself as very distinct from the labour movement, and vice versa; both distinguish themselves from the indigenous movement or the ecological movement; and so on and so forth. All these distinctions and separations have actually translated themselves into very practical differences, even into contradictions that contribute to bringing the movements apart and to fostering rivalries and factionalisms. Therefrom derives the fragmentation and atomization that are the dark side of diversity and multiplicity.

This dark side has lately been pointedly acknowledged by the movements and NGOs. The truth is, however, that none of them individually has had the capacity or credibility to confront it, for, in attempting it, it runs the risk of falling prey to the situation it wishes to remedy. Hence the extraordinary step taken by the WSF. It must be admitted, however, that the aggregation/association made possible by the WSF is of low intensity. The goals are limited, very often circumscribed to mutual knowledge or, at the most, to recognizing differences and making them more explicit and better known. Under these circumstances, joint action cannot but be limited.[2]

The challenge that counter-hegemonic globalization faces now may be formulated in the following way. The forms of aggregation and articulation made possible by the WSF were sufficient to achieve the goals of the phase that may be now coming to an end. Deepening the WSF's goals in a new phase requires forms of aggregation and articulation of higher intensity. Such a process includes articulating struggles and resistances, as well as promoting ever more comprehensive and consistent alternatives. Such articulations presuppose combinations among the different social movements and NGOs that are bound to question their very identity and autonomy as they have been conceived of so far. If the project is to promote counter-hegemonic practices that combine ecological, pacifist, indigenous, feminist, workers' and other movements, and to do so in a horizontal way and with respect for the identity of every movement, an enormous effort of mutual recognition, dialogue and debate will be required to carry out the task.

This is the only way to identify more rigorously what divides and unites the movements, so as to base the articulations of practices and knowledges on what unites them, rather than on what divides them. Such a task entails a wide exercise in translation to expand reciprocal intelligibility without destroying the identity of the partners of translation. The point is to create, in every movement or NGO, in every practice or strategy, in every discourse or knowledge, a *contact zone* that may render it porous and hence permeable to other NGOs, practices, strategies, discourses and knowledges. The exercise of translation aims to identify and reinforce what is common in the diversity of counter-hegemonic drive. Cancelling out what separates is out of the question. The goal is to have host-difference replace fortress-difference. Through translation work, diversity is celebrated, not as a factor of fragmentation and isolationism, but rather as a condition of sharing and solidarity.

In the following I provide some illustrations of translation work.

The work of translation concerns both knowledges and actions (strategic goals, organization, styles of struggle and agency). Of course, in the practice of the movements, knowledges and actions are inseparable. For the purposes of translation, however, it is important to distinguish between contact zones in which the interactions depend mainly upon knowledges, and contact zones in which interactions depend mainly upon actions.

Translation of knowledges Translation of knowledges consists of interpretation work between two or more cultures – those to which the different movements/organizations in the contact zone see themselves as belonging – to identify similar concerns or aspirations among them and the different responses they provide to them. For instance, the concern with and the aspiration to human dignity seem to be present, albeit in different ways, in different cultures. In Western culture the idea of human dignity is expressed today by the concept of human rights. If we look at the thousands of movements and organizations that gather at the WSF we will observe that many of them don't formulate their concerns in terms of human rights and many may even express a hostile stance against the idea of human rights. Does this mean that these movements don't care for human dignity? Or is it rather the case that they formulate their concerns for human dignity through a different set of concepts? I think that the latter is the case, and accordingly I have been proposing a translation of concerns for human dignity between the Western concept of human rights, the Islamic concept of *umma* (community) and the Hindu concept of *dharma* (cosmic harmony involving human and all the other beings) (Santos 1995: 327–65; 2002b: 257–301).[3]

In this case, the work of translation will reveal the reciprocal shortcomings or weaknesses of each of these conceptions of human dignity, once viewed from the perspective of any other conception. Thereby, a space is opened in the contact zone for dialogue, mutual knowledge and understanding and for identification, over and above conceptual and terminological differences, of commonalities from which practical combinations for action can emerge. A few examples will clarify what I mean. Seen from the perspective of *dharma*, human rights are incomplete in that they fail to establish the link between the part (the individual) and the whole (cosmic reality), or even more strongly in that they focus on what is merely derivative, on rights, rather than on the primordial imperative, the duty of individuals to find their place in the order of the entire society, and of the entire cosmos.[4] Seen from the perspective of *dharma* and, indeed, from that of *umma* also, the Western conception of human rights is plagued by a very simplistic and mechanistic symmetry between rights and duties. It grants rights only to those from whom it can demand duties. This explains why, according to Western human rights, nature has no rights: because it cannot have any duties imposed on it. For the same reason, it is impossible to grant rights to future generations: they have no rights because they have no duties.

On the other hand, seen from the perspective of human rights, *dharma* is also incomplete, owing to its strong bias in favour of the harmony of the social and religious status quo, thereby occulting injustices and totally neglecting the value of conflict as a way towards a richer harmony. Moreover, *dharma* is unconcerned with the principles of democratic order, with individual freedom and autonomy, and it neglects the fact that, without primordial rights, the individual is too fragile an entity to avoid being run over by powerful economic and political institutions. Moreover, *dharma* tends to forget that human suffering has an irreducible individual dimension: societies don't suffer, individuals do.

At another conceptual level, the same work of translation can be attempted between the concept of human rights and the concept of *umma* in Islamic culture. The passages in the Koran in which the word *umma* occurs are so varied that its meaning cannot be rigidly defined. This much, however, seems to be certain: it always refers to ethnic, linguistic or religious bodies of people who are the objects of the divine plan of salvation. As the prophetic activity of Muhammad progressed, the religious foundations of *umma* became increasingly apparent and consequently the *umma* of the Arabs was transformed into the *umma* of the Muslims. Seen from the perspective of *umma*, the incompleteness of individual human rights lies in the fact that on their basis alone it is impossible to ground the collective linkages, duties and solidarities without which no society can survive, and much less flourish. Herein lies the difficulty in the Western conception of human rights in terms of accepting collective rights of social groups or peoples, be they ethnic minorities, women or indigenous peoples. Conversely, from the perspective of individual human rights, *umma* over-emphasizes duties to the detriment of rights and, for that reason, is bound to condone otherwise abhorrent inequalities, such as the inequality between men and women and between Muslims and non-Muslims.

In sum, the work of translation in the intercultural contact zone among movements/organizations expounding different conceptions of human dignity allows us to identify the fundamental weakness of Western culture as consisting in dichotomizing too strictly between the individual and society, thus becoming vulnerable to possessive individualism, narcissism, alienation and anomie. On the other hand, the fundamental weakness of Hindu and Islamic culture lies in the fact that they both fail to recognize that human suffering has an irreducible individual dimension, which can only be adequately addressed in a society not hierarchically organized.

The recognition of reciprocal incompleteness and weakness is a condition *sine qua non* of a cross-cultural dialogue. The work of translation builds both on local identification of incompleteness and weakness and on its translocal intelligibility. In the area of human rights and dignity, the mobilization of social support for the emancipatory claims they potentially contain is achievable only if such claims have been appropriated in the local cultural context. Appropriation, in this sense, cannot be obtained through cultural cannibalization. It requires cross-cultural dialogue by means of translation work.

In light of the political and cultural characteristics of the movements/ organizations present at the WSF two other exercises of translation strike me as important. I just mention them here without going into details of translation. The first focuses on the concern for productive life as it is expressed in the modern capitalist conceptions of development and in Gandhi's conception of *swadeshi*.[5] The conceptions of productive life deriving from capitalist development have been reproduced by conventional economics and are often implicitly or explicitly accepted by social movements and NGOs, particularly in the Global North. Such conceptions are based on the idea of infinite growth reached through the increasing subjection of practices and knowledges to mercantile logic.[6] The *swadeshi*, in turn, is based on the idea of sustainability and reciprocity that Gandhi defined in 1916 in the following way:

> [...] swadeshi is that spirit in us which restricts us to the use and service of our immediate surroundings to the exclusion of the more remote. Thus as for religion, in order to satisfy the requirements of the definition I must restrict myself to my ancestral religion [...]. If I find it defective I should serve it by purging it of its defects. In the domain of politics I should make use of the indigenous institutions and serve them by curing them of their proven defects. In that of economics, I should use only things that are produced by my immediate neighbours and serve those industries by making them efficient and complete where they might be found wanting. (Gandhi 1941: 4–5)

This brief description of *swadeshi* and the weight it carries among NGOs and movements in South Asia, as could be observed at the WSF in Mumbai, shows how important the work of translation might be to bring about North/South and East/West coalitions among NGOs and movements concerned with development or production. Through such reciprocal translation the monoculture of capitalist production will be replaced by the ecology of productivities.

The other exercise of translation in the knowledge-based contact zone among NGOs/movements focuses on philosophies of life, on concerns for wisdom and enabling world-views. It may seem strange to speak of philosophy when dealing with the knowledges of grassroots movements fighting for 'another possible world'. After all, in the Western culture at least, philosophy is the utmost expression of elitist knowledge. The fact of the matter is that, however implicitly, philosophical ideas are often the driving force behind grassroots mobilization and it is not uncommon for the leaders of movements and the latter's organic intellectuals to become involved in vivid debates on philosophical ideas to ground both their divergences and their convergences. The work of translation must take place between Western conceptions of philosophy and the African concept of sagacity.[7] The latter underlies the actions of many African movements and organizations.[8] It resides in a critical reflection on the world that has as its protagonists what Odera Oruka calls *sages*, be they poets, traditional healers, storytellers, musicians or traditional authorities. According to Oruka, sage philosophy

> [...] consists of the expressed thoughts of wise men and women in any given community and is a way of thinking and explaining the world that fluctuates between popular wisdom (well known communal maxims, aphorisms and general commonsense truths) and didactic wisdom, an expounded wisdom and a rational thought of some given individuals within a community. While popular wisdom is often conformist, didactic wisdom is at times critical of the communal set-up and the popular wisdom. Thoughts can be expressed in writing or as unwritten sayings and argumentations associated with some individual(s). In traditional Africa, most of what would pass as sage-philosophy remains unwritten for reasons which must now be obvious to everyone. Some of these persons might have been partly influenced by the inevitable moral and technological culture from the West. Nevertheless, their own outlook and cultural well-being remain basically that of traditional rural Africa. Except for a handful of them, the majority of them are 'illiterate' or semi-illiterate. (Oruka 1990: 28)

The work of translation among knowledges starts from the idea that all cultures are incomplete and can, therefore, be enriched by dialogue and confrontation with other cultures. In my view, the WSF has granted this idea a new centrality and a higher urgency. To acknowledge the relativity of cultures does not imply the adoption of relativism as a cultural stance (the idea that all cultures are equally valid and that no judgement can be passed on them from the perspective of another culture). It does imply, however, conceiving of universalism as a Western peculiarity, whose idea of supremacy does not reside in itself, but rather in the supremacy of the interests that sustain it. As I mentioned above, the critique of universalism derives from the critique of the possibility of a general theory. The work of translation presupposes, rather, what I designated above as negative universalism, the shared idea of the impossibility of cultural completeness and, concomitantly, the impossibility of a general theory capable of accounting for the whole diversity of the world and its progressive transformation.

Once the exchange of experiences begins – this has been the most profound accomplishment of the WSF so far – the idea and feeling of want and incompleteness create motivation for the work of translation among social groups. In order to bear fruit, translation must be the coming together of converging motivations with their origins in different cultures. The Indian sociologist Shiv Vishvanathan formulated eloquently the notion of want and motivation that I here designate as the work of translation. Says Vishvanathan (2000: 12): 'My problem is, how do I take the best of Indian civilization and at the same time keep my modern, democratic imagination alive?' If we could imagine an exercise of translation conducted by Vishvanathan and a European or North American intellectual/activist or social movement, it would be possible to think of the latter's motivation for dialogue formulated thus: 'How can I keep alive in me the best of modern and democratic Western culture, while at the same time recognizing the value of the world that it designated autocratically as non-civilized, ignorant, residual, inferior or unproductive?'

Translation of practices The second type of translation work is undertaken among social practices and their agents. All social practices imply knowledge, and as such they are also knowledge practices. When dealing with practices, however, the work of translation focuses specifically on mutual intelligibility among forms of organization, objectives, styles of action and types of struggle. What distinguishes the two types of translation work is, after all, the emphasis or perspective that informs them. The specificity of the translation work concerning practices and their agents becomes clearer in situations in which the knowledges that inform different practices are less distinguishable than the practices themselves. This happens particularly when the practices take place within the same cultural universe. Such would be the case of a work of translation between the forms of organization and the objectives of action of two social movements, say the feminist movement and the labour movement in a Western society.

The relevance of the work of translation as regards practices is due to a double circumstance. On the one hand, the WSF meetings have enlarged considerably the stock of available and possible social struggles against capitalism and neo-liberal globalization. On the other, because there is no single principle of social transformation, as the Charter of Principles emphasizes, it is not possible to determine in abstract the links or hierarchies among the different social struggles and their conceptions of social transformation, both the objectives of social transformation and the means to achieve them. Only by building concrete contact zones among concrete struggles is it possible to evaluate them and identify possible alliances among them. Reciprocal knowledge and learning are a necessary condition for agreeing on association and building coalitions. The counter-hegemonic potential of any social movement resides in its capacity to associate with other movements, their forms of organization and objectives. For these associations to be possible, the movements must be mutually intelligible.

The work of translation aims to clarify what unites and separates the different movements and practices so as to ascertain the possibilities and limits of association and aggregation among them. Because there is no single universal social practice or collective subject to confer meaning and direction to history, the work of translation becomes crucial to define, in each concrete and historical moment or context, which constellations of subordinate practices carry more counter-hegemonic potential. For instance, in Mexico, in March 2001, the Zapatista indigenous movement was a privileged counter-hegemonic practice inasmuch as it was capable of undertaking the work of translation between its objectives and practices and the objectives and practices of other Mexican social movements, including the civic and labour movements and the feminist movement. One consequence of that work of translation was the fact that the Zapatista leader chosen to address the Mexican Congress was a woman, Comandante Esther. By that choice, the Zapatistas wanted to signify the linkage between the indigenous movement and the women's liberation movement, and thus deepen the counter-hegemonic potential of both.

While showing the diversity of social struggles fighting against neo-liberal globalization all over the world, the WSF calls for a giant work of translation. On the one hand, there are local movements and organizations not only very different in their practices and objectives but also embedded in different cultures; on the other, transnational organizations, some from the South, some from the North, that also differ widely among themselves. How to build association, aggregation and coalition among all these different movements and organizations? What do the participatory budgeting practised in many Latin American cities and the participatory democratic planning based on *panchayats* in Kerala and West Bengal in India have in common? What can they learn from each other?[9] In what kinds of counter-hegemonic global activities can they cooperate? The same questions can be asked about the pacifist and the anarchist movements, or the indigenous and gay movements, the Zapatista movement, the ATTAC, the Landless Movement in Brazil, and the Narmada River movement in India, and so on and so forth. These are the questions that the work of translation aims to answer. It is a complex work, not only because the movements and organizations involved are many and diverse, but also because they are embedded in diverse cultures and knowledges.

Conditions and procedures of translation The work of translation aims to create intelligibility, coherence and association in a world that sees itself enriched by multiplicity and diversity. Translation is not a mere technique. Even its obvious technical components and the way in which they are applied in the course of the translation process must be the object of democratic deliberation. Translation is a work of dialogue and politics. It has an emotional dimension as well, because it presupposes both a nonconformist attitude vis-à-vis the limits of one's knowledge and practice and the readiness to be surprised and learn from the other's knowledge and practice.

The work of translation is based on the premise that for cultural, social and political reasons specific to our time it is possible to reach a broad consensus around the idea that there is no general, all-encompassing theory of social transformation. Without this consensus – the only kind of legitimate (negative) universalism, as mentioned above – translation is a colonial kind of work, no matter how post-colonial it claims to be. Once such a postulate is guaranteed, the conditions and procedures of the work of translation can be elucidated on the basis of the following questions: What to translate? From what and into what to translate? Who translates? When should translation take place? Why translate?

WHAT TO TRANSLATE? The crucial concept in answering this question is that concept of *cosmopolitan contact zone*. Building coalitions to further counter-hegemonic globalization presupposes the existence of contact zones conceived of as social fields in which different movements/organizations meet and interact to reciprocally evaluate their normative aspirations, their practices and knowledges. In view of the history of progressive politics in the twentieth century it is probably unavoidable that unequal relations of power are present in the first steps of the construction of contact zones. The work of translation will be possible to the extent that the unequal power relations yield to relations of shared authority. Only then will the cosmopolitan contact zone be constituted. The cosmopolitan contact zone starts from the assumption that it is up to each knowledge or practice to decide what is put in contact with whom. Contact zones are always selective because the movement's or NGO's knowledges and practices exceed what they are willing to put in contact. Indeed, what is put in contact is not necessarily what is most relevant or central. As the work of translation advances it becomes possible to bring into the contact zone the aspects of knowledge or practice that each NGO or social movement considers more central and relevant.

In intercultural contact zones, it is up to each cultural group to decide which aspects must be selected for intercultural confrontation and dialogue. In every culture, there are features deemed too central to be exposed and rendered vulnerable by the confrontation in the contact zone, or aspects deemed inherently untranslatable into another culture. These decisions are part and parcel of the work of translation itself and are susceptible to revision as the work proceeds. If the work of translation progresses, it is to be expected that more features will be brought to the contact zone, which in turn will contribute to further translation progress. In many countries of Latin America, particularly in those in which multicultural constitutionalism has been adopted, the indigenous peoples have been fighting for the right to control what in their knowledges and practices should or should not be the object of translation vis-à-vis wider society, the *sociedad mayor*. Once involved in the WSF process, the indigenous movements conduct a similar struggle vis-à-vis all the non-indigenous movements.

The issue of what is translatable is not restricted to the selection criterion adopted by each group in the contact zone. Beyond active selectivity, there is what we might call passive selectivity. It consists of what in a given culture has become unpronounceable because of the extreme oppression to which it was subjected for long periods. These are deep absences, made of an emptiness impossible to fill; the silences they produce are too unfathomable to become the object of translation work.

What to translate provokes one other question that is particularly important in contact zones between groups from different cultural universes. Cultures are monolithic only when seen from the outside or from afar. When looked at from the inside or at close range, it is easy to see that they are made up of various and often conflicting versions of the same culture. For example, when I speak, as I did above, of a possible intercultural dialogue about conceptions of human dignity, we can easily see that in Western culture there is not just one conception of human rights. Two at least can be identified: a liberal conception that privileges political and civic rights to the detriment of social and economic rights; and a radical or socialist conception that stresses social and economic rights as a condition of all the others. By the same token, in Islam it is possible to identify several conceptions of *umma*: some, more inclusive, going back to the time when the Prophet lived in Mecca; others, less inclusive, which evolved after the construction of the Islamic state in Medina. Likewise, there are many conceptions of *dharma* in Hinduism. They vary, for instance, from caste to caste.

The most inclusive versions, which hold a wider circle of reciprocity, are those that generate more promising contact zones; they are the most adequate to deepen the work of translation.

TO TRANSLATE FROM WHAT INTO WHAT? The choice of knowledges and practices among which the work of translation occurs is always the result of a convergence among movements/NGOs concerning both the identification of a lack or deficiency in one's knowledge or practice, and the refusal to accept it as a fatal flaw and the motivation to over- come it. It may emerge from an evaluation that current performances don't measure up to the group's expectations and from a sense of crisis developing therefrom. As an example, the labour movement, confronted with an unprecedented crisis, has been opening itself to contact zones with other social movements, namely civic, feminist, ecological and migrant workers' movements. In this contact zone, there is an ongoing translation work between labour practices, claims and aspirations, and the objectives of citizenship, protection of the environment, fighting discrimination against women and ethnic or migrant minorities. Translation has slowly transformed the labour movement and the other social movements, thus rendering possible constellations of struggles that until a few years ago would have been unthinkable.

WHEN TO TRANSLATE? In this case, too, the cosmopolitan contact zone must be the result of a conjugation of times, rhythms and opportunities. If there is no such conjugation, the contact zone becomes imperial and the work of translation a form of cannibalization. In the last two decades, Western modernity discovered the possibilities and virtues of multiculturalism. Accustomed to the routine of its own hegemony, Western modernity presumed that if it were to open itself to dialogue with cultures it had previously oppressed, the latter would *naturally* be ready and available to engage in the dialogue, and indeed only too eager to do so. Such presupposition has resulted in new forms of cultural imperialism, even when it assumes the form of multiculturalism. This I call reactionary multiculturalism. In contrast, the success of the WSF signals the emergence among social movements of a reciprocally experienced, widespread sense that the advancement of counter-hegemonic struggles is premised upon the possibility of sharing practices and knowledges globally and cross-culturally. Upon this shared experience it becomes possible to build the horizontal conjugation of times from which a cosmopolitan contact zone and the emancipatory work of translation may emerge.

WHO TRANSLATES? Knowledges and practices exist only as mobilized by social groups, both movements and NGOs. Hence the work of translation is always carried out among representatives of those social groups. The WSF is a facilitator of cosmopolitan contact zones among NGOs/movements and a meeting ground for their leaders and activists. The workings of the contact zone generate a new kind of citizenship, a cosmopolitan attitude of reflection and self-reflection, reaching beyond familiar territories, be they familiar practices or familiar knowledges. As argumentative work, the work of translation requires argumentative capacity. The partners in the cosmopolitan contact zone must have a profile similar to that of the philosophical sage identified by Odera Oruka in his quest for African sagacity. They must be deeply embedded in the practices and knowledges they represent, having both a profound and a critical understanding. This critical dimension, which Odera Oruka designates as 'didactic sageness', grounds the want, the feeling of incompleteness and the motivation to discover in other knowledges and practices the answers that are not to be found within the limits of a given knowledge or practice. Translators of cultures must be good cosmopolitan citizens, both individual and collective citizens. They are to be found both among the leaders of social movements and among the rank-and-file activists. In the near future, the decision about who translates is likely to become one of the most crucial democratic deliberations in the construction of counter-hegemonic globalization.

HOW TO TRANSLATE? The work of translation is basically an argumentative work, based on the cosmopolitan emotion of sharing the world with those who do not share our knowledge or experience. The work of translation encounters multiple difficulties. The first difficulty concerns the premises of argumentation. Argumentation is based on postulates, axioms, rules and ideas that are not the object of argumentation because they are taken for granted by all those participating in the same argumentative circle. They constitute what is evident to everyone, the *commonplaces* (*loci communes, topoi*), the basic consensus that makes argumentative dissent possible.[10] The work of translation has no commonplaces at the outset, because the available commonplaces are those appropriate to a given movement, hence not acceptable as evident by another movement. In other words, the commonplaces that each movement brings into the contact zone cease to be premises of argumentation and become arguments. As it progresses, the work of translation constructs the commonplaces adequate to the contact zone and the translating situation. It is a demanding work, with no safety nets and ever on the verge of disaster. The ability to construct commonplaces is one of the most distinctive marks of the quality of the cosmopolitan contact zone.

The second difficulty regards the language used to conduct the argumentation. It is not usual for the movements present in contact zones to have a common language or to master the common language equally well or in the same way. Furthermore, when the cosmopolitan contact zone is multicultural, one of the languages in question is often the language that dominated the colonial or imperial contact zone. The replacement of the latter by a cosmopolitan contact zone may thus be boycotted by virtue of this use of the previously dominant language. The issue is not just that the different participants in the argumentative discourse may master the language unequally. The issue is that this language is responsible for the very unpronounceability of some of the central aspirations of the knowledges and practices that were oppressed in the colonial contact zone.

The third difficulty concerns the silences. Not the things that are unpronounceable, but rather the different rhythms with which the different movements link words with silences and the different eloquence (or meaning) that is ascribed to silence by the different cultures to which the groups belong. To manage and translate silence is one of the most exacting tasks of the work of translation.

WHY TRANSLATE? This last question encompasses all the others. Very succinctly, the work of translation enables the social movements and organizations to develop a cosmopolitan reason based on the core idea that global social justice is not possible without global cognitive justice.

The work of translation is the procedure we are left with to give coherence and generate coalitions among the enormous diversity of struggles against neo-liberal globalization when there is no general theory of progressive social transformation (and none would be welcomed if it existed) to be brought about by a privileged historical subject according to centrally established strategies and tactics. When social transformation has no automatic meaning and neither history nor society or nature can be centrally planned, the movements have to create, through translation, partial collective meanings that enable them to join together in courses of action that they consider most adequate to bring about the kind of social transformation they deem most desirable.

It may be asked: if we do not know whether a better world is possible, what gives us legitimacy or motivation to act as if we did? The work of translation is a work of epistemological and democratic imagination, aiming to construct new and plural conceptions of social emancipation upon the ruins of the automatic social emancipation of the modernist project. There is no guarantee that a better world may be possible, nor that all those who have not given up struggling for it conceive of it in the same way. The objective of the translation work is to nurture among progressive social movements and organizations the will to create together knowledges and practices strong enough to provide credible alternatives to neo-liberal globalization, which is no less and no more than a new step on the past of global capitalism towards subjecting the inexhaustible wealth of the world to the mercantile logic. In the cosmopolitan contact zone, the possibility of a better world is imagined from the vantage point of the present. Once the field of experiences is enlarged, it is possible to evaluate better the alternatives that are possible and available today. This diversification of experiences aims to re-create the tension between experiences and expectations, but in such a way that they both happen in the present. The new nonconformity results from the verification that it would be possible to live in a much better world today rather than tomorrow. The possibility of a better future lies therefore not in a distant future, but rather in the reinvention of the present as enlarged by the sociology of absences and by the sociology of emergences, and rendered coherent by the work of translation. To affirm the credibility and sustainability of this possibility is, in my view, the most profound contribution of the WSF to the counter-hegemonic struggles.

The work of translation permits the creation of meanings and directions that are precarious but concrete, short-range but radical in their objectives, uncertain but shared. The aim of translation between knowledges is to create cognitive justice from the standpoint of the epistemological imagination. The aim of translation between practices and their agents is to create the conditions for global social justice from the standpoint of the democratic imagination.

The work of translation creates the conditions for concrete social emancipations of concrete social groups in a present whose injustice is legitimized on the basis of a massive waste of experience. The kind of social transformation that may be accomplished on the basis of the work of translation requires that the reciprocal learning and the will to associate and coalesce be transformed into transformative practices. In the following chapter I present a concrete proposal aimed at expanding, deepening and consolidating the work of translation.

Notes

1 A version of this path was proposed by Michael Albert, of ZNET (2003). Here are the main points of his proposal:

1. Emphasize local forums as the foundation of the worldwide forum process.
2. Have each new level of forums, from towns, cities, countries, to continents and the world, built largely on those below.
3. Have the decision-making leadership of the most local events locally determined.
4. Have the decision-making leadership at each higher level chosen, at least to a large extent, by the local forums within the higher entity. Italy's national forum leadership is chosen by the smaller local forums in Italy. The European forums' leadership is chosen by the national forums within Europe, and similarly elsewhere.
5. Mandate that the decision-making leadership at every level should be at least 50 per cent women.
6. Have the forums from wealthier parts of the world charge delegates and organizations and attendees a tax on their fees to apply to helping finance

the forums in poorer parts of the world and subsidize delegate attendance at the world forum from poorer locales.

7. Set the WSF attendance at 5,000–10,000 people delegated to it from the major regional forums around the world. Have the WSF leadership selected by regional forums. Mandate the WSF to share and compare and propose based on all that is emerging worldwide – not to listen again to the same famous speakers whom everyone hears worldwide all the time anyhow – and have the WSF's results, like those of all other forums, published and made public, and of course reported by delegates back to the regions.

8. Ensure that the WSF as a whole and the forums worldwide do not make the mistake of trying to become an International, a movement of movements, or even just a voice of the world's movements. To be a forum, the WSF and the smaller component forums need to be as broad and diverse as possible. But being that broad and that diverse is simply being too broad and too diverse to be an organization.

9. Mandate that the forums at every level, including the WSF, welcome people from diverse constituencies using the forums and their processes to make contacts and to develop ties that can in turn yield national, regional or even international networks or movements of movements which share their political aspirations sufficiently to work closely together, but which exist alongside one another, rather than reflecting the forum phenomenon.

2 A good example was the first European Social Forum held in Florence in November 2002. The differences, rivalries and factionalisms that divide the various movements and NGOs that organized it are well known and have a history that is impossible to erase. This is why, in their positive response to the WSF's request to organize the ESF, the movements and NGOs that took up the task felt the need to assert that the differences among them were as sharp as ever and that they were coming together only with a very limited objective in mind: to organize the Forum and a Peace March. The Forum was indeed organized in such a way that the differences could be made very explicit.

3 On the concept of *umma*, see, for example, Faruki (1979); An-Na'im (1995, 2000); Hassan (1996); on the Hindu concept of *dharma*, see Gandhi (1929/32); Zaehner (1982).

4 I analyse in greater detail the relationships between human rights and other conceptions of human dignity in Santos (2002a).

5 See Gandhi (1941, 1967). On *swadeshi* see also, among others, Bipinchandra (1954); Nandy (1987); Krishna (1994).

6 These conceptions are so prevalent that I have designated them as the monoculture of production in Chapter 2.

7 Similar conceptions may be found, for instance, among the indigenous peoples.

8 On sage philosophy see Oruka (1990, 1998) and also Oseghare (1992); Presbey (1997).

9 A concrete example of mutual learning in this field can be seen in Santos (2005).

10 On commonplaces and argumentation in general, see Santos (1995: 7–55).

8 | The World Social Forum and self-learning: the Popular University of the Social Movements

The work of translation analysed in Chapter 7 is a daunting task and it will not be accomplished easily. It involves a complex process of global self-knowledge and self-training aimed at increasing reciprocal knowledge among the movements and organizations. The ecologies of knowledges I referred to in Chapter 2 of this book, as one of the features of an epistemology of the South, will not emerge spontaneously. On the contrary, because they confront the monoculture of scientific knowledge, they will develop only through a sociology of absences whereby suppressed, marginalized and discredited knowledges are made present and credible. As I said, the sociology of absences is no conventional sociology and cannot be pursued in the conventional sites for the production of hegemonic scientific knowledge, i.e. the universities and research centres. This does not mean that in those sites counter-hegemonic scientific knowledge cannot be produced. It can, and the WSF has benefited from it. What such sites cannot produce is ecologies of knowledges, that is to say promoting meaningful dialogues among different kinds of knowledges (science being one of them, and an important one in many instances), identifying alternative sources of knowledge and alternative knowledge creators, and experimenting with alternative criteria of rigour and relevance in light of shared objectives of emancipatory social transformation. The ecologies of knowledges call for context-bound, situated, useful knowledges embedded in transformative practices. Accordingly, they can be pursued only in settings as close as possible to such practices, and in such a way that the protagonists of social action are also the protagonists of knowledge creation.

In this regard, at the 2003 WSF I proposed the creation of a Popular University of the Social Movements (PUSM) with the purpose of enabling the self-education of activists and leaders of social movements, as well as social scientists, scholars and artists concerned with progressive social transformation.[1] The designation of 'popular university' was used not so much to evoke the working-class universities that proliferated in Europe and Latin America in the early twentieth century, as to convey the idea that after a century of elitist higher education a popular university is necessarily a counter-university. Since 2003, the proposal has been discussed on several occasions with different groups and people involved in the WSF.[2] In the following, I present the original proposal and briefly describe the initiatives undertaken to carry it out.

A proposal for collective transformative self-learning: the Popular University of the Social Movements

What the PUSM is and isn't[3] PUSM is not a school for training cadres or leaders of NGOs and social movements. Although PUSM is clearly oriented towards action for social transformation, its aim is not to offer the kinds of skills and training that are usually provided by such schools. Nor is PUSM a think tank of NGOs and social movements. Although it highly values strategic research and reflection, PUSM rejects the distance that one and the other usually maintain vis-à-vis collective action.

The major objective of PUSM is to help make knowledge of alternative globalization as global as globalization itself, and, at the same time, to render actions for social transformation better known and more efficient, and its protagonists more competent and reflective. To meet its goals PUSM will have to be more international and intercultural than similar existing initiatives.

Rationale As I argued above, the movement for an alternative globalization is a new political phenomenon focused on the idea that the current phase of global capitalism, known as neo-liberal globalization, requires new forms of resistance and new directions for social emancipation. From within this movement, made up of a large number of social movements and NGOs, new social agents and practices are emerging. They operate in an equally new framework, networking local, national and global struggles. Present theories of social change, even those concerned with emancipatory social change, cannot adequately deal with this political and cultural novelty.

This gap between theory and practice has negative consequences both for genuinely progressive social movements and NGOs, and the universities and research centres, where scientific social theories have traditionally been produced. Both leaders and activists of social movements and NGOs feel the lack of theories enabling them to reflect analytically on their practice and clarify their methods and objectives. Furthermore, progressive social scientists/scholars/artists, isolated from these new practices and agents, cannot contribute to this reflection and clarification. They can even make things more difficult by

149

insisting on concepts and theories that are not adequate to these new realities.

The proposal for a PUSM is meant to contribute to filling this gap and correcting the two deficiencies it produces. Ultimately, its objective is to overcome the distinction between theory and practice by bringing the two together through systematic encounters between those who mainly devote themselves to the practice of social change and those who mainly engage in theoretical production.

The kind of training envisioned by PUSM is therefore two-pronged. On the one hand, it aims to enable self-education of activists and community leaders of social movements and NGOs, by providing them with adequate analytical and theoretical frameworks. The latter will enable them to deepen their reflective understanding of their practice – their methods and objectives – enhancing their efficacy and consistency. On the other hand, it aims to enable self-education of progressive social scientists/scholars/artists interested in studying the new processes of social transformation, by offering them the opportunity of a direct dialogue with their protagonists. This will make it possible to identify, and whenever possible to eliminate, the discrepancy between the analytical and theoretical frameworks in which they were trained and the concrete needs and aspirations emerging from new transformational practices.

In this two-pronged educational approach lies the novelty of PUSM. To achieve its objective, PUSM must overcome the conventional distinction between teaching and learning – based on the distinction between teacher and pupil – thus creating contexts and moments for reciprocal learning. Recognition of reciprocal ignorance is its starting point. Its end point is the shared production of knowledges as global and diverse as the globalization processes themselves.

Beyond the gap between theory and practice, PUSM intends to tackle two problems that currently permeate all movements for a counter-hegemonic globalization. First, the scarcity of reciprocal knowledge that still exists among movements/NGOs active in the same thematic area and operating in different parts of the globe. The WSF and all the other regional and thematic forums have been powerful instruments in highlighting this need and showing the importance of reciprocal knowledge. Given their sporadic nature and short lifespan, however, they have been unable to fulfil this need. Without this reciprocal knowledge, it is impossible to increase the density and complexity of movement networks. Without this expansion it is not possible to augment significantly the efficacy and consistency of transformational actions beyond what has been achieved so far.

The other problem is the lack of shared knowledge among movements/organizations active in different thematic areas and struggles. This gap is even wider than the previous one, and bridging it is equally important. Because, as I said in Chapter 7, a general theory globally encompassing all movements and practices in all thematic areas is impossible (and if possible it would be undesirable), we need to create conditions for reciprocal intelligibility among movements through the work of translation laid out above. The PUSM is a permanent workshop of translation aimed at enhancing the density and complexity of the movements' networks fighting against neo-liberal globalization.

Activities PUSM has three principal activities: pedagogical activities, research activities for social transformation, and activities for spreading capabilities and tools for inter-thematic, transnational and intercultural translation.

PEDAGOGICAL ACTIVITIES. PUSM will be structured on the basis of workshops, attended by a limited number of activists/movement leaders, and social scientists/scholars/artists. Each workshop will last two weeks on a full-time basis, alternating periods for discussion, study and reflection and leisure.

Each workshop will have about ten discussion sessions. Activists/movement leaders and social scientists/scholars/artists will take turns in preparing and running these sessions. Study materials will be of various kinds: oral narratives and documents presented by movements and organizations about both successful and unsuccessful campaigns/struggles, and theoretical and analytical texts proposed by social scientists/scholars, dramatic plays[4] and art objects and activities proposed by artists. Each workshop will have two coordinators, one an activist/leader and the other a scientist/scholar/artist. Both activist/leaders and artists/scholars/artists will work as consecutive translators, whenever needed and feasible.

Each workshop will consist of two phases: thematic and inter-thematic. The thematic phase will be concerned with deepening the theoretical and practical knowledge of movements and organizations working in a given area, be it labour, indigenous people, feminism, environment, peace, human rights, fair trade, land, peasant agriculture, intellectual property rights, and so on. The inter-thematic phase will be concerned with the sharing of experiences and knowledges between at least two fields of collective action and their respective movements and organizations.

To this effect, at least two workshops will be held at the same time at PUSM. The first week of each workshop will be dedicated to deepening the theme. In the second week, activists/leaders and social scientists/scholars/artists participating in two (or more) workshops will meet together.

In its thematic phase, workshop discussions will deal with, among other things, the following:

1. accounts and trajectories of organization and action;
2. reflection on successful and unsuccessful practices;
3. discussion of the most complex issues, the most deeply felt wants;
4. discussion of objectives, strategies and methodologies;
5. discussion of topics proposed in the ambit of the two other activities of PUSM (see below), deemed by the coordinators as having particular relevance for the NGOs and movements that participate in the workshops.

Activists/leaders in particular will discuss and reflect on the basis of their practices. In addition to their role as discussion facilitators, social scientists/scholars/artists will have the specific task of conveying the compared experience of movements and organizations that are not present, but which have accumulated relevant knowledge. Participation of social scientists/scholars/artists from the Global South is particularly desirable, as in general they have more experience in linking theory and practice.

At the conclusion of the thematic phase, workshop participants will define by consensus a set of issues to be discussed with the other workshop (or workshops). The two (or more) sets of issues – one set for each thematic workshop – will be the basis for the inter-thematic phase of the workshops.

At the conclusion of each workshop, a rapporteur chosen by the participants will present a detailed report on discussions and main conclusions. This report will be disseminated among all movements, associations and social scientists/scholars/artists who have joined the PUSM network.

Fellowships and grants will be available for movement leaders/activists and social scientists/scholars/artists unable to pay for their participation.

RESEARCH ACTIVITIES FOR SOCIAL TRANSFORMATION. Besides being a network of plural knowledges, PUSM aims to be a network for the creation of plural knowledges. As the pedagogical activities evolve, themes and problems deemed relevant but as yet little known and understood will emerge. Workshop participants will be encouraged to identify these topics and problems, forwarding them to the translation coordination unit. The selected topics and problems will be researched by the PUSM network in the light of various participatory methodologies.[5]

ACTIVITIES FOR THE DIFFUSION OF TRANSLATION CAPABILITIES AND TOOLS. These activities consist in the diffusion of the translation methods and the concrete results obtained with them in the different workshops, namely in terms of new knowledges, designations, concepts, principles and methods of collective action, etc. For example, the concepts of democracy, direct action, social emancipation, socialism, non-violence, sagacity, *Satyagraha*, human rights, *swaraj*, multiculturalism, strike action, sovereignty, revolution, *umma*, *dharma*, and so on and so forth. Every one of these items is less global than globalization from below. Some are current within a given regional or thematic ambit, but totally unknown within others. Some are valorized positively by given movements or NGOs, but rejected by others. Different items are adequate in different ways for different scales of action (local, national, global).

Based on the analysis of the final reports of the workshops, the translation coordination unit will propose criteria to assess the limits and potentialities of each item for inter-thematic, transnational and intercultural usage. Such proposals will be organized according to two large sets: the lexicons and the manifestos.

The *lexicons* concern items that are mainly discursive: designations, concepts, knowledges, classifications, etc.

The *manifestos* concern items that are predominantly performative: principles and methodologies of action, instances of successful links among practices, etc.

The proposals will be refined through the PUSM Network as well as through the set of networks that make up alternative globalization, namely those participating in the World Social Forum.

Organization

PUSM comprises two operative units: PUSM Headquarters and PUSM Network.

PUSM HEADQUARTERS. This unit will operate in a country of intermediate development (say, Brazil, India, South Africa, Mexico). It includes the coordinating committee, the translation coordination unit and the executive committee. The first workshops will take place at the headquarters. PUSM Network will be managed here as well.

The *coordinating committee* is constituted of representatives of all the movements and NGOs that are part of PUSM Network. Its job is to coordinate the activities of PUSM and select the translation coordination unit and the executive committee.

The functions of the *translation coordination* unit are:

1. selecting workshops and their participants;
2. supervising activities, both pedagogical and those relating to research for change;
3. generating materials for diffusion as translation capabilities and tools;
4. granting scholarships to activists/leaders and social scientists/ scholars/artists who are not self-funded.

The *executive committee* handles the administration of PUSM Headquarters, prepares and manages the budget, and takes care of fundraising.

PUSM Headquarters will establish a relationship of privileged collaboration (as regards training and rendering of services) with the cooperatives, organizations and movements of the city or region of its location.

PUSM NETWORK. PUSM Network is composed of the set of organizations and movements that adhere to PUSM's Charter of Principles, and engage significantly in any one of the three major kinds of activities that constitute PUSM. The charter will be drafted by the NGOs/social movements that take responsibility for the foundation of the PUSM.

The PUSM, 2003–06

The proposal was enthusiastically welcomed, which shows that the PUSM meets an objective need. Some social movements expressed a concern to keep the PUSM under the direct control of the social movements, to ensure that the university will really be a school *of*, and not *for*, the social movements. Behind this concern was the more or less explicit fear that the PUSM might end up being controlled by the NGOs, always suspected of having more financial resources and being politically less radical. The strongest resistance came from organizations already involved with similar educational initiatives, such as cadre schools, summer courses for activists, citizenship schools. The discussions had made it clear that the novelty of the PUSM resided in its inter-thematic character (most of the initiatives already in existence are organized by thematic movements) and its global scope (existing initiatives have a national or regional scope).[6] Far from aiming to compete with these other initiatives, the PUSM was intended to complement the efforts already made, focusing mainly on promoting the dialogue at the global level among different political cultures and traditions of activism. At the 2005 WSF, a group of about sixty organizations and movements committed themselves to bringing about the creation of the PUSM, and a technical secretariat was constituted to coordinate the actions to be taken to that effect.[7] One of the organizations in favour of the proposal, Euralat, offered to set up an international meeting in Rome to discuss the proposal in greater detail and plan the first steps leading to the creation of the PUSM. The meeting, bringing together twenty-six organizations, took place in Rome in September 2005.[8]

The Rome meeting was decisive in stimulating the actual process of creation of the PUSM. Its objectives, methodology and structure were identified more rigorously, and the first steps leading on to its effective creation were agreed upon.

Objectives

1. The theoretical and analytical deficit in the majority of the social movements is quite obvious, as is the crisis in the social sciences; hence the need for rigorous processes of production of new knowledges, resulting from constructive dialogue between social movements and democratic intellectuals/social scientists, and from the systematization of the rich experience of the said movements.

2. It is imperative to ameliorate the political action of the social movements. Their understanding of contemporary phenomena can be improved, as can their capacity to propose and contribute to the construction of a more just world and society. In view of the crisis in political practice in the world today, the question of how to strengthen the social and political impact of the social movements must be constantly addressed.

3. The priority of the PUSM is not the training of movement leaders, which is already the task of several institutions in various continents. To be sure, systematizing experience and building new knowledges will necessarily contribute to forming social leadership as well. It is highly probable that setting up this initiative will end up having a positive impact on the current training programmes for social cadres and leaders.

4. Much elaboration and synthesis is being carried out in many parts

of the world, of which the social movements elsewhere are unaware. The purpose of the PUSM is to contribute to rendering this work visible.

5. The PUSM aims at promoting strategic alliances not only among the social movements themselves, but also between the social movements and democratic intellectuals/social scientists who are also eager to contribute to social transformation. A good number of the intellectuals and social scientists who participate in or are very close to the WSF are also social and political activists, or would like to be. The PUSM is an excellent space for such people.

6. With regard to relations with the intellectuals/social scientists, the question of the PUSM's stance vis-à-vis the existing universities, whether conventional or alternative, and particularly vis-à-vis the public universities, also needs to be addressed.

7. The PUSM must guard against ethnocentrism, careful not to presume uniformity where there are significant historical and cultural differences among the social movements and regions. Since identities are not immutable essences but rather relations, it is to be expected that they will change gradually, along with changes in knowledge, mutual recognition and joint action.

Methodology

1. The work of translation between knowledges and practices is the main method of accomplishing the objectives of the PUSM.

2. The formation of translators, both inside the movements and in the academic world, occurs through confrontational dialogues to encourage an action–reflection–action process. The ultimate objective is not to reach total mutual intelligibility or transparency. It is rather to foster the level of inter-knowledge and trust capable of generating joint actions.

3. The struggle in a hegemonic system implies disputing meanings and concepts often deeply embedded in common sense, such as the naturalization of the economy and the political and military system. The actions and programmes of the different social movements do not confront each other in an empty space. They occur in a field of relations of hegemony, in which other collective actors (political, social or intellectual) have projects and strategies that are dissonant from or even antagonistic to those of the social movements. It befits the PUSM to recognize and analyse this situation, bearing in mind both the necessary confrontation and the possible alliances.

4. The work of translation is no mere analytical and rational work. It

also fosters the emotions and affections that permit progress from a relation of trust to the decision to share collective actions, which may eventually turn out to be risky.

Organization

1. A balance between in-person and electronic interaction (PUSM Headquarters and PUSM Network) must be attempted.

2. The same goes for the three kinds of activities that characterize the PUSM: pedagogical activities; research activities for social transformation; activities for the diffusion of translation capabilities and tools. The PUSM will organize its activities autonomously. As a network, it will integrate in its activities all the activities carried out by the organizations and movements that subscribe to the Charter of Principles. Such activities may embrace schools, universities, summer courses, training sessions, research projects, etc.

3. If possible, the work of translation should be introduced on an experimental basis in ongoing or planned dialogues among movements. The aim is to obtain information to help design the activities that the PUSM organizes autonomously, namely its first pilot workshops.

4. The PUSM comprises an assembly, a technical secretariat and a methodological working group. The assembly is constituted by all the movements/organizations that subscribed to the Charter of Principles. The task of the assembly is: to choose the thematic and inter-thematic dialogues, bearing in mind, whenever possible, concrete requests of the WSF, namely of its International Council; to define the criteria of participation in the workshops organized autonomously by the PUSM; to designate the technical secretariat.

   The technical secretariat is made up of representatives of at least five geographically and culturally distinct organizations. Their task is to organize the activities of the PUSM and manage its resources. Their term is two years with a limit of two terms.

   The methodological working group is made up of people with pedagogical and knowledge-building experience in or with the social movements. Its role is to develop the translation method: to propose themes, pedagogies and methodologies; to prepare evaluations of the thematic and inter-thematic workshops to be discussed at the assembly.

Plan of activities 2006

1. To implement the translation method in the 'South–South Dialogue'

currently taking place between movements/organizations that constitute SADC (Southern African Development Community) and the southern cone of Latin America (Mercosur).[9]

2. To prepare the first pilot workshop of the PUSM.

3. To prepare the Charter of Principles.

4. To systematize the ongoing experiences of collective and transformative self-learning, namely the experiences of Andean leaders' training, and the experiences of popular education in the ambit of the struggles against the FTAA and the bilateral free trade treatises in Latin America.

5. To identify movements/organizations interested in joining the PUSM.

6. To accept as an activity of the PUSM the proposal 'Histories of Possible Worlds: international competition on experiences of struggle and social change', presented by the Università Popolare di Roma.[10]

7. To add representatives of movements/organizations from Africa and Asia to the technical secretariat appointed at the WSF 2005 (whose term lasts until the first meeting of the assembly of the PUSM).

8. To create the PUSM website.

The PUSM is under way. In the short term, the most important substantive task is to proceed with the work of intercultural and transpolitical translation in the ambit of the South–South Dialogue, with two meetings scheduled for 2006. The evaluation of the results will provide valuable indications as how to advance with the PUSM project.

Notes

1 The proposal was published for the first time in *Terraviva* (IBASE), 14 January 2003, pp. 78–83.

2 It was discussed in Madrid, on 25 April 2003, at the headquarters of ACSUR-Las Segovias, with Pedro Santana, Tomas Villasante, Juan Carlos Monedero and several other activists of Spanish and Latin American NGOs; in Amsterdam, on 18 May, at the meeting of fellows of the Transnational Institute; in Cartagena de Indias, on 16–20 June, during the Thematic World Social Forum on Democracy, Human Rights, Wars, and Narcotraffic, in a workshop coordinated by Pedro Santana, Giampero Rasimelli, Moema Miranda and myself; in Rio de Janeiro, on 2 September, at the IBASE headquarters, with Cândido Grzybowski, Moema Miranda, several other members of IBASE and Jorge Romano of Actionaid; in Mumbai at the 2004 WSF and in Porto Alegre at the 2005 WSF; in Rome, on 13–15 September 2005, in an international meeting convened by Euralat, UPTER/Universitá Popolare di Roma and Associazione ONGs Italiane; and in Caracas at the 2006 polycentric WSF.

3 There is no consensus on the name to be given to the proposed institution. Some consider the term 'university' elitist. Others think that the term

'popular university' entails identification with initiatives of communist parties and other left organizations of the first decades of the twentieth century. School? Academy? Open University of the Social Movements? Global University of Social Movements? Global Network of Knowledges? School for Global Citizenship? The organizations that decided at the 2005 WSF to take upon themselves the task of actually creating the popular university adopted the original name, adding as a kind of subtitle 'Global Network of Knowledges'.

4 For example, the Theatre of the Oppressed, the methodology proposed by Augusto Boal and used today in seventy countries.

5 One such methodology could be that developed by the Institute of Liberation Philosophy (Brazil) after Paulo Freire's pedagogy.

6 One initiative, among the most recent ones, must be highlighted: the creation of the Florestan Fernandes School for the formation of MST cadres in Brazil. In 2004, a proposal was made to create the Urban Popular University. The initiative came from the International Alliance of Inhabitants (IAI), one of the founding organizations of the PUSM. The objectives of the Urban Popular University are: (1) to respond to the need for research on and reflection about a global strategy of justice concerning the social construction of habitat and addressing housing issues; and (2) to encourage, facilitate and strengthen the organizational development of the various members of IAI (information obtained at: <www.habitants.org/article/articleview/1100/1/208/>, accessed 22 January 2006).

7 The secretariat was composed of five organizations: CES – Centre for Social Studies, Coimbra University; Euralat – Eurolatinamerican Observatory on Democratic and Social Development; IBASE – Brazilian Institute for Economic and Social Analysis; ICAE – International Council for Adult Education; IPF – Institute Paulo Freire.

8 The following organizations participated in the Rome meeting: Alianza Internacional de los Habitantes; CAFOLIS (Ecuador); Central Argentina de Trabajadores; Centro de Estudios y Publicaciones Alforja – Centroamerica; Centre for Judicial and Legal Training (Mozambique); CIMAS – Grupo de Trabajo de la Universidad Complutense de Madrid (Spain); Consejo de Educación de Adultos de América Latina (CEAAL); International Council of the World Education Forum; Corporación Región (Medellin, Colombia); Corporación Viva la Ciudadanía (Colombia); Centre for Social Studies (Coimbra University, Portugal); EURALAT – Eurolatinamerican Observatory on Democratic and Social Development; Federación Colombiana de Educadores (FECODE); FIPEC – Federazione Italiana per l'Educazione Continua; IBASE; International Council for Adult Education (ICAE); Instituto de Gobierno y Políticas Públicas de la Universidad Autónoma de Barcelona (Spain); Instituto Paulo Freire (Brazil); Laboratorio de Politica Publica do Rio de Janeiro e Buenos Aires; RAAB; Rede Mova (Brazil); UNISANGIL (Colombia); Universidad General Sarmiento, Instituto de Estudios Económicos (Argentina); Universidad Pedagógica Nacional de Colombia; UPTER – Università Popolare di Roma.

9 This initiative may be accessed at <www.ibase.org.br>.

10 This may be accessed at <www.upter.it>.

9 | The left after the World Social Forum

The majority of movements and organizations that have energized the WSF consider themselves to be on the left, even though, as I said at the beginning, they disagree to a large extent on what it means to be on the left these days. As I have indicated throughout this book, these disagreements are reflected in the debates carried out at the Forum, whether concerning organizational issues or issues of political theory and action. In this chapter, I engage in an inverse kind of enquiry: into the Forum's impact on left thinking and practice. Given the short period of the Forum's maturation, this enquiry cannot but be somewhat speculative. It is, none the less, possible to identify some of the problems of the left highlighted by the WSF, as well as some of the solutions made possible or more credible in the light of its experience. By its very nature, the WSF does not have an official line on its own impact on the left's future, and I suspect that many of the movements and organizations involved in it are not concerned about it. What I present next is a personal reflection drawn from my own experience of the WSF.

The phantasmal relation between theory and practice

The WSF has shown that the gap between left practices and classical theories of the left is broader today than ever. Of course, the WSF is not alone in this – as witness the political experiences in the region where the WSF emerged, Latin America. From the EZLN in Chiapas to Lula's election in Brazil, from the Argentinean *piqueteros* to the MST, from the indigenous movement in Bolivia and Ecuador to Uruguay's Frente Amplia, and to the successive victories of Hugo Chavez as well as, more recently, the election of Evo Morales, from the continental struggle against ALCA[1] to the alternative project of regional integration led by Hugo Chavez, we are faced with political practices that are in general recognized as leftist, but which were not foreseen by the major leftist theoretical traditions, or which even contradict them. As an international event and meeting point of so many resistance practices and projects of alternative society, the WSF has given a new dimension to this mutual blindness – of the practice vis-à-vis the theory and of the theory vis-à-vis the practice – and created the conditions for an ampler and deeper reflection on this problem. This is what I propose to engage in here.

The blindness of the theory results in the invisibility of the practice, hence its sub-theorization, whereas the blindness of the practice results in the irrelevance of the theory. The blindness of the theory can be seen in the way the conventional left parties and the intellectuals at their service have stubbornly not paid any attention to the WSF, or have minimized its meaning. The blindness of the practice, in turn, is glaringly present in the contempt shown by the great majority of the activists of the WSF for the rich leftist theoretical tradition, and their militant disregard for its renewal. This mutual misencounter yields, on the practice side, an extreme oscillation between revolutionary spontaneity and innocuous, self-censured possibilism, and, on the theory side, an equally extreme oscillation between *post-factum* reconstructive zeal and arrogant indifference to what is not included in such a reconstruction.

In such conditions, the relation between theory and practice assumes strange characteristics. On the one hand, the theory is no longer at the service of the future practices it potentially contains, and rather serves to legitimize (or not) the past practices that have emerged in spite of itself. Thus, avant-garde thought tends to tag along in the rearguard of practice. It stops being orientation to become ratification of the successes obtained by default or confirmation of pre-announced failures. On the other hand, the practice justifies itself by resorting to a theoretical *bricolage* focused on the needs of the moment, made up of heterogeneous concepts and languages which, from the point of view of the theory, are no more than opportunistic rationalizations or rhetorical exercises. From the point of view of the theory, theoretical *bricolage* never qualifies as theory. From the point of view of the practice, a posteriori theorization is mere parasitism.

This phantasmal relation between theory and practice yields three political facts, all of them made evident by the WSF, that are decisive for our understanding of the present situation of the left. The first is that the discrepancy between short-term certainties and medium- and long-term uncertainties has never been so wide. A certain insistence on tactics prevails, therefore, which can either be revolutionary or reformist, or can even go beyond such dichotomy. This insistence on tactics has been conditioned by the metamorphoses of the enemy of the left. For the last three decades, neo-liberal capitalism has been subjecting social relations to the law of the market to an extreme until recently unthinkable: it includes the commodification of culture, leisure, solidarity and even self-esteem, along with the reduction or elimination of the non-marketable interactions on the basis of which the modern social state was built (education, health, welfare). The brutal worsening of exploitation and exclusion – hence of social inequalities – brought about by the dismantling of the juridical and political mechanisms of regulation, which until very recently seemed irreversible, confers to the resistance struggles an urgency that allows for ample convergences regarding short-term goals (from the struggles against savage privatizations to the blockage of the World Trade Organization or the FTAA). What remains unclear is whether the struggle is aimed at capitalism in general on behalf of socialism or some other post-capitalist future, or, on the contrary, against *this* capitalism on behalf of a capitalism with a more human face.

This lack of clarity is not a new problem. On the contrary, it remained with the left throughout the twentieth century. But it now gains a new urgency. The impetus of neo-liberal capitalism is so overwhelming that what actually ends up conniving with it can be seen as struggling against it. By the same token, the uncertainty regarding the long term now has a new dimension: and that concerns whether there is indeed a long term at all. That is to say, the long term has become so uncertain that conflicts about it cease to be important or mobilizing. As a consequence, the short term lengthens, and the concrete political polarizations occur in the light of the short-term certainties and urgencies. If, on the one hand, discrediting the long term favours tactics, on the other it prevents the polarizations about the long term from interfering with the short-term polarizations. It permits a total opening up to the future on which consensuses are easy. If until recently dissent concerning the long term was strong, energies of convergence being concentrated on the short term, today, once the long term has been discredited, strong dissent has moved to the short term, where there are certainties. Now certainties, because they are different for different groups, are at the root of strong dissent.

The increasing uncertainty and open-endedness of the long term has a long trajectory in leftist thought. It is expressed in the transition from the certainty of the socialist future as the scientific result of the development of the productive forces, in Marx, to the dichotomy of socialism or barbarism, formulated by Rosa Luxemburg, to the various conceptions of socialism after the schism in the workers' movement at the beginning of the First World War, and, after many intermediate transitions, to the idea that 'another world is possible', which dominates the WSF.

The long term has always been the clear horizon of the left. In the past, the greater the difference in that horizon from the landscapes of present-day capitalism, the more radical the means necessary to reach it. Hence the cleavage between revolution and reform. Nowadays, this cleavage is suffering an erosion similar to that of the long term. It is still there, but it no longer has its former consistency and consequences. It has become a relatively loose signifier, prone to contradictory appropriations. There are reformist processes that seem revolutionary (Hugo Chavez in Venezuela), revolutionary processes that seem reformist (Zapatistas in Mexico) and reformist processes that don't even seem reformist (the PT government in Brazil 2002–06).

The second fact that derives from the phantasmal relation between theory and practice is the impossibility of a consensual account regarding the performance of the left. If, for some, the left has undergone an ebbing of the class struggle since the 1970s, for others this was a period teeming with innovation and creativity, in which the left renovated itself through new struggles, new forms of collective action, new political goals. According to the latter position there was certainly an ebbing, but it involved rather the classical forms of political organization and action, and it was thanks to this ebbing that new forms of political organization and action emerged. For those who sustain the idea of the general ebbing, the balance is negative and the supposed novelties result from the struggles' deviation from primary objectives (class struggle in the domain of production) to secondary objectives (identity, culture – in a word objectives in the domain of social reproduction). This was no more than a yielding to the enemy, no matter how radical the discourses of rupture. For those who support the idea of innovation and creativity, the balance is positive, because the blocking dogmatisms have been shattered, the forms of collective action and the social bases supporting them have been enlarged, and, above all, because the struggles, by their forms and range, have managed to reveal new vulnerabilities in the enemy. Among the participants in the WSF, the latter position prevails, even though the former, arguing the idea of the general ebbing, is quite visible in the participation of some organizations (mainly trade unions). Theirs is, however, a participation that verges on despair, with an unhappy awareness of the minimal dreams that history allowed to be fulfilled. In this argument about the assessment of the last thirty years, both positions resort to the fallacy of hypothetical pasts, be it to show that, if the class struggle had prevailed, the results would have been better, be it to show, on the contrary, that without the new struggles the results would have been much worse.

all still (?) class (not gender, race, sexuality?)

The third fact derived from the phantasmal relation between theory and practice concerns the new theoretical extremism. It concerns polarizations that are simultaneously much larger and much more inconsequent than those that characterized the theoretical arguments of thirty years ago. Unlike the latter, the current polarizations are not directly linked to concrete, political organizations and strategic forms. Compared with the more recent ones, the extreme positions of the past seem less removed from each other. And yet choosing among them yielded far more concrete consequences in the lives of the organizations, militants and societies than is apparent today. There are three main dimensions of present-day theoretical extremism.

As regards the *subjects of social transformation*, the polarization is between a well-defined historical subjectivity, the working class and its allies, on the one hand, and, on the other, indeterminate and unlimited subjectivities, be they all the oppressed, 'common people therefore rebels' (Sub-comandante Marcos),[2] or the *multitude* (Hardt and Negri 2000).[3] Until thirty years ago, the polarization occurred 'only' in the delimitation of the working class (the industrial avant-garde versus retrograde sectors), in the identification of the allies, whether the peasants or the petite bourgeoisie, in the move from 'class in itself' to 'class for itself', and so on and so forth.

Concerning the *goals of the social struggle*, the polarization is between the seizure of power and the total rejection of the concept of power, that is to say between the statism that has always prevailed in the left, one way or the other, and the most radical anti-statism, as in John Holloway's belief that it is possible to change the world without seizing power (Holloway 2002). Until thirty years ago, the polarization occurred around the means of seizing power (armed struggle or direct peaceful action versus institutional struggle) and the nature and goals of the exercise of power once seized (popular democracy/dictatorship of the proletariat versus participatory/representative democracy).

Concerning *organization*, the polarization is between the centralized organization in the party and the total absence of centralism and even organization, beyond that which emerges spontaneously in the course of the collective action, by the initiative of the actors themselves as a whole. Until thirty years ago, the polarization occurred between communist and socialist parties, between one single party and a multi-party system; it addressed the relation between the party and the masses or the forms of organization of the workers' party (democratic centralism versus decentralization and right of tendency).

We are facing, therefore, polarizations of a different kind, between new and more demarcated positions. It doesn't mean that the previous ones have disappeared; they have just lost their exclusivity and centrality. The new polarizations do have consequences for the left; but they are certainly more diffuse than those of previous polarizations. The reason is twofold. On the one hand, the aforementioned phantasmal relation between theory and practice contributes to rendering the latter relatively immune to theoretical polarizations or to encouraging it to use them selectively and instrumentally. On the other, actors in extreme positions do not dispute the same social bases, do not mobilize for the same objectives of struggle, do not militate in the same organizations, nor even in rival organizations. The contours of the left, therefore, look rather like the parallel lives of the left. Such disjunctions, however, have an important consequence: they make the acceptance of plurality and diversity difficult, and their conversion into motors of new forms of struggle, of new coalitions and associations impossible. This is an important consequence, particularly if we bear in mind that the extreme positions in the new polarizations go beyond the universe of the culture of the left as we know it. We face very distinct cultural, symbolic and linguistic universes and, without a translation procedure among them, it will not be possible to reach a mutual intelligibility. If, on one side, the talk is about class struggle, power relations, society, modern rationality, the state, reform, revolution, on the other the talk is about love, dignity, solidarity, community, rebellion, spirituality, emotions and sentiments, transformation of subjectivity, 'a world to encompass all the worlds'. There is, therefore, a cultural, as well as an epistemological fracture.[4] These fractures have a sociological basis in the emergence of collective actors from subordinate, indigenous, feminist, Asian, African and African-American cultures, which were ignored, if not antagonized, by the classical left throughout the twentieth century.

Considering this last aspect of the phantasmal relation between theory and practice (theoretical extremism), the following question is quite legitimate: how was the WSF possible? To my mind, this virulent, if inconsequent, theoretical extremism gradually lost contact with the practical aspirations and options of the activists engaged in concrete political action. Between concrete political action and theoretical extremism, a vacuum, a *terra nullius*, was formed, wherein gathered a diffuse will to join forces against the avalanche of neo-liberalism and to admit that this would be possible without having to sort out all the pending political debates. The urgency of the action turned against the purity of the theory, as it were. The WSF is the result of this Zeitgeist of the left, or rather of the lefts, at the end of the twentieth century.

The twenty-first-century left: depolarized pluralities

Does the WSF mean that a synthesis of the new and old extremisms of the left is possible? Certainly not. As I said above, such a synthesis is not only not possible but also undesirable. The search for a synthesis requires the idea of a totality that brings diversity back to unity. Now, the WSF shows eloquently that no totality can contain the inexhaustible diversity of the theories and practices of the world left today. Rather than a synthesis, the WSF suggests a call for *depolarized pluralities*. The aim is to reverse a tradition with deep roots in the left, based on the idea that to politicize differences is to polarize them. On the contrary, the WSF allows for politicization to occur by means of depolarization. It consists of giving priority to constructing coalitions and associations for concrete collective *practices* and discussing the theoretical differences exclusively in the ambit of such construction. The goal is to turn the acknowledgement of differences into a factor of cohesion and inclusion, by robbing differences of the possibility of thwarting collective actions, thus creating a context of political strife in which acknowledgement of differences goes hand in hand with the celebration and use of similarities. In other words, the point is to create contexts for debate, in which the drive for union and similarity may have the same intensity as the drive for separation and difference. Collective actions ruled by depolarized pluralities stir up a new conception of 'unity in action', to the extent that unity stops being the expression of a monolithic will to become the more or less vast and lasting meeting point of a plurality of wills.

The conception of depolarized pluralities counters all the automatisms of political strife inside the left. Hence it will not be easy to apply. Two important facts recommend its application, however. The first is the current predominance, mentioned above, of the short term over the long term, with the result that the long term has never conditioned the short term so little as it does today. In the past, when the long term was the great factor of political polarization inside the left, the short term – whenever it was conceived with some autonomy vis-à-vis the long term – played a depolarizing role (the old distinction between tactics and strategy). In view of this, the tacticism that results from the current predominance of the short term may facilitate an agreement to give priority to the concrete collective actions, in order to discuss plurality and diversity, but only in the context of the said collective actions. In the short term, every revolutionary action is potentially reformist, and every reformist action may eventually escape reformist control. Concentration on short-term certainties and urgencies, therefore, does not only imply neglecting the long term; it implies as well that the long term be conceived of as being open enough to include diffuse consensuses and complicities. That the long term remains indefinite may well encourage depolarization.

The other factor favourable to the construction of depolarized pluralities is the recognition, obvious today after the Zapatista uprising and after the WSF, that the left is multicultural. What this means is that the differences that divide the left escape the political terms that formulated them in the past. Underlying them are the cultural differences that an emergent global left cannot but acknowledge, since it would make no sense to fight for the recognition and respect of cultural differences 'outside', in society, and not to recognize or respect them 'at home', within the organizations and movements. A context is thereby created to act under the assumption that differences cannot be erased by means of political resolutions. Better to live with them and turn them into a factor of collective strength and enrichment.

The next step will be to analyse in some detail the fields and procedures behind the construction of depolarized pluralities. The goal is to highlight new paradigms of transformative and progressive action guided by the operative principle of depolarized pluralities. The construction of depolarized pluralities is carried out by collective subjects involved, or willing to become involved, in collective actions. The priority conferred on participation in collective actions, by means of association or coalition, allows for the suspension of the question of the subject in the abstract. In this sense, if only concrete actions are in progress, only concrete subjects are in progress as well. The presence of concrete subjects does not annul the issue of the abstract subject, be it the working class, the party, the people, humanity or common people, but it prevents this issue from interfering decisively in the conception or unfolding of the collective action. Indeed, the latter can never be the result of abstract subjects. Giving priority to participation in concrete collective actions means the following:

1. Theoretical disputes must take place in the context of concrete collective actions.
2. Each participant (movement, organization, campaign, etc.) stops claiming that the only important or correct collective actions are those exclusively conceived or organized by it. In a context in which the mechanisms of exploitation, exclusion and oppression multiply and intensify, it is particularly important not to squander any social experience of resistance on the part of the exploited, excluded or oppressed, and their allies.

167

3. Whenever a given collective subject has to put in question its participation in a collective action, withdrawal must proceed in such a way as to weaken as little as possible the position of the subjects still involved in the action.

4. Since resistance never takes place in the abstract, transformative collective actions begin by occurring on the ground and in terms of the conflicts established by the oppressors. The success of the collective actions is measured by the ability of collective action to change the ground and terms of the conflict during the struggle. Success, in turn, assesses the correctness of the theoretical positions assumed. The pragmatic conception of theoretical correctness creates willingness towards the depolarization of the pluralities while the action is taking place.

There are three major dimensions of the construction of depolarized pluralities within transformative collective actions: depolarization through intensification of mutual communication and intelligibility; depolarization through searching for inclusive organizational forms; depolarization through concentration on productive issues. To the first two I refer here only briefly, since the previous chapters have already suggested how depolarization may be undertaken. I will analyse in more detail depolarization achieved through concentration on productive issues.

Depolarization through intensification of mutual intelligibility This form of depolarization is that in which the contribution of the WSF is most consistent. The WSF has been a meeting point of movements and organizations from all over the world. In many cases, the relations therein established last way beyond the events, and are reflected in ever more consistent linkages in global transformative action. The progress made in the past few years is particularly remarkable in some areas: the struggle against external debt and predatory free trade; transcontinental feminist agendas; peasant movements, namely through the Via Campesina; and indigenous movements, mainly in the Americas. As I said above, the diversity of the associations, of the sociological, political and cultural profile of the movements and organizations, as well as of the traditions of resistance, renders impossible, and if possible undesirable, a general theory capable of giving global coherence to the wealth of meetings and initiatives. Inspired by the experience of the WSF, I proposed in Chapter 7 that the search for a general theory be replaced by the consequent elaboration of processes of translation aimed at deepening mutual intelligibility without putting in question the autonomy of current movements and organizations. The translation procedure, while safeguarding and even deepening diversity, contributes to turning it into a factor of inter-group proximity and enrichment of collective action.

Depolarization by searching for inclusive organizational forms In this domain, the role of the WSF has been to show that the will to collective action made manifest in dozens of forums for the past few years can be concretized only through new forms of political organization and association. The forms traditionally available to the left – national generalist parties and sectoral local movements – are insufficient in themselves, but are above all deficient vis-à-vis the exclusive and exclusionary policies they generated. As I have mentioned before, in many countries the collaboration between parties and social movements has been blocked by two opposed and symmetrical fundamentalisms, each with deep roots: the anti-movement fundamentalism on the part of the parties and the anti-party fundamentalism on the part of the social movements. Furthermore, all these organizational forms were designed in terms of their specific objectives and contexts, whether national or local, or general or thematic. It is not easy on the basis of these, and particularly on the basis of the political culture of which they are the product, to create new exigencies and new activisms, inter-thematic (among feminists, workers, peasants, ecologists, indigenous people, gays and lesbians, pacifists, activists for human rights, etc., etc.) and multi-scalar associations (local, national, regional and global).

The very organization of the WSF and of the different forums to which it has given rise is in itself a remarkable innovation, and their limits and difficulties, which I have pointed out in the previous chapters, have more to do with its success than its failure. What is at stake is the design and the actual carrying out of collective actions made possible and urgent by the action of the WSF, for which new organizational forms are necessary: forms that maximize internal democracy, guarantee efficacy at the level of the different scales of intervention, respect diversity and sustainability, and allow for the accumulation of anti-capitalist energy and collective memory. Such organizational forms must be different according to the goals in question: from mere exchange of information and experience to planning and carrying out global collective actions, involving different movements and organizations in different continents, operating in very distinct political and cultural contexts from quite unequal milieux. How to combine autonomy with working together? How

vs Socialism

to guarantee equality and respect for difference when the resources available to the different participants are so different? How to link particular agendas, contextualized locally and legitimized by well-defined social bases, with new transnational or translocal initiatives, formulated in different languages, whose connection with the particular agendas is neither obvious nor transparent to all members of the organization? How to assume and measure the risks of innovation, organization and action in such often difficult contexts, holding such precarious internal equilibriums? How to decide whether what is gained by the new activism makes up for the losses of the old one? What is the impact of the change of scale or thematic objective on the transparency and accountability of the organization vis-à-vis its members and target audience?

The major achievement of the WSF so far has been to put this issue on the agenda of the social forces interested in the emancipatory transformation of the societies and the world, and interested as well in the concretization of collective actions conceived within the WSF but to be carried out beyond it. I strongly believe that the relationships among parties, social movements and NGOs must change radically to prevent the expectations created by the WSF process from being frustrated.[5]

Depolarization by concentration on productive issues I consider productive issues those whose discussion has direct consequences for the conception and unfolding of collective action and for the conditions under which it takes place. All the others are unproductive issues. Without being necessarily neglected, they must be left to a level of indecision or state of suspension allowing for different responses. Many of the issues that incensed the left in the past and led to the best-known polarizations do not pass this test today, and must therefore be considered unproductive. The experience of the WSF, namely as regards the political cleavages inside the Forum analysed in Chapter 6, permits one to identify some productive and some unproductive issues. Among the latter, I highlight the following.

Unproductive issues

THE ISSUE OF SOCIALISM. That is to say, the kind of society model that will succeed socialism. This issue suffered a tremendous impact with the fall of the Berlin Wall. If it could be considered productive before, to the extent that the socialist future was on the political agenda, at least in some countries, and could, therefore, have practical consequences at the level of collective action, the same is not true today, with the exception of Cuba. As an unproductive issue, it must be left in a state of indecision, whose most eloquent formulation is the idea that 'another world is possible'. This formulation permits one to separate the current radical critique and the struggle for a post- or anti-capitalist horizon – one and the other constitutive of the collective actions – from the commitment to a specific model of future society.

REFORMISM OR REVOLUTION. This issue stirs up various productive issues that will be mentioned below, but in itself it is unproductive, since the conditions under which the option between reform and revolution turned into a decisive political battlefield are no longer in place. As I argue in Chapter 6, the issue was one of a principled option between legal and illegal means of seizing power, hence between a gradual and peaceful and an abrupt and potentially violent seizure. In either case, the seizure of power aimed as constructing the social- ist society, and was in fact its precondition. Actually, neither strategy succeeded, and as a result the opposition between them became com- plicity. Whenever power was actually seized, it was either to govern capitalism or to build societies that only with the utmost complacency could be deemed socialist. Another form of complicity between the two principles is that historically they have always existed in reciprocal complementarity. On the one hand, revolution has always been the founding act of a new cycle of reformism, since the first revolutionary acts – as witness the Bolsheviks – were to stop new revolutions, legis- lating reformism as the only future option after them. On the other hand, reformism had credibility only while the revolutionary alterna- tive existed. This is why the fall of the Berlin Wall brought about both the end of revolution and the end of reformism, at least in the forms available to us throughout the twentieth century. Moreover, in view of this, and in view of the changes implemented by capitalism in the last thirty years, the two terms of the dichotomy suffered such a drastic sem- antic evolution that they have become scarcely trustworthy as guiding principles of social struggle. Lately, reformism has been the object of a brutal attack on the part of the political forces at the service of global capitalism. This attack started out by being illegal (as when Salvador Allende was toppled in Chile in 1973). With the neo-liberal turn in the 1980s, it began resorting to the 'legal' means of structural adjustment, external debt, privatization, deregulation, and liberalization of trade. Reformism is, therefore, reduced today to a miniature caricature of what it used to be, as illustrated by the cases of Tony Blair's England, Thabo Mbeki's South Africa and Lula's Brazil. In its turn, revolution, which started out by symbolizing a maximalist seizure of power, ended

171

Nine

up evolving semantically towards conceptions of rejection of seizure of power, if not indeed of radical rejection of the idea of power, as illustrated by John Holloway's highly polemical interpretation of the Zapatistas (2002). Throughout the twentieth century, between the two extremes of seizure of power and total erasure of power, there were many intermediate views concerned with the idea of a change of power, such as, very early on, the Austro-Marxists' non-Leninist conceptions of revolution.[6]

For all these reasons, it does not seem productive to debate between reform and revolution. By virtue of its past, the discussion is polarizing. By virtue of its present and near future, it is inconsequent. In the absence of other terms, I propose to leave this issue in abeyance, which in this case means to recognize that social struggles are never essentially reformist or revolutionary. They may eventually assume either one or the other characteristic in view of their consequences (some of them intentional, some not), in tandem with other social struggles and according to the resistance of the forces that oppose them. In other words, abeyance entails here changing reform and revolution from guiding principles of future actions into evaluating principles of past actions. As I suggest in Chapter 6, the WSF points to the advantages of this state of suspension.

THE STATE: PRIVILEGED OR IRRELEVANT OBJECTIVE. Linked with the previous issue, there is another that I also consider unproductive. It consists in arguing whether the state is relevant or irrelevant to a leftist politics and, consequently, whether the state should be the object of social struggles, or not. The option is between social struggles aiming at the power of the state in its many forms and levels, and social struggles aiming exclusively at the powers that circulate in civil society and which determine the inequalities, exclusions and oppressions. Whether the state should be defended or attacked is not the question; rather it is to decide whether the social struggles should have goals other than to defend or attack the state. This issue can also unfold into a few productive issues, as I will show below, but in itself it is an unproductive issue. Related to it is the issue, broached above, of whether power must be seized or extinguished, as well as the issue, approached in Chapter 6, of whether the state is an ally or an enemy of the emancipatory social movements (one of the cleavages of the WSF).

That the issue of the relevance or irrelevance of the state is unproductive has to do with the fact that the modern capitalist state exists only in relation with civil society. The two of them, far from being external

172

to each other, are the two faces of the *grundnorm*, that is to say of the fundamental political relation in capitalist societies. From another perspective, the three pillars of modern social regulation are the state, the market and the community (Santos 1995: 1–5; 2002b: 1–4), and it is not possible to conceive of either one outside their relations with one another. Finally, since the state is a social, hence historical, relation, its relevancy or irrelevancy cannot be established regardless of the result of the social struggles that in the past had it as their object. To neutralize its potential for polarization I suggest the following level of indecision or state of suspension: the social struggles may have the power of the state or the powers that constitute civil society as their privileged objective, but, in either case, the powers not privileged are always present, affect the results of the struggles and are affected by the struggles.

Productive issues Likewise, in light of the experience of the WSF, I will next give some examples of productive issues, that is to say issues which, once discussed, may yield the depolarization of the pluralities that today constitute the thought and action of the left.

THE STATE AS AN ALLY OR AS AN ENEMY. Unlike the unproductive issue of the state's relevance or irrelevance, this issue is productive precisely because it does not take the state's relevance in the abstract. It confers to it a specific political meaning. The transformations undergone by the state throughout the entire twentieth century, both in core countries and in countries liberated from colonialism, and the contradictory role it played in the processes of social transformation, give historical and practical consistency to this issue. The experiences of social struggle, of parties and social movements in the different countries, are in this respect widely diversified and very rich, and cannot be reduced to a general principle or recipe.

The WSF, convening movements and associations with the most diverse experiences of relations with the state, is today an eloquent manifestation of this wealth of social struggles. The possibility of constructing in this domain a depolarized plurality resides precisely in the fact that, as I say in Chapter 6, the majority of movements and associations refuse to take a rigid, principled stance in their relations with the state. The experiences of struggle show that the state, being often the enemy, can also be, particularly in peripheral and semi-peripheral countries, a precious ally – for instance, in the struggle against transnational impositions. If in some situations confrontation with the state is justified, in others collaboration is advisable. In others still it is

173

appropriate to combine the two – witness the strategy of the MST in Brazil, a strategy that can be described as autonomous and confrontational cooperation. The choice of a given kind of interrelation with the state depends on a multiplicity of factors: history and dimension of the movement or organization; kind of political regime; structure of opportunities for direct or institutional action; national or local traditions of social struggle; level of complexity of the claims gauged by the kind and number of dimensions involved (social, political, cultural, ethnic, religious); kind and orientation of public opinion; international context. The most important factor is perhaps the structure of the opportunities: political opportunities (the larger or smaller fractures in the social and political basis of the state's action; the greater or lesser permeability to social contestation and political opposition; the level of social and political exclusion of the social groups engaged in the struggle); institutional opportunities (greater or lesser penetration and functionality of public administration, more or less availability, independence and efficacy of the judicial system, legalism or discretionary power in the way the repressive police and military forces take action); and ideological opportunities (receptivity of public opinion, relation between politics and ethics or religion, criteria to define the limits of tolerance and of what is negotiable).

The conception of the state as a contradictory social relation creates the possibility of contextualized discussions on what position to take vis-à-vis the state on the part of a certain political party, organization or movement, in a given social field, in a concrete country and historical moment. It also permits evaluation of comparatively different positions assumed by different parties, organizations or movements in different areas of intervention or in different countries or historical moments. Hence the possibility of the recognition of the existence of different strategies, all of them contextual and not free of risk, and, above all, none of them susceptible to becoming a general principle. This is what depolarized plurality consists of.

LOCAL, NATIONAL AND GLOBAL STRUGGLES. The issue of the relative priority of local, national or global collective actions is today amply debated, and in this case, too, the diversity of leftist practices is enormous. As I say in Chapter 6, this issue is present in the political options of the majority of the organizations and movements that participate in the WSF. To be sure, the theoretical tradition of the left was moulded on the national scale. The local struggles were traditionally considered minor, or else the germ of national struggles, to the detriment of the internationalist goals. The vicissitudes of internationalism, in turn, were evidence of the priority of national struggles and interests. The national scale presided over the formation of leftist parties and unions, and continues to structure their activism to this day.

In the second half of the twentieth century, particularly after the 1970s, as a result of the emergence of the new social movements, the local scale of social struggles assumed an unprecedented relevance. The organizational tradition of the left prevented the emancipatory potential of the association between local and national struggles to be explored to the utmost. The building processes of the African National Congress, in South Africa, and of the PT in Brazil were perhaps the most successful. From the 1990s on, particularly with the Zapatista uprising, the rallies in Seattle in 1999 and the WSF in 2001, the possibility of coalitions of local, national and global struggles gained unprecedented credibility. On the other hand, the field of concrete experiences of struggles on different scales broadens considerably, thus making possible contextualized debates on the different scales of collective action, their relative advantages, organizational demands and possibilities of association. Such a debate is ongoing these days in the WSF, and is one of the most productive, mainly regarding the specific instruments of association among different scales of action.

As has been made clear in the preceding chapters, the WSF gathers together social movements and organizations with different views of the relative priority of the different scales of action. While the WSF itself is a collective action on the global scale, many of the movements and organizations that participate in it have had experiences only of local and national struggles until recently. Even though they all view the WSF as the chance to enlarge their scales of action, they ascribe, as we have seen, very different priorities to the different scales of action. If, for some, the global scale of struggle will become more and more important as the struggle against globalization intensifies, for others the WSF is only a meeting point or a cultural event, no doubt useful, but in no way changing the basic principle that the 'real struggles', those really important for the welfare of populations, continue to be fought at the local and national level. There are still other movements and organizations that systematically link in their practices the local, national and global scales (the MST, for example, and, outside the WSF, the Zapatistas). As I said, however, for the vast majority of the movements, even if each concrete political practice is organized according to a given scale, all the others must be involved as a condition of success. The productive issues in this domain concern the way in which this involvement must take place.

The wealth of experiences of social struggle in this regard is thus huge, and allows for contextualized, hence productive, debates. The possibility that depolarized pluralities may emerge in this domain derives from the fact that, in light of recent experience, it makes increasingly less sense to give absolute or abstract priority to any of the scales of action. The space is thus opened to valorize the coexistence of social struggles on different scales and the variable geometry of links among them. The decision that determines the scale to be privileged is a political decision that must be taken according to concrete political conditions.

INSTITUTIONAL ACTION, DIRECT ACTION, CIVIL DISOBEDIENCE. Unlike the issue of choice between reform and revolution, the issue concerning the option between institutional action and direct action or resorting to civil disobedience is a productive issue in that it can be discussed in practical contexts of collective action. The question concerns what is to be privileged in the concrete conditions in which a given collective struggle or action is carried out: the use of legal means, – i.e. political or juridical work inside the institutions and dialogue with those in power – or, in contrast, illegality and confrontation with the state institutions. In the case of direct action, a distinction must be made between violent and non-violent action, and, in the case of violent action, between violence against human and non-human (property) targets.[7] In the case of institutional action, a distinction must be made between institutional action in the ambit of the power of the state (whether national or local) and institutional action in the ambit of parallel powers, namely by creating parallel institutionalities that avoid direct confrontation with the state or take place in regions not penetrated by the state. Parallel institutionality is a hybrid type of collective action in which elements of direct action and elements of institutional action are combined. The institutions of autonomous local power created by the Zapatists in Chiapas (*caracoles, juntas de buen gobierno*) and the forms of government in the *assentamentos* of the MST are forms of parallel institutionality.[8] Both courses of action (direct and institutional) have costs and benefits that can only be assessed in concrete contexts, demanding, of course, different kinds of organization and mobilization. What in general may be said of any other kind of collective action is not enough to make decisions upon contextualized discussions about them. The context is not limited to the immediate conditions of action, it also involves surrounding conditions – indeed, the same factors that condition relations with the state, mentioned above. The institutional

176

disobedience (handwritten)

action tends to take better advantage of the power contradictions and the fissures among the elites, but it is liable to the cooptation and emasculation of its conquests. It has difficulty as well in maintaining high levels of mobilization, because of the disjunction between the pace of the collectivization of claims and protests, on the one hand, and the judicial or legislative pace, on the other. Direct action tends to be better at exploring the inefficiencies of the power system and the fragilities of its social legitimizion, but has difficulty formulating credible alternatives and is liable to repression. If excessive, repression may actually compromise mobilization and even organization. While institutional action tends to call for association with the political parties, whenever they exist, direct action tends to be hostile to such associations.

Civil disobedience (whether individual or collective) is a form of non-violent direct action with a long history (Thoreau, Tolstoy, Gandhi, Einstein, Bertrand Russell, Martin Luther King, etc.). It is being widely discussed again in the wake of the WSF.[9] One of the movements with some presence in Europe is the *tute bianche*, which after 2001 came to be designated as the Movement of the Disobedient (*Disubbedienti*). The 'new' civil disobedience combines various traditions of direct action: anarchism, grassroots Christianity, communitarianism, the Paris Commune and utopian socialism. But it also exemplifies some new features, such as its performativity, recourse to the media, and manipulation of symbols. Civil disobedience has stirred up a lively debate, deriving mainly from two factors, which I consider very productive. On the one hand, the transition from revolution to rebellion, mentioned in Chapter 3, meant the substitution of the idea of partial ruptures, exactly those derived from actions of civil disobedience, for the idea of total rupture with the existing society.[10] On the other, the movements and organizations that participate in the WSF act in countries with different political regimes and cultures, differences that decisively condition the debates on the legitimacy, opportunity and efficacy of civil disobedience. For example, one of the debates concerns whether in liberal democratic societies, where legal resistance is allowed, collective civil disobedience is legitimate. Such a debate has led to another concerning the quality and limits of democracy. On the one hand, there are political regimes that are formally democratic but have so many limitations to the expression and organization of the opposition that, in practice, the democratic conflict and lawful resistance are banned. Such are the low-intensity democracies to which I allude in Chapter 3. On the other, even in more credible democracies, under the excuse of the fight against terrorism some legislation has been promulgated restricting the fundamental

The left after the WSF

liberties to such an extent that some scholars speak of the emergence of a new state of exception.[11] In this framework, the possibilities of legal resistance become more and more limited, which in turn leads to a reassessment of the role and legitimacy of illegal resistance.

The possibility of depolarization in terms of the option for either the legality or the illegality of the actions of resistance, when the world, in all its political and cultural diversity (including different conceptions of legality and violence), is taken as the unit of analysis, is once again grounded in the wealth of the leftist struggles of the past thirty years. This wealth is today condensed most eloquently in the WSF. The Charter of Principles contains, however, an important limitation: it excludes movements and organizations that advocate armed struggle as a form of political action. Violent direct action against people is, therefore, excluded. As I say in Chapters 4 and 5, the WSF brings together movements and organizations with very distinct experiences in this regard. If many privilege institutional actions, as many privilege direct actions. But what is most significant, in terms of depolarizing potential, is the experience of many movements and organizations which, in different struggles or different moments of the same struggle, resort to both kinds of action. Again, a good example is the MST: direct action against property (land occupation) and institutional action (legalization of the *assentamentos* and financial participation of the state in their government). Even though it is not physically present in the WSF, the EZLN opened up a horizon of convergent possibilies in this regard and exerts nowadays a strong influence, even if not too well known, in the movements, especially in Latin America. In the struggles of the EZLN there are clearly moments of violent direct action (the uprising of 1994), non-violent direct action (the march from Chiapas to Mexico City in 2001), institutional action (the Santo Andrés Accords, lobbying in the Mexican congress), and parallel institutional action (*caracoles, juntas de buen gobierno*). Once conditions for systematic evaluation are created, this vast experience will yield every condition to give credibility to the formation of depolarized pluralities.

STRUGGLES FOR EQUALITY AND STRUGGLES FOR RESPECT OF DIFFERENCE. The issue concerning the relative priority of the struggles for equality and struggles for respect of difference has been part of leftist struggles since the end of the nineteenth and the beginning of the twentieth centuries. It started with the first wave of feminism and gained a new impetus in the 1950s and 1960s with the civil rights movement of African-Americans in the USA. But it could be said that up to the 1970s and 1980s it was a marginal issue in leftist debates. Since then, however, it has acquired some centrality, mainly because of the impact of the new feminist, indigenous and LGBT movements, as well as the movements of Afro-descendants in the Americas and Europe. Organized on the basis of discriminated identities, these movements came to contest the conception of equality that presided over the social struggles of the previous periods, a conception focused on class (workers and peasants), based on the economy and hostile to the recognition of politically significant differences among the working classes. Identity movements, without contesting the importance of class inequalities, argue for the political importance of inequalities based on race, ethnicity, sex and sexual orientation. According to them, the principle of equality tends to homogenize differences and thus to conceal the hierarchies established in their midst. Such hierarchies are translated into discriminations that irreversibly affect the opportunities for personal and social fulfilment of the discriminated. On the basis of the principle of equality alone, they achieve no more than a subordinate, decharacterizing social inclusion. To avoid this, alongside equality the acknowledgement of difference must be considered a principle of social emancipation as well.

Linking the principles of equality and recognition of difference is no easy task. But also in this regard the diversity of the social struggles for the past thirty years makes possible the formation of depolarized pluralities. There are, to be sure, extreme positions that reject the validity of one of the principles or, recognizing the validity of both, give total priority in the abstract to one or the other. The majority of the movements, however, try to find concrete forms of linkage between the two principles, even if giving priority to one of them. This is quite apparent in the labour movement, certainly founded on the principle of equality, but increasingly sensitive to the recognition of the importance of ethnic and sexual discriminations and favourable to associations with identity movements in concrete struggles. It is likewise apparent in the identity movements, particularly in the feminist movement, in view of the increasing acknowledgement and politicization of class difference inside the movement.

In this domain, as well, the conditions are created for the formation of depolarized pluralities. Once again, the WSF offers a wide space where opportunities may be generated to construct associations and coalitions among movements with different conceptions of social emancipation. Inter-knowledge is a necessary condition of mutual recognition. Progress in this regard is allowing for the discussion concerning the two principles of emancipation not to occur in the abstract and between radical positions; rather it should occur between concrete options in the configuration of concrete struggles capable of engaging the movements without forcing on them fundamental changes in their basic cultural, philosophical or political conceptions.

Notes

1 In English, Free Trade Area of the Americas – FTAA.

2 '*Somos mujeres y hombres, ninos y ancianos bastante comunes, es decir, rebeldes, inconformes, incómodos, soñadores*' (Sub-comandante Marcos, La Jornada, 4 August 1999).

3 'We are all communists,' proclaimed Michael Hardt in his intervention in the 2005 WSF.

4 Referring to the Zapatistas, Ana Esther Ceceña speaks precisely of a 'new libertarian epistemology' (2004: 11). Similarly, in Chapter 2, I speak of the emergence of 'an epistemology of the South'.

5 Wainright (2003: 196–200) calls our attention to recent experiences of mutually enriching relations between parties and movements and to the emergence of new hybrid movement/party organizations. On this issue and, in general, on the challenges facing the left as we enter the twenty-first century, see Harnecker (2006: 289ff); Rodriguez-Garavito et al. (2004).

6 See Adler (1922); and Bauer (1924). In general, on the contributions of the Austro-Marxists, see Bottomore and Goode (1978).

7 The topic of violence was absent from leftist debates in the developed capitalist world during the second half of the twentieth century. It returned in the first decade of the twenty-first as a result of the brutal attacks on the Twin Towers in New York City on 11 September 2001, and the reactions thereby emerging. The concept, kinds, degrees, legitimacy, efficacy and opportunity of violence are now discussed. When there is mention of the violence of the movements' direct action, what is usually meant is a restrictive concept of violence: physical violence. Whereas the violence against which the movements fight may be physical, symbolic, structural, psychological, etc. Recourse to violence in a given direct action may derive from the original plan of action or emerge as a response to the state's violent repression by means of police or military forces.

8 In revolutionary or pre-revolutionary contexts, the forms of parallel or dual power assume specific characteristics. This was the case in Russia between February and October 1917, when the provisional government and the Soviets existed side by side (Lenin 1978: 17ff; Trotsky 1950: 251ff). The cases of Germany (Broué 1971: 161ff), Spain (Broué and Témime 1961: 103ff), Latin America (Mercado 1974), and Portugal (Santos 1990: 29ff) have also been analysed. The current most salient case is Venezuela, where the government of Hugo Chavez, faced with the inertia or blockage of public administration, created the *misiones* to make basic public services (subsidized education, health and food) available to the working classes.

9 A good summary of the debate can be found in Buey (2005: 211–64).

10 This does not mean that the movements that resort to civil disobedience accept the global legitimacy of the established order. It just means
that resistance against the established order is not conceived of as global,
illegal resistance.

11 On this subject, see Agamben (2004).

Conclusion

The translation of utopia into politics is not, in the case of the WSF, merely the translation of the long-range into the medium- and short-range. It is also the translation of the new into the old. This means that divergences about concrete political options are often mixed up with divergences about the codes and languages of political options.

It should be stressed, however, that the novelty of the utopia has managed so far to overcome the emergence of severe political divergences. In light of the argument developed in this book it is adequate to distinguish between high-intensity cleavages and low-intensity cleavages. The former are the cleavages in which radical discursive differences translate themselves into some form of factionalism, be it collective splits and abandonment of the political organization or organized tendencies within the organization; the latter, by contrast, are those in which the discursive differences, no matter how radical, do not preclude continued participation in the organization. So far, the divergences or cleavages within the WSF have been of the low-intensity kind. Contrary to what happened in the thinking and practice of the left in Western capitalist modernity throughout the twentieth century, the WSF managed to create a style and an atmosphere of inclusion of and respect for divergences that made it very difficult for the different political factions to exclude themselves from the start with the excuse that they were being excluded. The WSF's 'minimalist' programme, stated in its Charter of Principles, contributed decisively to this effect: emphatic assertion of respect for diversity; access denied only to movements or groups that advocate political violence; no voting or deliberations at the Forum as such; no representative entity to speak for the Forum. It is almost like a tabula rasa where all forms of struggle against neo-liberalism and for a more just society may have their place. Confronted with such openness, those who choose to exclude themselves find it difficult to define what exactly they are excluding themselves from.

All this has contributed to making the WSF's power of attraction greater than its capacity to repel. For all these reasons, the desire to highlight what the movements and organizations have in common has prevailed over the desire to underscore what separates them. The manifestation of tensions or cleavages has been relatively tenuous and, above all, has not resulted in mutual exclusions. It remains to be seen for how long this will to convergence and this chaotic sharing of differences will last.

This does not mean that there are no strong disagreements. There are, and they have become louder and louder in recent years. This raises several issues. Is it possible to link up the different peoples of the WSF as an embryonic form of a counter-hegemonic civil society? How to transform the areas of widely shared consensuses into calls for collective action? How better to explore the implications of both the agreements and the disagreements? Should disagreements be the object of specific discussions in the WSF? How to conceive of the relationship between participants and organizers (the IC and the IS)? How to link such diversity with the common core upon which the WSF builds its identity and eventually develops its capacity to act?

These questions lurk behind most formulations of most cleavages manifested within the WSF. In Chapter 6 I identified the following main strategic cleavages: reform or revolution; socialism or social emancipation; the state as enemy or as ally (potentially, at least); priority to be given to national or to global struggles; direct action or institutional action or relations between them; priority to be given to the principle of equality or to the principle of respect for difference; the WSF as a space or as a movement. With the exception of the last, these cleavages belong to the historical legacy of the social forces that for the past two centuries have struggled against the status quo for a better society. The specificity of the WSF resides in the fact that the different cleavages are important in different ways for the different movements and organizations, and none of them is present in the practices or discourses of all the movements and organizations. When cleavages are acknowledged, the different movements and organizations distribute themselves among them in a non-linear way. Movements that oppose one another in a given cleavage may well be on the same side in another cleavage. Thus, the different strategic alliances or common actions featured by each movement tend to have different partners. But, on the whole, all the movements and organizations have room for action and discourse in which to agree with all the other movements or organizations, whatever the cleavages among them. In this way, the accumulation and strengthening of divergences that could result from the alignment of the movements in multiple cleavages are precluded. The cleavages end up neutralizing or disempowering one another. At the same time as they tend towards factionalism, they liberate the potential for consensus. Herein has lain, in the last instance, the WSF's cohesive power.

The Forum's future is doubly open, since the institutional changes and even its very survival may result either from its success or from its failure. This question is further complicated if a prior question is asked about what counts as success or failure. If we take some of the features most commonly attributed to the WSF – its organizational and programmatic novelty, global reach and style of consensus-building – we can reasonably argue that the WSF is a success. And yet, either because of this or in spite of this, the question of the WSF's future has become recurrent. In my view, there are two main reasons for this recurrence. The first is the WSF's novelty itself. Because the left's political thinking and practice have been historically moulded by three traditional forms of organization (leftist parties, labour unions and the Internationals), the WSF has been carrying a permanent burden of proof as to its sustainability. The permanent questioning of its future has generated an impulse for innovation which I don't see in any other organization of its size. Indeed, as I have stressed throughout this book, the WSF has been reinventing itself from the very beginning and shows no sign of exhaustion. The organizers may be exhausted, not the WSF, a fact that may recommend the renovation of the organizing movements and organizations. The second reason behind the recurrent questioning of the WSF's future is the fact that the factors that account for its success have solved as many problems as they have created. The new problems account for the ambivalence in the evaluation of the past and for the uncertainty as to the future. They can be formulated in terms of strong questions.

The question of efficaciousness. As I showed above, this is one of the most divisive questions, since efficaciousness can be measured in terms of different criteria and there is no consensus about which to adopt. The evaluation of the efficaciousness of the WSF is one of the exercises that best discloses the confrontation between new and old conceptions of social transformation. From the point of view of the old ones, the WSF cannot but be assessed negatively. Evaluated in terms of the new conceptions of social transformation it advocates, the WSF cannot but be positively assessed. The emergence of a global consciousness among movements and NGOs, regardless of the scope of their action, has been crucial in creating a certain symmetry of scale between hegemonic globalization and the movements and NGOs that fight against it. The dozens of forums held since 2001 bear witness to how precious this consciousness is, and to how much remains to be done in order to preserve and strengthen it. This explains, ultimately, why the factors of attraction and cohesion prevail over those of repulsion and divisiveness. The question remains, however, as to how this global consciousness and the potential it has generated can be best put to the task of bringing about progressive social transformation on a global scale. On the other hand, in light of the trans-scale nature of the struggles encompassed by the WSF, it is inadequate to assess its efficaciousness exclusively in terms of global changes. It has to be assessed as well in terms of local and national changes. Given all the levels involved, the evaluation of the WSF's efficaciousness is undoubtedly complex, but for that very reason it does not allow for rash assessments.

The questions of representation and organization. The novelty of the WSF is consensually attributed to its absence of leaders and hierarchical organization, its emphasis on cyberspace networks, its ideal of participatory democracy, and its flexibility and readiness to engage in experimentation. But, of course, the reality is much more complex and, as I have discussed in the previous chapters at length, the questions of representation and participation are likely to remain wide open in the foreseeable future. Even if the limits of the world dimension of the WSF are pushed back as much as possible, the issue of representation will always be there until the selection criteria are more transparent and democratic and the conditions for participation more equally distributed. It will definitely help to adopt a broad conception of the WSF, turning it into a permanent process and promoting continuity among its many initiatives, so as to transform the WSF into 'an incremental process of collective learning and growth', as stated in the resolutions adopted at IC meetings during the 2003 WSF.

The WSF's utopia is one of emancipatory democracy. Since the WSF claims to be a large collective process for deepening democracy, it is no wonder that the issue of internal democracy has become more and more pressing. In the coming years, the WSF's credibility in its struggle for democracy in society will depend more and more on the credibility of its internal democracy.

The question of how to combine the celebration of diversity with the construction of strong consensuses leading to collective action. The celebration of diversity is one of the most cherished characteristics of the WSF. I identified above some of the outstanding cleavages that divide the social movements and organizations and showed how, in spite of them, the cohesive power of the WSF has so far remained

Conclusion

185

intact. For how long? The problems for the future in this regard can be formulated in terms of the following questions:

a) Through the celebration of diversity and its cohesive power the WSF has managed to liberate a tremendous energy: is it now making the best use of such energy? Is it possible that the process that has liberated so much energy may also be the one that neutralizes or stifles it for failing to keep pace with the changes produced by the energy itself?

b) Since aggregation of movements and organizations is not a value in itself, what is its political objective? Can we build strong consensuses on the basis of the celebration of diversity? And if so, what to do with such consensuses?

c) Having been at its inception a highly political phenomenon, is the WSF renovating and strengthening its political potential or is it rather being transformed into a politically diluted umbrella organization for more or less depoliticized forms of collective action?

These problems reveal in my view the current vitality of the WSF, and there is no reason to believe that it will not respond successfully to the challenges confronting it. It seems clear, however, that, in order to do so, the WSF has to undergo a demanding process of self-learning guided by the following normative orientations: all possible measures must be taken to make the WSF as global as its name indicates; its organization must be guided by the very same idea of participatory democracy that the WSF has been advocating for society at large; internal 'schools' of global self-knowledge and self-training must be created, aimed at increasing reciprocal knowledge among the movements and organizations; strong sectoral consensuses must be promoted, capable of sustaining global struggles and durable collective actions.

The implementation of these orientations may give rise to new institutions and practices that will take us beyond the WSF. Though the WSF does not seem to believe in dialectics, the movements and organizations gathered around it do not exclude the possibility that the very accomplishments of the WSF will lead us beyond the organization as part and parcel of the ever unfinished historical tasks of the left.

At any rate, as I mentioned in the previous chapter, the WSF has already contributed significantly to the renovation of leftist thinking and practice. I highlight two instances, one concerning scale, the other concerning political philosophy. The internationalist left at the end of the nineteenth and beginning of the twentieth centuries, far from being a global left, was a European and North Atlantic one. From the

1950s on, it broadened its range, along with the anti-colonial liberation movements and the movement of the non-aligned countries. The profound differences between the European societies and the societies of the emerging 'Third World', however, did not allow for a consistent dialogue between leftists in both regions, not least because a large part of the European left had been colonialist, and never assumed a post-colonial stance, not even after the independence of the colonies. Furthermore, the beginning of the cold war deepened the divergences both within the European left and the left of the Global South. For all these reasons, the emergence of a global left was precluded. The WSF may be considered the first manifestation, however embryonic, of such a left. Its global nature does not derive, at least for now, from positions or actions of global range, but from serious reflection about its own possibilities, from inter-knowledge that is exponentially superior to what existed before, and from the construction of local and national political agendas, maintaining relevance of its global impacts and the experiences and teachings of the agendas of other leftists in other parts of the world. Second, the WSF's contribution to the emergence of one or several global lefts has to do with political philosophy. It concerns the new political culture whose major features I traced in Chapter 9. A new relationship within the various lefts is in question, between the theories and emotions of separation, on the one hand, and the theories and emotions of union, on the other. This new relationship is based on the general idea of politicization by means of depolarization. The principal elements of such an idea are: concentration on productive issues, i.e. the issues that maximize the capacities for resistance against and the formulation of alternatives to the exclusions, inequalities and discriminations created or worsened by global capitalism; recognition of the very diverse and intercultural character of leftist thinking and practice when the world is taken as the unit of analysis and action; a pragmatic conception of the aggregation of wills that makes possible regional linkages (as is notably the case in Latin America), and even global linkages, without loss of autonomy and identity on the part of the movements, parties or organizations therein engaged; consensus on the need to construct new political organizations devoted to global action, and to reinvent the relations between parties, unions, social movements and progressive organizations, bearing in mind that no one holds the monopoly of organized representation of interests.

All these contributions will bear fruit in the anti-capitalist and anti-imperialist struggles, both in the Global South and the Global North, no matter what the future of the WSF may be.

187

Annexe I: Composition of the International Council of the WSF (2005)

Members

International Secretariat of the World Social Forum, <www.forumsocialmundial.org.br>, e-mail: <fsminfo@forumsocialmundial.org.br>

Brazilian Organizing Committee, e-mail: <fsmcoordesc@forumsocial mundial.org.br>

Indian Organizing Committee, <www.wsfindia.org>, e-mail: <wsfindia@vsnl.net>

50 Years Is Enough!, <www.50years.org>, e-mail: <50years@50years.org>

ABONG – Associação Brasileira de ONGs (Brazilian Association of NGOs), <www.abong.org.br>, e-mail: <abong@uol.com.br>

ACTU – Australian Council of Trade Unions, <www.actu.asn.au/>, e-mail: <mailbox@actu.asn.au>

AEC – Assemblée Européenne des Citoyens (European Citizens' Assembly), <www.cedetim.org/AEC/>, e-mail: <cedetim@globenet.org>; <aec@globenet.org>

AFL-CIO – American Federation of Labour-Congress of Industrial Organizations, <www.aflcio.org>, e-mail: <feedback@aflcio.org>; <Tbeaty@aflcio.org>

Africa Trade Network, <twnafrica.org/networks/ATN/atn-index.asp>, e-mail: <contact@twnafrica.org>; <dkeet@iafrica.com>; <aidc@iafrica.com>

AIDC – Alternative Information on Development Center, <www.aidc.org.za/>, e-mail: <info@aidc.org.za>

ALAI – Agencia Latinoamericana de Información (Latin American Information Agency), <www.alainet.org>, e-mail: <info@alai.ecuanex.net.ec>; <info@alainet.org>

ALAMPYME – Associação Latino-Americana de Pequenos e Médios Empresários (Latin American Association of Small and Median Entrepreneurs), www.apyme.com.ar>, e-mail: <apyme@rcc.com.ar>

All Arab Peasants and Agricultural Cooperatives Union, e-mail: <F76arab@maktoob.com>

Alliance for a Responsible, Plural and United World, <www.alliance21.org>, e-mail: <paris@fph.fr>; <gustavo@alliance21.org>

ALOP – Associação Latino-Americana de Organismos de Promoção (Latin American Association for the Promotion of Regional Cooperation), <www.alop.or.cr/index.htm>, e-mail: <info@alop.or.cr>; <eballon@desco.org.pe>

Alternative Information Center, <www.alternativenews.org/>, e-mail: <aic@alt-info.org>; <sergio@alt-info.org>

Alternatives (Action and Communication Network for International Development), <www.alternatives.ca>, e-mail: <alternativesqc@alternatives.ca>; <marcela@alternatives.ca>

Alternatives Russia, <www.alternativy.ru/> e-mail: <dhrr@online.ru>; <alternativy@tochka.ru>

APC – Association for Progressive Communications, <www.apc.org>, e-mail: <webeditor@apc.org>; <anriette@apc.org>

APC – Asamblea de los Pueblos del Caribe (Assembly of the Caribbean People), <www.movimientos.org/apcaribe>, e-mail: <habitatcarib@hotmail.com>; <pedroarg@tricom.net>

APM – Agricultures paysannes, sociétés et mondialisation (Peasants' agriculture, societies and globalization), <www.zooide.com/apm>, e-mail: <pvuarin@fph.fr>

APRODEV (Association of World Council of Churches Related to Development Organizations in Europe), www.aprodev.net>, e-mail: <admin@aprodev.net>; <aprodev@aprodev.net>

Arab NGO Network for Development, <www.annd.org>, e-mail: <annd@cyberia.net>; <lbannd@cyberia.net.lb>; <zmajed@assafir.com>; <zmajed@hotmail.com>

ARENA – Asian Regional Exchange for New Alternatives, <www.arenaonline.org>, e-mail: <arena@asianexchange.org>

Articulación Feminista MarcoSur (Feminist Articulation MarcoSur), <www.mujeresdelsur.org.uy>, e-mail: <mujeresdelsur@mujersur.org.uy>; <cotidiann@cotidianmujer.org.uy>

ASC – Aliança Social Continental (Continental Social Alliance), <www.asc-hsa.org>; <www.web.ca/comfront>, e-mail: <comfront@web.ca>; <asc@laneta.apc.org>; <cilas@laneta.apc.org>

Assembly of the United Nations of the People (Tavola della Pace), <www.perlapace.it/tavola.htm>, e-mail: <flavio@perlapace.it>; <info@tavoladellapace.it>

ATTAC – Brazil (Association for the Taxation of Financial Transactions for the Aid of Citizens – Brazil), <www.attac.org/brasil>, e-mail: <attacsaopaulo@attac.org>; <cida@that.com.br>; <antoniomartins@yahoo.com>; <tiburcio@uol.com.br>; <jcleite@dglnet.com.br>

ATTAC – France (Association for the Taxation of Financial Transactions for the Aid of Citizens – France), <www.attac.org>, e-mail: <attac@attac.org>; <bernard cassen@monde_diplomatique.fr>; <aguiton@ras.eu.org>; <attacint@attac.org>

Babels, <www.babels.org>, e-mail: <wsfsm@babels.org>; <info@babels.org>

Bankwatch Network, <www.bankwatch.org>, e-mail: <jozseff@bankwatch.org>

CADTM – Comité pour l'Annulation de la Dette du Tiers Monde (Committee for the Cancellation of the Third World Debt), <www. cadtm.org>, e-mail: <cadtm@skynet.be>; <info@cadtm.org>

Caritas Internationalis, <www.caritas.org>, e-mail: <caritas. internationalis@caritas.va>

CBJP – Comissão Brasileira de Justiça e Paz (Brazilian Justice and Peace Commission), <www.cbjp.org.br>, e-mail: <intercom@cidadanet.org. br>; <cbjp@cbjp.org.br>; <cbjpcnbb@gns.com.br>

CCSCS – Coordenadora de Centrais Sindicais do Cone Sul (Coordination of Trade Unionist Federations of the Southern Cone), <www. sindicatomercosul.com.br/>, e-mail: <eduardo@aebu.org.uy>

CEAAL – Consejo de Educación de Adultos de América Latina (Latin American Council of Adult Education), <www.ceaal.org>, e-mail: <ceaal@laneta.apc.org>; <czarco@laneta.apc.org>

CEDAR Internacional (Forum for the Implementation of Economic, Social and Cultural Rights – Centre for Dignity and Rights), <www. cedarinternational.net/>, e-mail: <cedar@asser.nl>; <goldewijk. cedar@asser.nl>

CEDETIM – Centre d'Études et d'Initiatives de Solidarité Internationale (Research and Initiative Centre for International Solidarity), <www. cedetim.org/>, e-mail: <cedetim@globenet.org>; <cedetim@reseau-ipam.org>

Central de Trabajadores Argentinos (Argentinean Trade Union), <www. cta.org.ar>, e-mail: <cta@roc.com.ar>; <alaris@sinectis.com.ar>

CETRI (Tricontinental Centre) , <www.cetri.be>, e-mail: <cetri@cetri.be>; <houtart@espo.ucl.ac.be>

CIDSE – Coopération Internationale pour le Développement et la Solidarité (International Cooperation for Development and Solidarity), <www.cidse.org>, e-mail: <postmaster@cidse.org>

CIOSL – Confederação Internacional de Organizações Sindicais Livres (International Confederation of Free Trade Unions), <www.cioslorit. org>, e-mail: <info@cioslorit.org>; <sedeorit@cioslorit.org>; <internetpo@icftu.org>

CIVES –Associação Brasileira de Empresários pela Cidadania (Brazilian Association of Entrepreneurs for Citizenship), <www.cives.com.br> e-mail: <cives@cives.com.br>

CLACSO – Consejo Latinoamericano de Ciencias Sociales (Latin American Council of Social Sciences), <www.clacso.org>, e-mail: <clacsofsm@clacso.edu.ar>

CLC – Canadian Labour Congress, <www.clc-ctc.ca>, e-mail: <sbenedict@clc-ctc.ca>

CMT – Confederação Mundial do Trabalho (World Confederation of Labour), <www.cmt-wcl.org>, e-mail: <info@cmt-wcl.org>

Coligação para a Justiça Económica (Colligation for Economic Justice), e-mail: <viriato@zebra.uem.mz>

COMPA – Convergencia de los Movimientos de los Pueblos de las Américas (Convergence of the People's Movements of the Americas), <www.sitiocompa.org>, e-mail: <colectivoredom_@hotmail.com>; <rgf@alum.vassar.edu>

CONAIE – Confederación de Nacionalidades Indígenas del Ecuador (Confederation of Indigenous Nationalities of Ecuador), <www.conaie. org>, e-mail: <info@conaie.org>

Congresso Nacional Indígena do México (Indigenous National Congress of Mexico), e-mail: <ceatl@laneta.apc.org>

Conselho Mundial de Igrejas/World Council of Churches, <www.wcc-coe. org>, e-mail: <info@wcc-coe.org>

Coordination du Forum 'L'Autre Davos', <www.otherdavos.net/index. html>, e-mail: <Page2@fastnet.ch>

Corpwatch, <www.corpwatch.org>, e-mail: <corpwatch@corpwatch.org>

COSATU – Congress of South African Trade Unions, <www.cosatu.org.za>, e-mail: <cosatu@wn.apc.org>; <florinah@cosatu.org.za>

Council of Canadians, <www.canadians.org>, e-mail: <Jdunn@canadians. org>

CRID – Centre de Recherche et d'Information pour le Développement (Research and Information Centre for Development), <www.crid.asso. fr>, e-mail: <info@crid.asso.fr>

CUT – Central Única dos Trabalhadores (Central Trade Union Federation), <www.cut.org.br>, e-mail: <sri-cut@uol.com.br>

DAWN – Development Alternatives with Women for a New Era, <www. dawn.org.fj>, e-mail: <dawn@is.com.fj>

Encuentros Hemisféricos contra el ALCA (Hemisphere Meetings against the FTAA), <www.alcaabajo.cu/>, e-mail: <joel@mlking.sld.cu>

ENDA – TM Environnement et Développement du Tiers-Monde (Environment and Development Action in the Third World), <www. enda.sn>, e-mail: <taoufik@enda.sn>

ETUC – European Trade Union Confederation, <www.etuc.org/>, e-mail: <etuc@etuc.org>; <jmoreno@ccoo.es>

EURALAT – Observatorio Eurolatinoamericano sobre el Desarrollo Democrático y Social (Eurolatinamerican Observatory on Democratic and Social Development), <www.euralat.org>, e-mail: <criera@aepdc. org>

Euromarchés (European Marches), <www.euromarches.org>, e-mail: <euromarches@ras.eu.org>

FAMES (Forum des Femmes Africaines pour un Monde de l'Economie), e-mail: <rabia@enda.sn>

FCOC – Frente Continental de Organizações Comunitárias (Continental Front of Community Organizations), <www.movimientos.org/fcoc>; <www.siscom.or.cr/aso/fcoc/fcoc.htm>, e-mail: <mlongoria@laneta. apc.org>

FDIF – Fédération Démocratique Internationale des Femmes (World

Democratic Federation of Women), <www.fdif.eu.org>, e-mail: <fdif@fdif.eu.org>

Federación Mundial de Juventudes Democráticas (World Federation of Democratic Youth), <www.wfdy.org>, e-mail: <wfdy@wfdy.org>

FIAN – Food First International Action Network, <www.fian.org>, e-mail: <fian@fian.org>

FIDH – Fédération International de Droits Humaines (Internationale Federation of Human Rights), <www.fidh.org>, e-mail: <rsanchez@fidh.org>

Focus on the Global South, <www.focusweb.org>, e-mail: <admin@focusweb.org>

Forum Dakar, e-mail: <Residel.kaolack@sentoo.sn>

Forum Mondial des Alternatives (World Forum of Alternatives), <www.alternatives-action.org/fma>, e-mail: <ftm@syfed.refer.sn>

Forum of the Poor, <www.thai.to/aop>, e-mail: <fopthai@asiaaccess.net.th>

Fórum Social Italiano (Italian Social Forum), e-mail: <vagnoleto@lila.it>

Friends of the Earth International, <www.foei.org>, e-mail: <foe@foe.org>; <manus@foenl.antenna.nl>

GLBT South–South Dialogue, e-mail: <phumim@ecuanex.net.ec>

Global Exchange, <www.globalexchange.org>, e-mail: <admin@globalexchange.org>

Global Policy Network, <www.globalpolicynetwork.org>, e-mail: <gpn-listowner@epinet.org>

Greenpeace, <www.greenpeace.org>, e-mail: <greenpeace.brazil@dialb.greenpeace.org>

Grito dos Excluídos (Cry of the Excluded), <www.movimientos.org>, e-mail: <gritoexcluidos@uol.com.br>

Grupo de Trabalho Amazónico (Amazonian Working Group), <www.gta.org.br/>

Habitat International Coalition, <www.hic-net.org>, e-mail: <hic-al@hic-al.org>

IATP – Institute for Agriculture and Trade Policy, <www.iatp.org>, e-mail: <khoff@iatp.org>

IBASE – Instituto Brasileiro de Análises Sociais e Económicas (Brazilian Institute for Economic and Social Studies), <www.ibase.br>, e-mail: <ibase@ibase.br>

ICAE – International Council for Adult Education, <www.icao.org.uy/spa/sindex.html>, e-mail: <icae@icae.ca>

IFAT – International Federation of Alternative Trade, <www.ifat.org>, e-mail: <ifat@ifat.org.uk>

IFG – International Forum on Globalization, <www.ifg.org>, e-mail: <ifg@ifg.org>

IFTDH – The International Federation Terre des Hommes, <www.terredeshommes.org>, e-mail: <info@terredeshommes.org>

INSP – International Network of Street Papers, <www.street-papers.com>, e-mail: <l.maclean@bigissuescotland.com>

International Gender and Trade Network, <www.genderandtrade.net>, e-mail: <secretariat@coc.org>

IPB – International Peace Bureau, <www.ipb.org>, e-mail: <mailbox@ipb.org>

IPF – Instituto Paulo Freire (Institute Paulo Freire), <www.paulofreire.org>, e-mail: <ipf@paulofreire.org>

IPS – Inter Press Service, <www.ips.org>, e-mail: <kosi@ips.org>; Africa – <mail@ipsafrica.org>; Asia-Pacific – <ipsasia@loxinfo.co.th>; Caribbean – <ipskin@cwjamaica.com>; Europe – Middle East – <eurodesk@ips.org>; Latin America – <latam@ipsenespanol.org>; USA and Canada – <latam@ipsenespanol.org>

IUS – International Union of Students, <www.ius-uie.org>, e-mail: <ius@cfs-fcee.ca>

Jubilee South – Africa, <www.jubileesouth.org>, e-mail: <aidc@iafrica.com>

Jubilee South – Asia, <www.jubileesouth.org>, e-mail: <vinod.raina@vsnl.com>

Jubilee 2000, <www.jubilee2000uk.org/jubilee2000/links.html>; <www.aidc.org.za/j2000/index.html>, e-mail: <kitazawa@jca.apc.org>

Jubileu Sul América Latina (Jubilee South – Latin America), <www.jubileusul.hpg.com.br>, e-mail: <keeneba@wamani.apc.org>

KCTU – Korean Confederation of Trade Unions, <www.kctu.org>, e-mail: <inter@kctu.org>

KOPA (Korean People's Action against the FTA and the WTO), <wwwantiwto.jinbo.net/eroom/index.html>, e-mail: <kopa@jinbo.net>

Land Research Action Network, e-mail: <wellington@nlc.co.za>

MST – Movimento dos Trabalhadores Rurais Sem Terra (Landless Rural Workers Movement), <www.mst.org.br>, e-mail: <srimst@uol.com.br>

Narmada, <www.narmada.org>, e-mail: <subbu@narmada.org>

National Network of Autonomous Women's Groups, e-mail: <shahnandita@redifmail.com>

NIGD – Network Institute for Global Democratization, <www.nigd.org>, e-mail: <katarina@nigd.u-net.com>

North–South Centre, <www.coe.int/T/E/North-South_Centre>, e-mail: <Fifi.BENABOUD@coe.int>

OATUU – Organization of African Trade Unions Unity, e-mail: <oatuu@ighmail.com>

OCLAE – Organización Continental Latinoamericana y Caribeña de Estudiantes (Continental Organization of Latin America and Caribbean Students), <www.oclae.org>, e-mail: <oclae@jcce.org.cu>

Oneworld, <www.unimondo.org>; <www.oneworld.org>, e-mail: <jason.nardi@unimondo.org>

ORIT – Organización Regional Interamericana de Trabajadores

(Interamerican Regional Workers' Organization), <www.orit-ciosl.org>, e-mail: <info@cioslorit.org>

OXFAM Internacional, <www.oxfam.org>; <www.oxfaminternational.org>, e-mail: <information@oxfaminternational.org>

Palestinian Grassroots Anti-apartheid Wall Campaign, <www.stopthewall.org>, e-mail: <mobilize@stopthewall.org>

Peace Boat, <www.peaceboat.org>, e-mail: <y-nami@peaceboat.gr.jp

PIDHDD – Plataforma Interamericana de Derechos Humanos, Democracia y Desarrollo (Interamerican Platform of Human Rights, Democracy and Development), <www.pidhdd.org>, e-mail: <regional@pidhdd.org>

PNGO – Palestinian Non-governmental Organizations Network, <www.pngo.net>, e-mail: <bisanrd@palnet.com>

Project K, <www.projet-k.org/, e-mail: <salvatore.cannavo@flashnet.it; <ilpanelerose@hotmail.com>

Public Citizen, <www.citizen.org>, e-mail: <tgerson@citizen.org>

Rede CONSEU – Conferencia de Naciones sin Estado de Europa (Conference of Nations without State in Europe), e-mail: <activitats@ciemen.org>

Rede de Solidariedade Ásia Pacífico (Solidarity Network Asia Pacific), e-mail: <intl@dsp.org.au>

Rede Latinoamericana e Caribenha de Mulheres Negras (Network of Black Women from the Caribbean and Latin America), <www.criola.ong.org>, e-mail: <criola@alternex.com.br>

Rede Mulher e Habitat (Women and Shelter Network), <www.redmujer.org.ar>, e-mail: <gem@agora.com.ar>

Rede Social de Justiça e Direitos Humanos (Social Network for Justice and Human Rights), <www.social.org.br>, e-mail: <rede@social.org.br>

Redes Socioeconomia Solidaria (Networks for Socieconomic Solidarity), <www.reasnet.com>, e-mail: <creintjes@ideas.coop>

REMTE – Red Latinoamericana Mujeres Transformando la Economía (Latin American Network of Women Transforming the Economy), <www.movimientos.org/remte/>, e-mail: <mleon@interactive.net.ec>; <remte@fedaeps.org>

REPEM – Red de educación popular entre mujeres (Network of Popular Education Among Women), <www.repem.org.uy>, e-mail: <repem@repem.org.uy>

Réseaux Sous-régional sur la Dette et les DSRP (Sub-regional Network on Debt and DSRP), e-mail: <jubilecad-mali@cefib.com>; <barryaminatou@yahoo.fr>

SIGTUR – Southern Initiative on Globalisation and Trade Union Rights, e-mail: <rlambert@ecel.uwa.edu.au>

Social Watch, <www.socialwarch.org>, e-mail: <socwatch@chasque.net>

Solidar, <www.solidar.org>, e-mail: <solidar@skynet.be>

Solidarity Africa Network in Action, e-mail: <njoki@igc.org>

TNI – Transnational Institute, <www.tni.org>, e-mail: <tni@tni.org>

Transform Network!, e-mail: <elgauthi@internatif.org>

TWN – Third World Network, <www.twnside.org.sg>, e-mail: <twn@igc.apc.org>

UBUNTU – Foro Mundial de Redes de la Sociedad Civil (World Forum of the Networks of Civil Society), <www.ubuntu.upc.es>, e-mail: <ubuntu@ubuntu.upc.es>

Via Campesina, <www.ns.rds.org.hn/via/>, e-mail: <viacam@gbm.hn>

Women's Global Network for Reproductive Rights, <www.wngrr.org>, e-mail: <office@wngrr.nl>

World Association of Community Radio Broadcasters – AMARC, <www.amarc.org>, e-mail: <amarc@amarc.org>

World March of Women, <www.marchemondiale.org/>; <www.ffq.qc.ca/marche2000/en/index.html>, e-mail: <dmatte@ffq.qc.ca>

Znet, <www-zmag.org>, e-mail: <sysop@zmag.org>

Observers

FNTG – Funders Network on Trade and Globalization, <www.fntg.org>, e-mail: <mark@fntg.org>

Organizing Committee of the African Social Forum, e-mail: <taoufik@enda.sn>

Organizing Committee of the Americas Social Forum, <www.forosocialamericas.org>, e-mail: <fsmcontinental@fsmecuador.org>

Organizing Committee of the European Social Forum, <www.fse-esf.org>, e-mail: <wsf@fse-esf.org>

Organizing Committee of the Mediterranean Social Forum, e-mail: <activitats@ciemen.org>; <fsmedi@terra.es>

Organizing Committee of the Pan-Amazonic Social Forum, <www.fspanamazonico.com.br>, e-mail: <cri-pmb@belem.pa.gov.br>

Organizing Committee of the Thematic Social Forum: Democracy, Human Rights, War and Drug Traffic, <www.fsmt.org.co>, e-mail: <forosocialtematico@cable.net.co>

Annexe II

Comparison between the Charter of Principles, the WSF India policy statement[1] and the Charter of Principles and Values of the African Social Forum[2]

Approved charter

Approved and adopted in São Paulo, on April 9, 2001, by the organizations that make up the World Social Forum Organizing Committee, approved with modifications by the World Social Forum International Council on June 10, 2001.

1. The World Social Forum is an open meeting place for reflective thinking, democratic debate of ideas, formulation of proposals, free exchange of experiences and interlinking for effective action, by groups and movements of civil society that are opposed to neo-liberalism and to domination of the world by capital and any form of imperialism, and are committed to building a planetary society directed towards fruitful relationships among Humankind and between it and the Earth.

2. The World Social Forum at Porto Alegre was an event localized in time and place. From now on, in the certainty proclaimed at Porto Alegre that 'another world is possible', it becomes a permanent process of seeking and building alternatives, which cannot be reduced to the events supporting it.

3. The World Social Forum is a world process. All the meetings that are held as part of this process have an international dimension.

4. The alternatives proposed at the World Social Forum stand in opposition to a process of globalization commanded by the large multinational corporations and by the governments and international institutions at the service of those corporations' interests, with the complicity of national governments. They are designed to ensure that globalization in solidarity will prevail as a new stage in world history. This will respect universal human rights, and those of all citizens – men and women – of all nations and the environment and will rest on democratic international systems and institutions at the service of social justice, equality and the sovereignty of peoples.

5. The World Social Forum brings together and interlinks only organizations and movements of civil society from all the countries in the world, but intends not to be a body representing world civil society.

6. The meetings of the World Social Forum do not deliberate on behalf of the World Social Forum as a body. No one, therefore, will be authorized, on behalf of any of the editions of the Forum, to express positions claim-

ing to be those of all its participants. The participants in the Forum shall not be called on to take decisions as a body, whether by vote or acclamation, on declarations or proposals for action that would commit all, or the majority, of them and that propose to be taken as establishing positions of the Forum as a body. It thus does not constitute a locus of power to be disputed by the participants in its meetings, nor does it intend to constitute the only option for interrelation and action by the organizations and movements that participate in it.

7. Nevertheless, organizations or groups of organizations that participate in the Forum's meetings must be assured the right, during such meetings, to deliberate on declarations or actions they may decide on, whether singly or in coordination with other participants. The World Social Forum undertakes to circulate such decisions widely by the means at its disposal, without directing, hierarchizing, censuring or restricting them, but as deliberations of the organizations or groups of organizations that made the decisions.

8. The World Social Forum is a plural, diversified, non-confessional, non-governmental and non-party context that, in a decentralized fashion, interrelates organizations and movements engaged in concrete action at levels from the local to the international to build another world.

9. The World Social Forum will always be a forum open to pluralism and to the diversity of activities and ways of engaging of the organizations and movements that decide to participate in it, as well as the diversity of genders, ethnicities, cultures, generations and physical capacities, providing they abide by this Charter of Principles. Neither party representations nor military organizations shall participate in the Forum. Government leaders and members of legislatures who accept the commitments of this Charter may be invited to participate in a personal capacity.

10. The World Social Forum is opposed to all totalitarian and reductionist views of economy, development and history and to the use of violence as a means of social control by the State. It upholds respect for Human Rights, the practices of real democracy, participatory democracy, peaceful relations, in equality and solidarity, among people, ethnicities, genders and peoples, and condemns all forms of domination and all subjection of one person by another.

11. As a forum for debate, the World Social Forum is a movement of ideas that prompts reflection, and the transparent circulation of the results of that reflection, on the mechanisms and instruments of domination by capital, on means and actions to resist and overcome that domination, and on the alternatives proposed to solve the problems of exclusion and social inequality that the process of capitalist globalization with its racist, sexist and environmentally destructive dimensions is creating internationally and within countries.

12. As a framework for the exchange of experiences, the World Social

Forum encourages understanding and mutual recognition among its participant organizations and movements, and places special value on the exchange among them, particularly on all that society is building to centre economic activity and political action on meeting the needs of people and respecting nature, in the present and for future generations.

13. As a context for interrelations, the World Social Forum seeks to strengthen and create new national and international links among organizations and movements of society, that – in both public and private life - will increase the capacity for non-violent social resistance to the process of dehumanization the world is undergoing and to the violence used by the State, and reinforce the humanizing measures being taken by the action of these movements and organizations.

14. The World Social Forum is a process that encourages its participant organizations and movements to situate their actions, from the local level to the national level and seeking active participation in international contexts, as issues of planetary citizenship, and to introduce on to the global agenda the change-inducing practices that they are experimenting in building a new world in solidarity.

Indian version

The consultation of Indian organizations and individuals that took place in the city of Bhopal in India, on April 19–20 2002, and that constituted the World Social Forum-India. It was decided that WSF's Charter for India needs to be evolved with certain additions required for India. It accordingly entrusted the task to the WSF India Working Committee.

Starting with the original Preamble to the WSF Charter of Principles, as prepared by the Brazil Organizing Committee, the following constitutes the revised text as prepared by the WSF India Working Committee.

1. The World Social Forum is an open meeting place for reflective thinking, democratic debate of ideas, formulation of proposals, free exchange of experiences and interlinking for effective action, by groups and movements of civil society that are opposed to neo-liberalism and to domination of the world by capital and any form of imperialism, and are committed to building *a world order centred on the human person.*

2. The World Social Forum at Porto Alegre – *held from January 25th–30th, 2001,* was an event localized in time and place. *With the Porto Alegre Proclamation* that 'another world is possible', it becomes a permanent process of seeking and building alternatives, which cannot be reduced to the events supporting it.

3. The World Social Forum is a world process. All the meetings that are held as part of this process have an international dimension.

4. The alternatives proposed at the World Social Forum stand in op-position to a process of *capitalist* globalization commanded by the large multinational corporations and by the governments and international

institutions at the service of those corporation's interests. They are designed to ensure that globalization in solidarity will prevail as a new stage in world history. This will respect universal human rights, and those of all citizens – men and women – of all nations and the environment and will rest on democratic international systems and institutions at the service of social justice, equality and the sovereignty of peoples.

5. The World Social Forum brings together and interlinks only organizations and movements of civil society from all the countries in the world, but intends neither to be a body representing world civil society *nor to exclude from the debates it promotes those in positions of political responsibility, mandated by their peoples, who decide to enter into the commitments resulting from those debates.*

6. The meetings of the World Social Forum do not deliberate on behalf of the World Social Forum as a body. No one, therefore, will be authorized, on behalf of any of the editions of the Forum, to express positions claiming to be those of all its participants. The participants in the Forum shall not be called on to take decisions as a body, whether by vote or acclamation, on declarations or proposals for action that would commit all, or the majority, of them and that propose to be taken as establishing positions of the Forum as a body.

7. Nevertheless, organizations or groups of organizations that participate in the Forum's meetings must be assured the right, during such meetings, to deliberate on declarations or actions they may decide on, whether singly or in coordination with other participants. The World Social Forum undertakes to circulate such decisions widely by the means at its disposal, without directing, *creating hierarchies*, censuring or restricting them, but as deliberations of the organizations or groups of organizations that made the decisions.

8. The World Social Forum is a plural, diversified, non-confessional, non-governmental and non-party context that, in a decentralized fashion, interrelates organizations and movements engaged in concrete action at levels from the local to the international – to build another world. *It thus does not constitute a locus of power to be disputed by the participants in its meetings, nor does it intend to constitute the only option for interrelation and action by the organizations and movements that participate in it.*

9. *The World Social Forum asserts democracy as the avenue to resolving society's problems politically. As a meeting place, it is open to pluralism and to the diversity of activities and ways of engaging of the organizations and movements that decide to participate in it, as well as the diversity of genders, races, ethnicities and cultures.*

10. The World Social Forum is opposed to all *authoritarian* and reductionist views of history and to the use of violence as a means of social control by the State. It upholds respect for Human Rights, for peaceful relations, in equality and solidarity, among people, *races*, genders and

peoples, and condemns all forms of domination and all subjection of one person by another.

11. *The meetings of the World Social Forum are always open to all those who wish to take part in them, except organizations that seek to take people's lives as a method of political action and those organizations that exclude groups/communities based on ethnic, racial, religious or caste considerations from the democratic world.*

12. *The WSF process in India must necessarily make space for all struggling sections of society to come together and articulate their struggles and visions, individually and collectively, against the neo-liberal economic agenda of the world and national elite, which is breaking down the very fabric of the lives of ordinary people all over the world and marginalizing the majority of the world people, keeping profits as the main criteria of development rather than society and destroying the freedoms and rights of all women, men, and children to live in peace, security, and dignity.[3] It must make space for workers, peasants, indigenous peoples, Dalits, women, hawkers, minorities, immigrants, students, academicians, artisans, artists and other members of the creative world, professionals, the media, and for local businessmen and industrialists, as well as for parliamentarians, sympathetic bureaucrats and other concerned sections from within and outside the state. Most importantly, it must make space for all the 'sections' of society that remain less visible, marginalized, unrecognized, and oppressed.[4]*

13. *In India today, all civil and political organizations/groups that are organizing around people's issues – economic, political, social, and cultural – are being profoundly challenged by the religious and political intolerance that is raging in the country, and increasingly across the world. There is the threat of growing communal fascism and fundamentalism. The WSF India will strive to encourage a process that allows all of those who are combating communal fascism and fundamentalism to come together, to hear and understand each other, to explore areas of common interest, and also our differences, and to learn from the experiences and struggles of people here and in other countries.*

14. *The WSF India process involves not only events but also different activities across the country. These processes, in the spirit of the WSF, would be open, inclusive and flexible and designed to build capabilities of local groups and movements. The process should also be designed to seek and draw out people's perceptions regarding the impact of neo-liberal economic policies and imperialism on their daily lives. The language of dissent and resistance towards these will have to be informed by local idioms and forms.*

15. *WSF [India] will strive as far as possible for self-reliance based on local resources generation in its activities. However, recognizing that global solidarity against the global neo-liberal agenda may involve international events. For such events and activities, resources may need to be mobilized from external resources.*

16. As a forum for debate, the World Social Forum is a movement of ideas that prompts reflection, and the *maximum possible* transparent circulation of the results of that reflection, on the mechanisms and instruments of domination by capital, on means and actions to resist and overcome that domination, and on the alternatives *that can be* proposed to solve the problems of exclusion and inequality that the process of capitalist globalization *currently prevalent* is creating *or aggravating*, internationally and within countries.

17. As a framework for the exchange of experiences, the World Social Forum encourages understanding and mutual recognition among its participant organizations and movements, and places special value on all that society is building to centre economic activity and political action on meeting the needs of people and respecting nature.

18. As a context for interrelations, the World Social Forum seeks to strengthen and create new national and international links among organizations and movements of civil society, that – in both public and private life – will increase the capacity for social resistance to the process of dehumanization the world is undergoing and reinforce the humanizing measures being taken by the action of these movements and organizations.

19. The World Social Forum is a process that encourages its participant organizations and movements to situate their actions as issues of *world* citizenship, and to introduce on to the global agenda the change-inducing practices that they are experimenting in building a new world.

African version

After evaluating the results obtained and hopes aroused by the two editions of the African Social Forum (ASF) (organized in Bamako in January 2002 and Addis Ababa in January 2003), the initiators of the ASF considered it necessary to define a Charter of principles and values which establishes the political and moral bases of this collective space, and provide guidance for the continuation of this initiative.

The Principles contained in this Charter, which shall be observed by all those desiring to participate in the Forum and organize activities within it, are in conformity with the ideals that guided the realization of the two editions of the African Social Forum and defined the new political and moral orientations.

This Charter was approved in Addis Ababa, in January 2003.

1. The African Social Forum is an open meeting space *aimed at deepening* reflections, democratic debate, formulating proposals, experiences and articulation of efficient actions, entities and *African* social movements which are opposed to neo-liberalism, *injustice* and the domination of the world by market forces.

2. *The Bamako Forum was a high point in the existence of the African social movement during which we agreed and proclaimed that 'another Africa is possible'. This creed, which is also our hobbyhorse, shall guide us in*

the search for and construction of alternatives to the domination and plundering of the continent.

3. The African Social Forum shall speak as a continental body. Thus all the meetings that contribute to this process shall also have a regional dimension.

4. The alternatives proposed *by the African Social Forum shall be focused on the human person and opposed to the merchandising of Africa and the selling off of its riches within the framework of neo-liberal globalization. The latter is particularly beneficial to the major multinational firms, rich nations and international institutions at the latter's service. The Forum thus objects to the programmes and initiatives launched on behalf of the continent which, in fact, establish the domination of the financial, political and cultural hegemonic forces.*

5. *The Forum shall, more specifically, campaign in favour of an interdependent African integration based, on the one hand, on the respect of the rights of men and women, minority rights, democracy, the principles of a sustainable development, and on the other, on democratic institutions at the service of interests of the continent, social justice, equality and people's sovereignty.*

6. The African Social Forum shall bring together and connect civil society entities and movements *from all African countries,* but shall not claim to be representative of the *African civil society or exclude from its debates political leaders, mandated by the peoples, who accept to make commitments resulting from this Charter.*[5]

7. Meetings of the *African Social Forum* do not have voting powers. No one shall therefore be authorized to speak on behalf of the Forum, no matter in what form, by presenting viewpoints claiming to be those of the ASF. As members of the Forum, participants shall not take decisions by vote or acclamation, nor approve declarations or proposals for action which bind the Forum.[6]

8. Entities partaking in the Forum proceedings should however be able to deliberate freely during these meetings, alone or with other participants, about declarations and actions which they decide to develop. The World Social Forum shall undertake to widely circulate these decisions, through the means at its disposal, without imposing directions, hierarchies, censures and restrictions, but as proceedings of entities or groups of entities which would have assumed them.[7]

9. The African Social Forum is a pluralist and diversified, non-confessional, non-governmental and non-partisan space, which links, in a decentralized way and in networks, entities and movements engaged in concrete actions, from the local to the international level, for the construction of *another Africa* and another world. *It shall therefore not establish itself as a governing body for participants during its meetings, nor shall it claim to be the only mode of articulation and action for entities and movements that participate in it.*[8]

10. As a meeting space, the Forum is open to pluralism and the diverse commitments and actions of participating entities and movements, such as gender, *racial*, ethnic and cultural diversity.[9]

11. *The African Social Forum believes in the power of democracy as the preferred channel for conflict renegotiation and resolution within societies and between States. Participants to the Forum shall undertake to strengthen participation and citizen control.*

12. The African Social Forum shall reject any form of totalitarian and reductionist vision of history and the use of violence by States *or any other social or political force*. It shall put forward the respect of Human Rights, equitable, interdependent and peaceful relations among peoples, sexes and *races*, and condemn all forms of domination as well as the subjugation of one human being by another.[10]

13. *Meetings of the African Social Forum shall always constitute open spaces for all those desiring to participate in them, with the exception of organizations known to have made an attempt on people's lives as a method of political action.*

14. As a space for debate, *the African Social Forum* is a movement of ideas which stimulates reflection and the maximum transparent circulation of the results of this reflection, on mechanisms and tools of economic domination, means and actions to resist this domination, and on the alternatives that can be proposed to resolve the problems of exclusion and inequality which the current globalization process has strengthened and aggravated both at continental level *and in each African country*.[11]

15. As a space for the exchange of experiences, the African Social Forum shall stimulate the knowledge and mutual recognition of participating entities and movements, by specifically enhancing the value of what African societies themselves build in order to streamline economic activity and political action on human needs and the respect of the environment.[12]

16. As a space of articulation, the *African Social Forum* shall seek to strengthen and create new national and international linkages between entities and civil society movements. The capacity to resist the economic and cultural impoverishment and dehumanization process, within the continent and the globe, is emerging.[13]

17. The *African Social Forum* is a process that stimulates entities and movements which contribute in defining their actions in the perspective of the creation of an *African* and global citizen, introducing, in the continental and global agenda, transforming practices which they experiment in order to build another society, *another Africa* and another world.[14]

18. *The African Social Forum is a process connected to other world processes aimed at building another world on the basis of the principles and values that we are adopting today. It is an integral part of the movement created by the World Social Forum. It shall seek to strengthen the solidarity*

between the movements and the entities working in Africa and those in other parts of the world.

Notes

1 Also adopted by the WSF 2006, Karachi.

2 The differences from the approved WSF charter are presented in italic.

3 In the WSF 2006 polycentric Forum held in Pakistan, it reads as follows: 'The WSF process in Pakistan must necessarily make space for all struggling sections of society to come together and articulate their struggles and visions, individually and collectively, against the neo-liberal economic agenda of the world and national elite, which is breaking down the very fabric of the lives of ordinary people all over the world and marginalizing the majority of the world people, keeping profits as the main criteria of development rather than society and destroying the freedoms and rights of all women, men, and children to live in peace, security, and dignity.'

4 In the WSF 2006 polycentric Forum held in Pakistan, this part constitutes another paragraph (13). It reads as follows: 'The WSF process in Pakistan must also make space for workers, peasants, indigenous peoples, Dalits, women, hawkers, minorities, immigrants, students, academicians, artisans, artists and other members of the creative world, professionals, the media, and for local businessmen and industrialists, as well as for parliamentarians, sympathetic bureaucrats and other concerned sections from within and outside the state. Most importantly, it must make space for all the "sections" of society that remain less visible, marginalized, unrecognized, and oppressed.'

5 Similar to para. 5 of the WSF-approved charter.

6 Similar to para. 6 of the WSF-approved charter.

7 Similar to para. 7 of the WSF-approved charter.

8 Similar to para. 8 of the WSF-approved charter.

9 Similar to para. 9 of the WSF-approved charter.

10 Similar to para. 10 of the WSF-approved charter.

11 Similar to para. 11 of the WSF-approved charter.

12 Similar to para. 12 of the WSF-approved charter.

13 Similar to para. 13 of the WSF-approved charter.

14 Similar to para. 14 of the WSF-approved charter.

Annexe III: Manifesto of Porto Alegre

Another world is possible: twelve proposals

Since the first World Social Forum held in Porto Alegre in January 2001, the social forums have spread to all continents on national and local planes. With the WSF, a public space for civil rights arose that spans the earth. The WSF proposes political alternatives to dictation of neo-liberal globalization advanced by the financial markets and multinational corporations. The military arm of these markets and corporations is the imperial power of the United States. In the meantime the movement for another world that gained strength through its diversity and the solidarity of activists and social movements has not made a difference worldwide.

The social movements generally accepted the proposals developed at the forums. The signatories of the manifesto of Porto Alegre that only voice their personal opinion and in no way speak in the name of the forum worked out twelve proposals that represent foundations for building another world. If they were implemented, citizens could finally begin to reappropriate their future together.

This minimal platform was presented for review to the WSF participants and the social movements of all countries. The struggles necessary for their realization must be waged on all planes, on the plane of the entire planet, the continents and the national and local planes. We have no illusions about the actual will of the governments and international institutions to implement these proposals.

I. Another world is possible: The right to life for all persons should be respected by means of new rules in the economy.

The following measures are necessary:

1. Cancelling the state debts of the countries of the southern hemisphere. These debts have already been paid several times. For the creditor states, credit institutes and international financial institutions, the debts represent the best and most effective means for dominating the majority of humanity and keeping them in poverty. The repayment of the giant sums withheld from their peoples by corrupt leaders is imperative.

2. An international taxation on financial transactions (e.g. the Tobin tax on currency speculation), direct investments abroad, consolidated profits of multinational firms, weapons trade and activities with strong emissions of greenhouse gases. State economic assistance should reach the level of 0.7 per cent of the gross domestic product of the rich countries. These funds would be used for the border-crossing control of

epidemics (including AIDS) and for assuring everyone's access to drinking water, housing, energy, health care, medicines, education and social security.

3. Gradual removal of all forms of tax-, legal- and bank account havens that are hideouts for organized criminality, corruption, every kind of illegal trade, fraud, tax evasion and criminal business deals of large corporations and governments.

These tax havens are not limited to certain states regarded as law-free zones. The laws of developed countries are also involved. Strongly taxing the capital movements that flow in or out of these 'havens' as well as the credit institutes, financial actors and others responsible for large-scale embezzlements would be a sensible first step.

4. The right of every inhabitant of this earth to work, social security and pension following the equality between man and woman as a founding element of all internal and international policy.

5. Promoting all forms of fair trade by rejecting the free trade rules of the WTO and instituting mechanisms that gradually adjust social and environmental norms upwards in the production of goods and the provision of services. Education, health care, social services and culture must be completely excluded from the scope of the General Agreement on Trade in Services (GATS) of the WTO.

In the agreement on cultural diversity currently negotiated in UNESCO, the right to culture and to public policy in favour of culture is explicitly given priority over commercial law.

6. Securing the right of every country or federation of countries to food security and sovereignty through promotion of rural agriculture. This requires both the complete abolition of subsidies for the export of agricultural products, particularly by the United States and the European Union and the possibility of taxing imports to prevent dumping practices. Every country or federation of countries should also have the unrestricted right to prevent the production and importation of genetically modified food.

7. Prohibiting every form of patenting knowledge and life (whether human, animal or plant life) and all privatization of the common property of humanity, especially drinking water.

II. Another world is possible: promoting 'cooperative life' in peace and justice
The following measures are necessary:

8. First of all, combating all forms of discrimination, sexism, hostility against foreigners, racism and anti-Semitism through different political measures.

9. Taking immediate steps to stop destruction of the environment and the danger of grave climate changes caused by the greenhouse effect and by the rapid growth of traffic and the squandering of non-renewable energy. Existing agreements and treaties should be implemented even

if they are inadequate. Another development model should be realized based on an energy-saving way of life and democratic controls on natural mineral resources, particularly drinking water.

10. Military bases of foreign countries should be closed. All foreign troops should be withdrawn except on the explicit mandate of the UN. This is important first of all for Iraq and Palestine.

III. Another world is possible: promoting democracy on local and global planes

The following measures are necessary:

11. Securing the right of individuals to information and to pass on information through legislation that
   1. ends the concentration of the media in gigantic communication conglomerates;
   2. assures the independence of journalists over against shareholders; and
   3. promotes a non-profit-oriented press, especially the alternative and cooperatively organized media.

Observation of these rights presupposes citizens developing counter-powers, particularly in the form of national and international media-tracking stations.

12. Reforming and democratizing international organizations by enforcing economic, social and cultural human rights in the sense of the Universal Declaration of Human Rights. This priority requires the inclusion of the World Bank, the IMF and the WTO in the decision-making system and the decision-making mechanisms of the United Nations. Amid the continuing violations of international laws by the United States, the headquarters of the United Nations should be transferred from New York to another country, preferably in the South.

Porto Alegre, January 29, 2005

Tariq Ali (Pakistan), Samir Amin (Egypt), Walden Bello (Philippines), Frei Betto (Brazil), Atílio Borón (Argentina), Bernard Cassen (France), Eduardo Galeano (Uruguay), François Houtart (Belgium), Armand Mattelart (Belgium), Adolfo Pérez Esquivel (Argentina), Riccardo Petrella (Italy), Ignácio Ramonet (Spain), Samuel Ruiz Garcia (Mexico), Emir Sader (Brazil), José Saramago (Portugal), Roberto Sávio (Italy), Boaventura de Sousa Santos (Portugal), Animata Traoré (Mali), Immanuel Wallerstein (United States)

Annexe IV

Organizations and institutions that have provided financial support to the World Social Forums

2001 (Porto Alegre) Droits et Démocratie; Ford Foundation; H. Boll Foundation; ICCO; Le Monde Diplomatique; Oxfam; RITS-Rede de Informação para o Terceiro Setor; Rio Grande do Sul State Government; Porto Alegre City Government.

2002 (Porto Alegre) RITS-Rede de Informação para o Terceiro Setor; EED; CCFD; NOVIB; OXFAM GB; North–South Centre; ActionAid; ICCO; Ford Foundation; Rio Grande do Sul State Government; Porto Alegre City Government; Procergs; World Forum of Alternatives.

2003 (Porto Alegre) ActionAid; Cafod; CCFD; EED; Fundação Banco do Brazil; H. Boll Foundation; ICCO; Misereor; Novib; Ford Foundation; Oxfam; Petrobras; Rio Grande do Sul State Government; Porto Alegre City Government.

2004 (Mumbai) Supporters of the World Social Forum 2004, in India ActionAid (United Kingdom); Alternatives (Canada); Attac Norge Solidarites (Norway); Comité Catholique Contre la Faim et pour le Développement (CCFD – France); Christian Aid (United Kingdom); Development and Peace (Canada); Evangelischer Entwicklungsdienst (EED – Germany); Funders Network on Trade and Globalization (FNTG – United States); Heinrich Boll Foundation (Germany); Humanist Institute for Cooperation with Developing Countries (HIVOS – Netherlands); Inter Church Organization for Development Cooperation (CCO – Netherlands); Oxfam International; Swedish International Development Cooperation Agency (SIDA – Sweden); Solidago Foundation (USA); Swiss Agency for Development Cooperation (SDC – Switzerland); Tides Foundation (USA); World Council of Churches (Switzerland); Members of India General Council for their solidarity contribution (India).

Sponsors and supporters of the WSF process in 2004: Petrobras; Fundação Banco do Brazil; Ford Foundation; A Caixa (Brazilian bank); Brazilian Post Office.

2005 (Porto Alegre) Rio Grande do Sul State Government; Porto Alegre City Government; Fundação Banco do Brazil; Federal Government of Brazil; Brazilian Ministry of Tourism; A Caixa (Brazilian bank); Brazilian Post Office; EED; Christian Aid; EletroBras; Comité Catholique

Contre la Faim et pour le Développement (CCFD); NOVIB; Petrobras; Catholic Agency for Overseas Development (CAFOD); Rockfeller Brothers Fund; Misereor; Infraero (Brazilian airports); ICCO; FURNAS.

Sources: <www.forumsocialmundial.org.br/dinamic.php?pagina= apoiadores_2005_por>; <www.forumsocialmundial.org.br/dinamic. php?pagina=apoiadores_2004_por>; <www.forumsocialmundial.org. br/dinamic.php?pagina=apoio_finan_india_po>; <www.wsf2006karachi. org/wsfstructure.html>

Bibliography

Adler, M. (1922) *Die Staatsauffassung des Marxismus*, VieNna: Verlag der Wiener Volksbuchhandlung.

Agamben, G. (2004) *State of Exception*, Chicago, IL: University of Chicago Press.

Albert, M. (2003) 'The WSF's future', *ZNET*, <www.zmag.org/content/showarticle.cfm?SectionID=41&ItemID=2956>, accessed 20 March 2003.

An-Na'im, A. (ed.) (1995) *Human Rights and Religious Values: An Uneasy Relationship?*, Amsterdam: Editions Rodopi.

— (2000) 'Human rights and Islamic identity in France and Uzbekistan: mediation of the local and global', *Human Rights Quarterly*, 22(4): 906–41.

ATTAC (2002) *Control of Financial Capital*, Library of Alternatives, World Social Forum, <www.forumsocialmundial.org.br/dinamic/eng_pcf_controle_fin.asp>, accessed 22 November 2002.

Bauer, O. (1924) *Die Nationalitätenfrage und die Sozialdemokratie* (2nd edn), Vienna: Verlag der Wiener Volksbuchhandlung.

Bennett, W. L. (2004) 'Communicating global activism: strengths and vulnerabilities of networked politics', in W. van der Donk, B. D. Loader, P. G. Nixon, D. Rucht (eds), *Cyberprotest: New Media, Citizens and Social Movements*, London: Routledge, pp. 123–46.

Bertinoti, F. (2002) 'Reinventing left politics: toward a socialist politics for the second globalization', *Transnational Alternativas*, <www.tni.org./tat/>, accessed 19 March 2003.

Bipinchandra, P. (1954) *Swadeshi & Swaraj (The Rise of New Patriotism)*, Calcutta: Yugayatri Prakashak.

Blin, A., L. Bouguerra, A. D. Cattani, E. Granet, P.-Y. Guihéneuf, Y. Hardy, A. Hernandez, V. Kleck, C. MacKenzie, P. F. Vizentini, M. A. Weissheimer (2006) *100 propositions du Forum social mondial*, Paris: Éditions Charles Léopold Mayer.

Bloch, E. (1995) *The Principle of Hope*, Cambridge, MA: MIT Press.

Bonafini, H. de (2002) *Discurso en la Marcha de las Madres de los días Jueves*, <http://lists.indymedia.org/mailman/public/www-it/2002-February/000496.html>, accessed 19 June 2003.

Bottomore, T. and P. Goode (eds) (1978) *Austro-Marxism*, Oxford: Oxford University Press.

Broué, P. (1971) *Révolution en Allemagne (1917–1923)*, Paris: Editions de Minuit.

Broué, P. and E. Témime (1961) *La Révolution et la guerre d'Espagne*, Paris: Editions de Minuit.

Buey, F. F. (2005) *Guía para una Globalización Alternativa: Otro Mundo Es Posible*, Barcelona: Byblos.

Calinicos, A. and C. Nineham (2005) 'Critical reflections on the Fifth World Social Forum', *ZNET*, <www.zmag.org/content/showarticle. cfm?ItemID=7197>, accessed 11 March 2005.

Ceceña, A. E. (2004) 'Los desafíos del mundo en que caben todos los mundos y la subversión del saber histórico de la lucha', *Chiapas*, 16: 9–29.

Dewey, J. (1960) *The Quest for Certainty*, New York: Capricorn Books.

Escobar, A. (2004) 'Other worlds are already possible: self-organization, complexity and post-capitalist cultures', in J. Sen, A. Anand, A. Escobar, P. Waterman (eds), *World Social Forum: Challenging Empires*, New Delhi: Viveka Foundation, pp. 349–58.

Faruki, K. A. (1979) *The Constitutional and Legal Role of the Umma*, Karachi: Ma'aref.

Fisher, W. F. and T. Ponniah (2003) *Another World is Possible: Popular Alternatives to Globalization at the World Social Forum*, London: Zed Books.

Gandhi, Mahatma (1929/32) *The Story of My Experiments with Truth*, vols 1 and 2, Ahmedabad: Navajivan.

— (1941) *The Economics of Khadi*, Ahmedabad: Navajivan.

— (1967) *The Gospel of Swadeshi*, Bombay: Bharatiya Vidya Bhavan.

Gobrin-Morante, C. (2002) 'The World Social Forum fights imperialist globalization', in L. Nisula and K. Sehm-Patomäki (eds), *We, the Peoples of the World Social Forum*, Network Institute for Global Democratization Discussion Paper 2, pp. 19–21.

Grzybowski, C. (2002) *Um Mundo Mais Feminino é Possível?*, Library of Alternatives, World Social Forum, <www.forumsocialmundial.org.br/dinamic/por_Candido_Mulheres.asp>, accessed 20 March 2003.

— (2003a) 'Por que pensar o Fórum Social Mundial?', *Terraviva*, 17 January, pp. 3–14.

— (2003b) 'Apresentação', in IBASE (ed.), *Colecção Fórum Social Mundial 2003*, Rio de Janeiro: IBASE, vol. 4, pp. 7–8.

Hardt, M. and A. Negri (2000) *Empire*, Cambridge, MA: Harvard University Press.

Harnecker, M. (2006) *Haciendo Posible lo Imposible: la izquierda en el umbral del siglo XXI*, Caracas: Fondo Editorial Tropykos.

Hassan, R. (1996) 'Religious human rights and the Qur'an', in J. Witte Jr and J. D. van der Vyver (eds), *Religious Human Rights in Global Perspective: Religious Perspectives*, The Hague: Martinus Nijhoff Publishers, pp. 361–86.

Hinkelammert, F. (2002) *Crítica de la Razón Utópica*, Bilbao: Desclée de Brouwer.

Holloway, J. (2002) *Change the World without Taking the Power: The Meaning of Revolution Today*, London: Pluto Press.

Houtart, F. (2001) 'The current state of globalization', *ALAI, América Latina en Movimiento*, 22 June, <http://alainet.org/active/show_text.php3?key=2372>, accessed 19 March 2003.

Bibliography

IBASE (2003) *Coleção Fórum Social Mundial 2003*, 5 vols, Rio de Janeiro: IBASE.

— (2006) *An X-ray of the Participation in the 2005 Forum: Elements for Debate*, Rio de Janeiro: WSF International Secretariat.

Koselleck, R. (1985) *Futures Past: On the Semantics of Historical Time*, Cambridge, MA: MIT Press.

Krishna, D. (1994) *Swadeshi View of Globalisation*, New Delhi: Swadeshi Jagaran Manch.

Lagunas, L. (2003) 'Mujeres demandan representación equitativa en el FSM', *Mujeres Hoy*, 23 January, <www.mujereshoy.com/secciones/199.shtml>, accessed 28 March 2003.

Lenin, V. I. (1978) *Obras Escolhidas*, vol. 2, Lisbon: Avante.

McAdam, D., J. D. McCarthy and M. N. Zald (eds) (1996) *Comparative Perspectives on Social Movements: Political Opportunities, Mobilizing Structures, and Cultural Framings*, New York: Cambridge University Press.

McAdam, D., S. Tarrow and C. Tilly (2001) *Dynamics of Contention*, New York: Cambridge University Press.

Marramao, G. (1985) *Potere e Secolarizazione. Le categorie del tempo*, Rome: Editori Reuniti.

Mercado, Z. (1974) *El Poder Dual en América Latina*, Mexico: Siglo Veintiuno.

Merleau-Ponty, M. (1947) *Humanisme et Terreur*, Paris: Gallimard.

Mignolo, W. (2000) *Local Histories/Global Designs: Coloniality, Subaltern Knowledges, and Border Thinking*, Princeton, NJ: Princeton University Press.

Nandy, A. (1987) *Traditions, Tyranny and Utopias*, New Delhi: Oxford University Press.

Obando, A. E. (2005) 'Sexism in the World Social Forum: is another world possible?', *WHRnet*, February, <www.iiav.nl/ezines/web/WHRnet/2005/February.pdf>, accessed 8 August 2005.

Oruka, H. O. (1990) 'Sage-philosophy: the basic questions and methodology', in H. O. Oruka (ed.), *Sage Philosophy: Indigenous Thinkers and Modern Debate on African Philosophy*, Leiden: Brill, pp. 27–40.

— (1998) 'Grundlegende Fragen der afrikanischen "Sage-Philosophy"', in F. Wimmer (ed.), *Vier Fragen zur Philosophie in Afrika, Asien und Lateinamerika*, Vienna: Passagen, pp. 35–53.

Oseghare, A. S. (1992) 'Sagacity and African philosophy', *International Philosophical Quarterly*, 32(1): 95–104.

Presbey, G. M. (1997) 'Who counts as a sage? Problems in the further implementation of sage philosophy', *Quest: Philosophical Discussions*, 11(1/2): 53–65.

Quijano, A. (2000) 'Colonialidad del poder y classificacion social', *Journal of World-Systems Research*, 6(2): 342–86.

Research Unit for Political Economy (RUPE) (2003) 'The economics and politics of the World Social Forum: lessons for the struggle against "globalisation"', *Aspects of India's Economy*, Mumbai, September, <http://globalresearch.ca/articles/RUP401A.html>, accessed 20 May 2004.

Rodríguez Garavito, C., P. S. Barrett and D. Chavez (eds) (2004) *La Nueva*

Izquierda en América Latina (sus orígenes y trayectoria futura), Bogotá: Grupo Editorial Norma.

Romano, J. (2003) 'Apresentação', in IBASE (ed.), *Colecção Fórum Social Mundial 2003*, Rio de Janeiro: IBASE, vol. 2, pp. 7–14.

Santos, B. de S. (1990) *O Estado e a Sociedade em Portugal (1974–1988)*, Oporto: Afrontamento.

— (1995) *Toward a New Common Sense: Law, Science and Politics in the Paradigmatic Transition*, New York: Routledge.

— (1998) 'Oppositional postmodernism and globalizations', *Law and Social Inquiry*, 23(1): 121–39.

— (2000) *A Crítica da Razão Indolente: Contra o Desperdício da Experiência*, Oporto: Afrontamento.

— (2001a) 'Nuestra America: reinventing a subaltern paradigm of recognition and redistribution', *Theory Culture and Society*, 18(2/3): 185–217.

— (2001b) 'Toward an epistemology of blindness: why the new forms of "ceremonial adequacy" neither regulate nor emancipate', *European Journal of Social Theory*, 4(3): 251–79.

— (2002a) 'Toward a multicultural conception of human rights', in B. Truyol (ed.), *Moral Imperialism: A Critical Anthology*, New York: New York University Press, pp. 39–60.

— (2002b) *Toward a New Legal Common Sense: Law, Globalisation and Emancipation*, London: Butterworth.

— (ed.) (2003a) *Conhecimento Prudente para uma Vida Decente: um 'Discurso sobre as Ciências' Revisitado*, Oporto: Afrontamento.

— (2003b) 'The Popular University of Social Movements', *Democracia Viva*, 14: 78–83.

— (2004a) 'Mumbai and the future', *Footnotes – Newsletter of the American Sociological Association*, 32(3).

— (2004b) 'A critique of lazy reason: against the waste of experience', in I. Wallerstein (ed.), *The Modern World-System in the Long Durée*, London: Paradigm Publishers, pp. 157–97.

— (ed.) (2005) *Democratizing Democracy: Beyond the Liberal Democratic Canon*, London: Verso.

— (2006a) 'The World Social Forum: where do we stand and where are we going?', in M. Glasius, M. Kaldor and H. Anheier (eds), *Global Civil Society 2005/6*, London: Sage, pp. 73–8.

— (2006b) 'The heterogeneous state and legal pluralism in Mozambique', *Law & Society Review*, 40(1): 39–75.

Sen, J. (2003a) 'Porto Alegre – Hyderabad – Porto Alegre: reflections on the past year of the World Social Forum process in India, and internationally', *Choike*, January, <www.choike.org/cgi-bin/choike/links/page.cgi?p=ver_informe&id=967>, accessed 7 July 2003.

— (2003b) 'The WSF as logo, the WSF as commons: take a moment to reflect on what is happening in the World Social Forum', *Choike*, May, <www.

choike.org/documentos/Jai_Sen_wsf2004_as_logo.pdf>, accessed 28 July 2004.

— (2004) 'A tale of two charters', in J. Sen, A. Anand, A. Escobar and P. Waterman (eds), *World Social Forum: Challenging Empires*, New Delhi: Viveka Foundation, pp. 72–5.

Sen, J., A. Anand, A. Escobar and P. Waterman (eds) (2004) *World Social Forum: Challenging Empires*, New Delhi: Viveka Foundation.

Teivainen, T. (2003) 'World Social Forum: what should it be when it grows?', *OpenDemocracy*, 10 July, <www.opendemocracy.net/debates/article-3-31-1342.jsp>, accessed 15 July 2003.

— (2004) 'Twenty-two theses on the problems of democracy in the World Social Forum', *Transform!*, 1, March, <www.transform.it/newsletter/news_transform01.html>, accessed 19 May 2004.

— (forthcoming) *Democracy in Movement: The World Social Forum as a Political Process*, London: Routledge.

Trotsky, L. (1950) *Histoire de la Révolution Russe*, vol. 1, Paris: Seuil.

Van der Wekken, R. (2005) *A Picture of the World/Africa Social Forum Process (September 2005)*, Network Institute for Global Democratisation (NIGD), <www.nigd.org/docs/WSFStudyACWSFRuby.pdf>, accessed 20 November 2005.

Vargas, V. (2002) 'Feminismo, globalización, y el movimiento de justicia y solidaridad global', *Transnational Alternatives*, <www.tni.org./tat/>, accessed 19 March 2003.

— (2003) *Informe del Seminario de Sistematización del Foro Social Mundial, 21 a 23 de Mayo, Rio de Janeiro*, E-mail, 29 May.

— (n.d.) *Los Aportes y los Retos Feministas en el Foro Social Mundial*, <http://alainet.org/publica/retosfem/aportes.html>, accessed 19 March 2003.

Visvanathan, S. (2000) 'Environmental values, policy, and conflict in India', Text presented to the seminar on 'Understanding values: a comparative study on environmental values in China, India and the United States' (sponsored by the Carnegie Council), <www.carnegiecouncil.org/pdf/visvanathan.pdf>, accessed 24 September 2001.

Vivas, E. (ed.) (2004) *Mumbai (Foro Social Mundial 2004): Balance y perspectivas de un movimiento de movimientos*, Barcelona: Icaria.

Wainwright, H. (2003) *Reclaim the State: Experiments in Popular Democracy*, London: Verso.

Wallerstein, I. and E. Balibar (1991) *Race, Nation, Class: Ambiguous Identities*, New York: Verso.

Waterman, P. (2003a) *First Reflections on the 3rd World Social Forum, Porto Alegre, Brazil*, Library of Alternatives, World Social Forum, <www.forumsocialmundial.org.br/dinamic.asp?pagina=balan_waterman2003in>, accessed 19 March 2003.

— (2003b) 'Place, space and the reinvention of social emancipation on a global scale: second thoughts on the third World Social Forum', Working Papers 378, The Hague: Institute of Social Studies.

— (2004) 'Globalization from the middle? Reflections from a margin', in J. Sen, A. Anand, A. Escobar and P. Waterman (eds), *World Social Forum: Challenging Empires*, New Delhi: Viveka Foundation, pp. 87–94.

Whitaker, F. (2002a) 'Lessons from Porto Alegre', in L. Nisula and K. Sehm-Patomäki (eds), *We, the Peoples of the World Social Forum*, Network Institute for Global Democratization, Discussion Paper 2/2002, pp. 13–16.

— (2002b) *Fórum Social Mundial: Origens e objetivos*, Library of Alternatives, World Social Forum, <www.forumsocialmundial.org.br/main. asp?id_menu=2_1&cd_language=12>, accessed September 2002.

— (2003) *Notas para o Debate sobre o Fórum Social Mundial*, Memorial, WSF 2003, 14 March, <www.forumsocialmundial.org.br/dinamic. php?pagina=bal_whitaker_por>, accessed 27 July 2004.

WSF – IC (2005) *Relatoría de la Reunión del Consejo Internacional del Foro Social Mundial en Barcelona*, 20–22 June 2005, São Paulo: Escritório do Fórum Social Mundial /World Social Forum Office.

Zaehner, R. C. (1982) *Hinduism*, Oxford: Oxford University Press.

Index

multiculturalism, 143, 144
multilateral institutions: involvement of WSF participants in, 98; participants' attitudes to, 92
multitude, concept of, 164
Mumbai: chosen as venue for 2004 WSF, 74, 75
Mumbai Committee, 73
Mumbai Resistance, 56, 75

national or global struggles, 115–17
Negri, Toni, 164
neo-liberalism, 2, 10, 11, 17, 112, 171
Network Institute for Global Democratization (NIGD), 122
new social movements, 8
non-governmental organizations (NGOs), 69, 70, 86, 90, 91, 95, 120, 122, 128, 129, 131, 132, 133, 136, 137, 149; WSF participants' involvement in, 93, 96
NGOization of WSF, 70, 96, 97
non-existence, 15, 16, 17; social forms of, 18
non-violence, 7, 176, 178
Not and Not Yet, 30–1

Obando, Ana Elena, 80
oppressed classes, absence of, from WSF, 99
organizational problems of WSF, 100, 120
Organizing Committee of WSF (OC), 46, 47, 54, 63, 66, 78, 89, 90, 100, 116, 117, 120; Brazilian composition of, 72; relations with International Committee, 48–51; tensions with social movements, 72
Oruka, Oders, 137

Palestine Thematic Forum, 36
Pan-Africanism, 117
Pan-Amazonian Forum, 35–6
panels: gender balance of, 64; organization of, 60–5; regional balance of, 64
parallel institutionality, 176, 178

participants in WSF, numbers of, 57, 58; social profiles of, 85–109
parties, political: collaboration with social movements, 169–70; involvement of WSF participants in, 91, 95, 96; relations with WSF, 55, 56, 117
peasant movements, 27
pluralism, 124
pluralities, depolarized, 166–80
polarizations, 164–5; removal of, 166–80
Popular University of the Social Movements (PUSM), 148, 149–54; Charter of Principles, 154, 157, 158; coordinating committee, 154; devlopment of, 154–8; executive committee, 154; headquarters, 153, 157; methodology of, 156–7; network, 154; objectives of, 155–6; organization of, 157; pedagogic activities of, 151; plan of activities, 157–8 (in research, 152–3); technical secretariat of, 157
Porto Alegre, 46, 49; people of, 88–94, 88 (social profile of, 94–9); thematic consultation in, 77–8 see also Manifesto of Porto Alegre and WSF, Porto Alegre meetings
Porto Alegre Charter of Principles, 7
Porto Alegre Consensus, 76, 86, 123
practices, translation of, 138
privatization, movements against, 27
productive issues, 173–80; concentration on, 170, 187
productivities, ecology of, 27–9
productivity, 28; monoculture of, 17
progress, concept of, crisis of, 32

race: as classification, 17; imbalances of, 100
reform or revolution, 111–13, 183; as unproductive issue, 171–2
regional representation of WSF: imbalances of, 60, 64, 67, 69, 104, 106
relativism, 20, 138
religion factor within WSF, 75–6; beliefs of WSF participants, 90

utopia, 10–11, 128, 182; conservative, 10, 11, 12, 17, 110; critical, 12; democratic, 110

Vargas, Virginia, 53, 60, 119–20
Venezuelan Organizing Committee, 56
violence, renunciation of, 3–4
Vishvanathan, Shiv, 138

Wall of Proposals, 79
Washington Consensus, 123
Waterman, Peter, 70
welfare systems, 118
Whitaker, Francisco, 46, 47, 121, 124
women: among guest speakers, 53; participation of, in WSF, 89; violence against, 79
women's movements, 60
Workers' Party (PT), 49, 55–6; attempt to use WSF, 56; electoral victory of, 93
workshops, organization of, 151–2
World Bank, 77
World Economic Forum (Davos), 35, 46, 55, 77, 123
World Forum of Judges, 35
World Parliamentary Forum, 35
World Social Forum (WSF): 2001 meeting, 175; 2003 meeting, 99, 120, 123, 148 (debates following, 68–72; evaluation of, 58–72); 2004 meeting, 87, 90, 116 (creates new challenges for WSF, 76; step towards globalization of WSF, 86; success of, 75); 2005 meeting (Mumbai), 35, 36, 47, 48, 57, 69, 72–80, 99, 102, 122, 123, 129, 137, 155 (social profile of, 94–9; methodological innovation in, 78; new organizational model, 102; stress on self-organization, 79; thematic terrain of, 98); 2006 meeting, preparation for, 80; accusation of reformist leadership, 112; as an expression of an elite, 90; as embryo of civil society, 125; as epistemology,

127, 132 (of the South, 13); as exercise in sociology of absences, 29; as insurgent cosmopolitan politics, 35–45; as movement of movements, 120; as open space, 77, 124; as political entity, 112; as polycentric forum, 58, 87; as power space, 72; as space or as movement, 120–5; as utopia, 127, 132, 185 (critical, 10); Charter of Principles, 12, 35, 36, 38, 49, 55, 56, 58, 63, 72, 85, 110, 116, 117, 121, 123, 125, 139, 178, 182, 196–204; counter-hegemonic nature of, 99; defining political nature of, 72; diversity of, 123; emergence of, 6; Facilitation Group, 48, 51; financial crisis of, 56; funding institutions of, 208–9; future of, 127–47; geographical representation of, 87; internal balkanization of, 70; internal democracy of, 129, 130, 131, 185; International Committee *see* International Committee of WSF; International Secretariat *see* International Secretariat of WSF; methodology and systematization team, 59; Mumbai demonstration, 72–80; organization of, 46, 58 (innovations in, 73; problems of, 47–8, 69, 80; structure of, 54, 185); Organizing Committee *see* Organizing Comittee of WSF; Porto Alegre meetings, 35, 36, 69, 130; representativeness of, 85–100; seen as an elite, 95; self-transformation capacity of, 72, 80, 81, 98, 103; social profile of participants, 24, 99, 129–30; success or failure of, 184; 'Thematic Consultation and Cohesion of Activities' report, 77; top-down organization of, 54
World Social Forum India, 116; policy statement of, 196–204
World Social Territory, 78, 95, 123
World Trade Unions Forum, 35